Governance in Higher Education

"This book stands as a beacon, cutting through the fog with its illuminating insights in an era where clarity is often clouded by the noise of information overload. Professors Yahchouchi and Azoury's talent in distilling complex ideas into digestible narratives is nothing short of remarkable. It's not just a book; it's a journey - a journey that takes you from the realm of the known to the realm of the unknown, leaving you with a richer understanding of the world around us."
—Georges Jabbour, *The George Washington University School of Business, USA*

"Professor Azoury has done an excellent job in gathering views on the future of Higher Education in the Middle East and North Africa - which, given online learning and international partnerships, is of global relevance."
—Jonathan Michie, *University of Oxford, UK*

Nehme Azoury · Georges Yahchouchi
Editors

Governance in Higher Education

Global Reform and Trends in the MENA Region

Editors
Nehme Azoury
Faculty of Business
Holy Spirit University of Kaslik
Jounieh, Lebanon

Georges Yahchouchi
American University
of the Middle East
Egaila, Kuwait

ISBN 978-3-031-40585-3   ISBN 978-3-031-40586-0   (eBook)
https://doi.org/10.1007/978-3-031-40586-0

This Palgrave Macmillan imprint is published by the registered company Springer Nature Switzerland AG
The registered company address is: Gewerbestrasse 11, 6330 Cham, Switzerland

Paper in this product is recyclable.

To all the passionate educators, students, and researchers who tirelessly contribute to the field of education, this work is dedicated to you. Your unwavering commitment and dedication to improving the learning experience inspire us all.

Foreword

Professors Nehme Azouri (Holy Spirit University of Kaslik—USEK) and George Yahchouchi (American University of the Middle East—AUM), along with an esteemed team of academics, industry professionals, consultants, and tech leaders, present this insightful volume on higher education reforms and trends in the Middle East and North Africa (MENA) region.

The MENA region, steeped in a rich historical tapestry, is home to some of the oldest higher education institutions in the world, symbolizing the region's early recognition of the value of advanced learning. Yet, despite this illustrious heritage, the region faces unique and pressing challenges. These range from the overarching political instability and unrest to those more specific to the higher education sector, a mirror to the global dilemma but intensified by the region's distinctive societal, cultural, and political dynamics. Furthermore, the drive toward academic excellence, underscored by international accreditation ambitions, lends further significance to the reforms discussed in the book.

Acknowledging these challenges and understanding the global shift in higher education, the authors embarked on a scholarly journey to address a gap in the existing literature. The book explores global education trends, examining them through the specific lens of the MENA region. It offers unique perspectives on several key issues: the transformation to hybrid learning due to the COVID-19 pandemic, the importance of inclusion and diversity in academia, and the transformative potential of artificial intelligence (AI) in the education sector.

The authors' exploration has unfolded during a time of exceptional technological advancements, particularly in the realm of AI. Recognizing AI's transformative potential, a dedicated chapter explores its implications on higher education, with a particular focus on personalized learning. This is emblematic of the team's agility in addressing emerging trends that hold immense significance for higher education reform.

The book takes the reader through a thorough examination of the MENA region's higher education landscape, beginning with an overview of the current system, discussing the shift to hybrid learning, and diving into the challenges and opportunities faced by students and faculty. It further explores the role of women in academia, the need for curriculum reform and program delivery restructuring, and discusses new tactics and tools for enhancing interactivity, engagement, and assessment in education. The text reflects on the changing role of governance, the quality of e-education, and discusses AI's potential to reshape higher education. Finally, it provides a comprehensive exploration of inclusion and diversity in the education sector.

The authors of this work are not mere observers of change but active catalysts in their respective domains. The professors, who are alumni of leading universities worldwide, have shaped minds and influenced educational policies. The industry professionals and tech leaders have driven innovation within the largest tech firms, while the consultants and policy leaders have navigated the complexities of shaping educational strategies amidst socio-political upheavals. Their rich experiences, diverse backgrounds, and deep insights converge in this seminal work, making it a beacon for those navigating the tumultuous seas of higher education reform.

Intended for education leaders, policymakers, and researchers interested in the MENA region, this book not only deepens understanding of the region's unique educational challenges and opportunities but also inspires potential solutions. The authors aspire for the readers to comprehend the MENA region's peculiar situation: home to the earliest seeds of higher education and currently a hub of unique challenges, requiring innovative solutions, particularly leveraging AI, for the advancement of higher education.

Their unique synthesis of perspectives, drawn from the highest echelons of academia, consulting, policymaking, and technology in the MENA region, Europe, and North America, forms a profound commentary on higher education's evolving landscape.

With its comprehensive exploration and analysis, this book contributes significantly to the global discourse on higher education reforms, and the authors hope it will stimulate impactful changes in the educational landscape.

Brussels, Belgium   Professor Eric Cornuel
                                                    President, EFMD Global

Prof. Eric Cornuel is the President of EFMD Global.

He holds a degree in Sciences Po from IEP Paris, an M.B.A. from HEC Graduate School of Management in Paris, and a DEA in strategy and management from Paris Nanterre University, together with a Doctoral Certificate in Strategy from HEC Paris and a Ph.D. in management, written on international network organizations, from Paris Dauphine University.

Prof. Cornuel started his career as an entrepreneur by setting up a hydro-electric power plant in France while he was still a student. He was also the Coordinator of the HEC Institute for Central and Eastern Europe. From 1997 to 1999, he served as Dean of KIMEP, at the time the leading business and economics school in Central Asia, where he was awarded an honorary professorship. He has taught for over 20 years at various management schools in Europe and Asia, holding the positions of Affiliate Professor at HEC Paris and Professor at the Catholic University of Louvain.

Prof. Cornuel received several awards, including, in 2018, the Magnolia Award from the city of Shanghai and the French National Order of the "Légion d'honneur". He also received awards from PRME and CEIBS, as well as the John Fernandes prize for entrepreneurship in management education and the Koźmiński University personality of the year award.

Acknowledgments

We would like to express our deepest gratitude to all those who have contributed to the realization of this book. Our heartfelt thanks go to the researchers, scholars, and experts who have generously shared their knowledge, insights, and experiences. We also extend our appreciation to the editorial team, reviewers, and support staff who have dedicated their time and expertise to ensure the quality and accuracy of this work. We are grateful for the encouragement, support, and guidance provided by our colleagues, friends, and family throughout this journey. Their unwavering belief in our vision has been instrumental in bringing this book to fruition. Lastly, we extend our sincere appreciation to the readers for their interest in this work. It is our hope that this book will contribute to meaningful discussions, innovations, and advancements in the field of education.

Contents

Notes on Contributors

Dr. Shaima AlHarmoodi is an Assistant Professor at Hamdan bin Mohamed Smart University. She has a Ph.D. in the field of innovation project management. She is also an innovation and entrepreneurship ecosystem developer aiming to inspire and support the next generation of entrepreneurs and provide them with the necessary means to succeed. She leads the development and implementation of the university's ecosystem long-term strategy that incorporates impactful projects and initiatives.

Dr. Shaima is also a Certified External Examiner by the Ministry of Education for licensure of higher education institutions and accreditation of their academic programs.

She also actively runs workshops, masterclasses, and seminars in areas related to innovation, creativity, entrepreneurship, and project management in addition to her interest in research that resulted in a number of publications in international journals and conferences.

Prof. Nehme Azoury is a Professor and previous Deputy-President of Research at the Holy Spirit University of Kaslik—USEK. Former Dean of the Faculty of Business, he lectures in the fields of marketing, strategy, and corporate governance in several universities, namely teaches strategic management and corporate governance. He obtained his Ph.D. in Business Sciences from Université Paris XI and the Holy Spirit University of Kaslik, USEK. He was the Secretary General of the Arab Society of Faculties of Business Administration (affiliated with the Association of Arab Universities and founded by the Arab League) and is one of the eight members of the scientific committee of Eduniversal, as a representative of the Eurasian region. He has been visiting Professor and Lecturer at various universities, including Panthéon-Assas (Paris II), Euromed-Marseille, La Rochelle, Lyon 3, HEC Montréal, and the George Washington University, which presented him with an appreciation award for Active Contribution to the Education of MSF Students. He is the author of several publications and editor-in-chief of the Arab Economic & Business Journal and the Lebanese Journal of Economics and Management. He is also a Managing Partner at Widein, a consultancy firm based in Lebanon. He has published with Palgrave Macmillan many books such as "Business and Education in the Middle East", "Business and Society in the Middle East- Exploring Responsible Practice", and Entrepreneurship and Social Entrepreneurship in the MENA Region Advances in Research". He also published, along with Prof. Frank Bournois within Cambridge Publications, a book entitled: "Crisis, Globalization, and Governance. How to draw lessons?".

Dr. Marwan Azouri Specialist in Marketing and Social Media studies. Currently holds the position of Assistant Professor at the Notre Dame University, Lebanon as well as chairperson of the Department of Marketing and Management. Active in research and holds a Ph.D. from the University of Burgundy, Dijon France in 2016. His course load evolves around: Fundamentals of Marketing, Digital Business, Business Research, Consumer Behavior, and Salesmanship. He has also taught in a multitude of universities in Lebanon and France.

Dr. Bettina Lynda Bastian earned her doctorate in Technology and Innovation Management (Corporate Strategy) from the Swiss Federal Institute of Technology Lausanne (EPFL), Switzerland. Since 2021, she serves as Dean at the College of Business and Law (CBL) at the Royal University for Women (RUW), Bahrain. Before this assignment, she served as Head of Academic Programs in Entrepreneurship and Innovation at the Holy Spirit University of Kaslik, Lebanon (USEK), and Head of Business Ethics programs at the American University of Beirut (AUB). She is editor-in-chief of the Arab Economic Business Journal (AEBJ) and guest editor of diverse special issues concerned with innovation management and entrepreneurship. Her research is internationally recognized for translating social science into work policies and practices that promote entrepreneurship and sustainable business, especially women's development and capacity building.

Dr. Lindos Daou is a holder of a Ph.D. in Marketing from USEK, he is currently an Assistant Professor at the Marketing Department at the College of Business—Effat University, Jeddah, KSA. Previously, he was an assistant Professor at the Faculty of Business at Notre Dame University (NDU). He used to teach at USEK Business School at the Holy Spirit University of Kaslik. He also occupied the position of Chairperson of Management, in addition to Transport and Logistics Departments. He has also published several Book chapters with Palgrave Macmillan and was a co-editor of the book "Business and Social Media in the Middle East" in 2020. In 2015, he participated in the Fulbright Junior Faculty Development Program for Lebanon at the University of Illinois, USA. In 2018, he was also a visiting Professor at Varna University of Management-Bulgaria.

Jacques Digout has a strong background in business development and digital strategy, currently serves as a Director of Campus at Toulouse Business School and the CEO of eKipage, a company dedicated to professional transition support and training and fostering professional practice communities. In his role at Toulouse Business School, he has a proven track record in developing and managing academic programs, with a particular focus on digital marketing. In addition to his role at Toulouse Business School, he is also the CEO of Ring Commerce, a consultancy specializing in digital strategy and e-commerce. Previously, he held academic positions at Université Paul Sabatier de Toulouse and was a Director at the Chamber of Commerce and Industry of Toulouse. He also has experience in software development and multimedia education from his time at Languages Informatique SA. He holds a Doctorate from Université Toulouse 3 and an Habilitation to Direct Research in Marketing from IAE de Nantes. He is academically qualified with accreditations from AERS, AMBA, AACSB, and EQUIS. He is a prolific author with several books and academic articles on digital marketing and e-commerce. He is fluent in French, English, and Spanish.

Antoine Habchi is an Associate Professor at the Faculty of Business and Commercial Sciences at USEK. He is a current member of the Lebanese parliament elected for the second mandate representing Baalbek-Hermel governorate. He holds a Ph.D. in History, Maters in Sociology of Development, BA in Clinical Psychology, and DEUG in Psychology. He founded the Middle East Institution for Research and Strategic Studies, an NGO involved in the publication of analytical reports and the preparation of round-table debates. He is also the founder of CHAINGE Consulting, a firm specialized in tailoring customized training programs and tackling managerial problems facing both private and public organizations. The Central Bank of Lebanon, the Association of Banks in Lebanon, and the Rosary School of Byblos are among the many organizations for which he has provided both training and consultancy. He also founded the Hotel Management department "L.T. Hotellerie" at Cortbawi Institute and has managed the Organizational Project of Aintoura College along with several educational institutions.

Cynthia El Hajj is a Senior Business Analyst at PFC International, a business consultancy firm with offices in Beirut, Australia, Oman, Qatar, Iraq, and Spain. She specializes in conducting feasibility studies, market assessments, financial analyses, and business development plans. She also manages a team of junior business analysts and interns at PFC International. She is currently pursuing a Ph.D. in Business Administration at the Holy Spirit University of Kaslik (USEK), where she also completed a Bachelor of Arts and Business Administration in Banking and Finance, as well as a Master of Science in Business Administration and Management, graduating with high distinction and ranked first in the faculty of business. In addition to her academic and professional achievements, Cynthia has published a chapter titled "The Metaverse for Education" in the book "Higher Education—Reflections from the Field—Volume 3", edited by Dr. Lee Waller and Dr. Sharon Waller.

She also acquired various certifications from international organizations, including McKinsey and Company, the University of Illinois, the University of Virginia, the University of London, and Elsevier Academy. These certifications cover topics such as entrepreneurship, leadership, finance, company management, and personal branding.

Steve Harvey is President of Harvey Education Management, and a Strategic Advisor for SuccessFinder, a company specializing in talent assessments. Prior to founding HEM Steve had a distinguished career spanning thirty years as Professor, Management Consultant, and Senior Leader across multiple appointments in Business and Higher Education. He was most recently dean of the Olayan School of Business at the American University of Beirut, and prior to this, he was dean of the John Molson School of Business at Concordia University, Montreal, and before then, dean at the Williams School of Business at Bishop's University.

Steve is a veteran of business education and is sought out in business, higher education, and by other business schools worldwide to provide thought leadership and strategy in a fast-changing context for business and education. He serves on multiple international committees for education and accreditation, and on the advisory boards of other business schools and organizations, and he continues to provide strategic consulting services and speak on matters cutting across the future of work and business schools and talent management.

Johnny Karam's career embodies a dynamic intersection of education, technology, and policy. With an academic foundation rooted in computer science, complemented by graduate studies in political science, he has carved out a unique niche, specializing in the application of technology within educational policy development. Spanning North Africa, the Levant, and the Middle East, his professional journey has firmly established him as a vanguard in the education technology industry. His graduate research in Political Science, with a specific focus on education reform through public policy, synergizes with his technological expertise, reinforcing his profound impact on the sector.

In his role as a regional education leader at Microsoft, his pioneering efforts in applying AI and cloud technology have been transformative across the region. He has enabled Higher Education institutions, Ministries of Education, and Global School networks to harness technology in innovative ways, solving critical educational challenges. By forging strategic relationships with key institutions, he has fostered a collaborative ethos, accelerating the adoption of digital practices. His transformative work has placed these organizations at the cutting edge of modern educational practices.

Prior to his tenure at Microsoft, he was a Senior Consultant with Oxford Policy Management, leading the digital transformation strategy in response to the COVID crisis for the Lebanese Ministry of Education and Higher Education. His strategic vision and ability to foster key relationships and lead critical negotiations proved instrumental in adopting innovative cloud solutions.

In addition to his extensive industry experience, his policy acumen was honed while serving as a Policy Advisor for several members of parliament. His background in Computer Science, coupled with his graduate studies in Political Science, provided a unique perspective that blended technology and public policy, proving invaluable in drafting educational policies and laws.

Johnny's commitment to education is evidenced by his extensive experience with both K12 and Higher Education institutions. With a rich background in educational management and curriculum development, he consistently encourages a transformative shift toward digital integration in educational settings. His career is a testament to his leadership and his deep understanding of the intertwined nature of education and technology, showcasing his ability to foster meaningful change. As he continues to shape the landscape of education technology, he remains a relentless advocate for innovation and progress, driven by his unwavering belief in the power of education to shape the future.

Dr. Rim El Khoury is an Associate Professor of Finance at the Lebanese American University, with a Ph.D. in International Finance from Sogang University, South Korea. She has taught at various universities and has held leadership roles in academic coordination and learning assessment. She has received several awards for her contributions to finance and actively serves as a reviewer for several esteemed journals. She has also guest-edited special issues in various journals. Her research work, including numerous peer-reviewed articles, is published in renowned academic journals, underlining her status as a respected researcher in finance.

Prof. Rock-Antoine Mehanna has 30+ years of academic, management, and consultancy experience in the USA, EU, and MENA regions in several industries, namely higher education, government, real estate, and hospitality. He is currently the Dean of the School of Business, Head of the Entrepreneurship Hub, and Professor of Strategy and Innovation at the Hamdan Bin Mohammed Smart University. He also serves as President of the World Economics Association—Lebanon Chapter. Prior to this, he served for 10 years as the Dean of the Business School at Sagesse University in Lebanon and founded its flagship Smart Center. He has also taught at major universities in the USA, Lebanon, UK, and France, as well as served on several corporate boards. He holds a Ph.D. in Business Strategy (USA), M.B.A. in Finance (USA), and B.S. in Management and Marketing. He has provided consultancy services to The World Bank, Boston Consulting Group, Saudi Aramco, Arab Planning Institute, and UAE Center for Strategic Studies and Research, among other multinationals. He has published 15 books, 38+ peer-reviewed articles, and 100+ conference papers. He serves on 5 editorial boards of professional journals and 3 NGOs. Dr. Mehanna is the recipient of 16 academic, research, and leadership awards.

Dr. Arpita Mehrotra, earned her doctorate in Commerce from India. Before her engagement with RUW, she served as the Director of Marketing as well as the Asst Director of Academics at MSB, India. Her interests lie in Learning and Teaching, Institutional Effectiveness, Quality Assurance, program management, and corporate training for industries. She is actively functioning in distinct roles as an Acting Dean for the College of Business and Financial Sciences, Head of the Department for Banking and Finance Department, Associate Professor, Internship coordinator, member of the quality assurance committee,

AACSB team lead, and a student advisor. Relatively, she has valuable academic experience in some of the most prestigious and renowned universities in the Kingdom of Bahrain and India. She has proven experience in leading and motivating a diverse team of academics and support staff to achieve set goals. The most commendable quality she brings to the table is the ability to adapt to diverse cultures in educational and business environments and the empirical approach to resolving business challenges.

Sareh Rotabi is an Executive Manager of Staff Development at the American University of the Middle East in Kuwait, with extensive experience in higher education, management, and financial analysis. Her research interests span a broad range of topics, including Behavioral Economics, Circular Economy, Entrepreneurship, and Sustainability. She is a recognized contributor to the academic community, having participated in numerous conferences and an exchange program.

Hady El Samra is a civil engineer and business analyst specializing in education, livelihood, human rights, health care, and agriculture. He has demonstrated expertise as a Business Analyst at PFC International, conducting comprehensive research and utilizing advanced data collection methods for feasibility studies, market assessments, financial analyses, grant proposals, and business development plans. His proficiency extends to primary research tools, feasibility studies, business plans, and market and vulnerability studies. He has practical experience in civil engineering, with a focus on skyscraper and residential projects, and has implemented ISO standards. He actively contributes to the field of higher education and research, with a particular emphasis on enhancing educational systems. He has attended multiple seminars on topics such as the evolution of teaching methodologies in relation to technological advancements. During his academic years, he engaged in various university departments, including the admissions office, student affairs office, and civil engineering laboratories, where he provided valuable assistance to fellow students.

Hady holds a master's degree from the University of Sydney and a BE degree from the Holy Spirit University of Kaslik (USEK). He has earned certificates in Leadership, Engineering, Real Estate, Quality

Assurance, Monitoring, and Evaluation. Currently, he is pursuing further training in trainers' studies related to Building Information Modeling and Entrepreneurship coaching for start-ups.

Dr. Nadia Shuayto is currently serving as an Assistant Professor of Marketing at the Dicke College of Business at Ohio Northern University. She teaches Principles of Marketing, Marketing Research, International Marketing, and other marketing courses.

During her time at the American University of Beirut, she founded and directed the Executive M.B.A. Program and served on the General Education Committee, Strategic Planning Committee, and AACSB task force, among others.

While at Lawrence Technological University, she served as the M.B.A. Program Chair, BSBA Program Director, and AACSB Coordinator. She served on the Faculty Senate, Faculty Council (President for one-year term), and strategic planning committee, and taught Global Marketing, Marketing Management, and International Business in the doctoral and M.B.A. programs.

She is a published award-winning author. She regularly attends and presents at regional, national, and international conferences. In her spare time, she enjoys gardening, traveling, and spending time with family and friends.

Filza Walters, M.B.A., FESD, FASHRAE is a Professor of Practice at Texas A&M University's College of Engineering, in the Department of Multidisciplinary Engineering, within the Architectural Engineering program. She develops courses, teaches, conducts applied research, and has published while serving on the department's Tenure & Promotion, Scholarship, and Strategic Planning committees.

Professor Walters is active in the Engineering Education Faculty Group (EEFG) and serves as an advisor for multiple student organizations. Externally, her service includes ASEE's Architectural Engineering Division, ASCE/AEI's Academic Council, and ASHRAE where she received both the Chapter and Regional Distinguished Service Awards.

Prior to joining TAMU, Walters was the founding director of a 5 year, integrated baccalaureate master's degree at Lawrence Technological

University in Southfield, Michigan, and served as Interim Director of Graduate Studies in the College of Architecture and Design.

Walters has over 18 years of industry experience as a consulting engineer, project manager, and owner's representative, for commercial, institutional, health care, industrial, and educational facilities. She holds a Master of Business Administration in International Business from LTU and a 5-Year Bachelor of Science in Architectural Engineering from Kansas State University with an emphasis on building mechanical systems. Professor Walters was elevated to Fellow of ASHRAE (American Society of Heating, Refrigerating and Air-Conditioning Engineers and the Engineering Society of Detroit). In 2019, Crain's Detroit Business recognized Walters as a Notable Woman in Education Leadership.

Prof. Georges Yahchouchi as president of the American University of the Middle East, Prof. Georges Yahchouchi is committed to excellence in higher education and expertise in academic leadership and has had a broad educational background and exposure to multicultural environments during his educational and professional career. He is Professor in Business Administration, and he received his Ph.D. in Business Administration from Montesquieu Bordeaux University, France, in 2004 and earned a Post-graduate Certificate in Learning and Teaching in Higher Education from the University of Chester, UK in 2013. He completed the Professional Education Certificate in Institute for Educational Management (IEM Class of 2019) offered by the Harvard Graduate School of Education. He is the author of several research papers in business, leadership, and educational management.

List of Figures

List of Tables

1

Introduction

Nehme Azoury

Technology improvements, cultural changes, and the changing demands of students and instructors are driving a dramatic revolution in the higher education scene. The Middle East and North Africa (MENA) area is the primary focus of this book's exploration of these shifts, which also offers a thorough examination of the present situation and potential developments in higher education.

As higher education systems continue undergoing rapid transformations driven by student realities. Changes on both individual and structural levels must be accompanied by extensive reflection. This book provides readers with a comprehensive overview of MENA's governmental/regulatory frameworks within public and private educational institutions. The many challenges faced by universities navigating today's landscape are also examined in depth so that educators may be best

N. Azoury (✉)
School of Business, Holy Spirit University of Kaslik (USEK), Jounieh, Lebanon
e-mail: nehmeazoury@usek.edu.lb

positioned to respond effectively. Hybrid learning modalities represent one such significant development that is currently coming into view—requiring vast shifts within prevailing organizational structures/regulations/decision-making processes. This book examines how institutions may remain relevant amid ongoing advancements and evolve through reevaluation continually.

Finally, this book offers insights into "the metaverse," a virtual realm where real-time communication could revolutionize Education as we know it. Through deep global research/analysis—including exploring governance issues—readers will gain valuable perspective regarding how this dynamic technology can shape teaching practices going forward. However, it is crucial to consider the potential and problems it brings in order to properly adopt and control this new strategy. The book offers a thorough examination of the governance frameworks and procedures required to enable the metaverse in education, giving educators and decision-makers the knowledge and skills, they need to effectively explore this fascinating new territory.

Also covered are inclusion and diversity in higher education. The necessity of developing an accepting and encouraging learning environment is becoming more widely acknowledged. The book addresses the difficulties institutions confront in fostering diversity and inclusion and evaluates the efficacy of tactics including affirmative action laws, diversity training courses, and focused recruiting campaigns.

The possibilities and issues that the current higher education system brings to both students and teachers are also covered in the book. It draws attention to how governance affects student experiences and gives suggestions for how educational leaders and legislators may successfully navigate the challenges of hybrid learning in this rapidly evolving context.

Anyone interested in the future of higher education should read this book, which is written for management and international business professionals, academics, stakeholders, deans, instructors, and administrators. It provides a thorough grasp of the situation of higher education today and its prospects for the future, with a special emphasis on the

MENA area. It seeks to provide readers with the skills they need to successfully traverse the intricacies of the higher education environment and contribute to its continued development and improvement via its thorough analysis and observations.

Part I

Current Status of the Higher Education System in the MENA Region

2

Overview of the Current Higher Education System in the Middle East and North Africa

Nehme Azoury and Antoine Habchi

Introduction

The higher education system evolved throughout history as a technical tool to answer society's economic needs and cultural challenges. This is why the higher education institutions (HEIs) shaped their management and governance system to answer the evolution of the market, mainly the technical complexity of the national and international production system. The industrial revolution in the eighteenth century, followed by the technological one in the twentieth century, complexified and diversified the production system in a way that impacted higher education to answer the market needs. Indeed, the information and its use became an essential target of the higher education system in order to provide

N. Azoury · A. Habchi (✉)
Faculty of Business, Holy Spirit University of Kaslik (USEK), Jounieh, Lebanon
e-mail: Antoinehabchi@usek.edu.lb

N. Azoury
e-mail: nehmeazoury@usek.edu.lb

N. Azoury and G. Yahchouchi (eds.), *Governance in Higher Education*,
https://doi.org/10.1007/978-3-031-40586-0_2

the skills and competencies needed in the society, to improve production institutions, and to keep the competitive edge. Globalization and internationalization of the market induced internationalization of the higher education institutions which increased the challenges that arose mainly with the COVID-19 pandemic and the need for technical tools to implement the distant learning. It is also worth mentioning the use of artificial intelligence which is playing a bigger role in the production process to decrease its cost and ensure its competitiveness.

The higher education institutions in the Middle East and North Africa (MENA) region and mainly in the Arab world are invited to revise not only their capacity to adapt to the change in the production system but also to the deep cultural and political transformations within their countries. The Arab Spring, the COVID-19 pandemic, and the need for a new economic era in the Middle East (based on a productive economy in different sectors) urged the need to remodel the higher education institutions in order to face the new challenges that are multifaced: ensure the productive economic process without neglecting the cultural evolution needed to integrate the openness to the international system. After the Arab Spring, aspirations of youth became a must to be considered in the political system, to avoid the societal clash between the traditions and the aim for a modern productive society. Higher education institutions are at the core of this evolution, affecting and affecting this long process of transformation; facing challenges is a key condition to grab opportunities and achieve successful adaptation to the increasing technical complexity of the market and its internationalization. This chapter will provide a review of the higher education system in the MENA region, its historical evolution, its challenges, and opportunities. This overview underlies the necessity of understanding the complexity of the higher education system through a deep analysis of governance and management of higher education institutions.

History of Higher Education in MENA

From the thirteenth to the fifteenth centuries, the number of universities worldwide increased steadily from 16 to 38 to 72. Religious institutions were the principal owners of these universities until the nineteenth century when the state began to supplant religious organizations (Bowman, 1962). In the emergent Soviet Union, and following the 1917 Russian Revolution, the communist party gained political influence over the higher education system (Heyneman, 1997).

The MENA area was a global pioneer in the establishment of higher education institutions. Middle Eastern institutions, such as Al-Karaouine University in Morocco, which has been awarding degrees since 859 A.D., are among the world's oldest. The Library of Alexandria was a learning hub in Egypt under the Ptolemaic dynasty that attracted intellectuals from all across the ancient world (Devarajan, 2016). It is worth noting that higher education in the Arab world is established on confessions and implemented through confessional teachings, such as Al Azhar University in Egypt, which was created in the tenth century. Egypt established higher education institutions influenced by the European model, particularly the French model, throughout the Ottoman Empire and during the reign of Mohammad Ali.

Since the late seventeenth century, Protestants and European missionaries have played an important role in the creation of HEIs throughout the MENA area. The growth of HEIs in the MENA area occurred in the second half of the twentieth century, mostly following World War II. Before this time, there were only 14 universities. By the end of the twentieth century, about 600 universities in both the commercial and public sectors had been created throughout the Arab world. During this time, Arab republics were gaining independence and leaving European colonialism. Promoting development, economic progress, and social welfare influenced the newly independent governments' political legitimacy toward their population (Cohen, 2004). In this sense, higher education was critical not just as a technical instrument for market adaptation and economic growth, but also as a weapon for centralizing government authority and generating social mobility (Cohen, 2004), extending the middle class and controlling its political ideology (Mazawi,

2005). The government guaranteed free university admission and jobs for university graduates while also regulating access to higher education through rigorous high school exams (Anderson, 1987; Teixeira, 2009). This rule of state control for higher education had two exceptions in the Middle East, for Lebanon and Palestine (Buckner, 2011).

In the case of Lebanon, the confessional struggle and political instability weakened the state's ability to construct a state higher education institution, and is currently still unable to do so. Hence, the reason behind the fragmentation of the private higher education system, according to religious belonging, flourished (El-Ghali, 2010). With the civil war, the expansion of private colleges accelerated, giving birth to a decentralized private higher education system (Bashshur, 2006, Nahas, 2009).

In the case of Palestine, since the beginning, higher education has been mostly private and decentralized, allowing each university to set its own admission rules independent of any central or national direction (Mazawi, 2005, Nakhle, 2006).

These two cases of operating a state-controlled higher education system in the Arab world demonstrate that decentralization is a critical indicator for growing enrollment in higher education institutions, as was the case in Palestine and Lebanon between 2005 and 2010 (Schofer & Meyer, 2005). (Fig. 2.1).

During the first decade of the twenty-first century, Arab governments were urged by the World Bank and the International Monetary Fund to liberalize their economies and include the public–private partnership, which influenced the whole education sector in these countries (Guazzone and Pioppi, 2009). The transition of these states from conventional economies to knowledge economies necessitated the need for higher-quality education in HEIs (Altbach & Peterson, 2007) to integrate their workforce into the global economy (Kabbani & Salloum, 2009) (World Band, 2008). This new trend resulted in a growth of the Arab world's higher education system (Fig. 2.2) due to a rise in enrollment generated by new higher education providers, including private colleges (Fig. 2.3) (Abdesallem, 2009; Buckner & Saba, 2010).

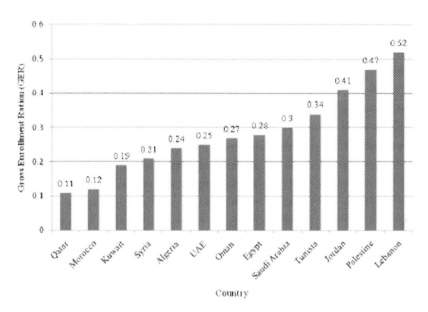

Fig. 2.1 Gross enrollment rations in Arab states (*Source* UNESCO Institute of Statistics 2005–2010; Syria data from Syrian Central Bureau of Statistics, 2010)

Overview of Higher Education in MENA

Globalization has influenced the worldwide higher education system, particularly in the Arab world, where higher education is responding to the need for economic growth to be more competitive in the global economy (Buckner, 2022, pp. 34–100). This new direction dedicates higher education to "the creation of the knowledge society" (Stromquist, 2002, p. xiii). Education policies were revised to meet the new goal of integrating skilled employees into the global economy (Kabbani & Salloum, 2011; Mazawi, 2007; World Bank, 2008). The new educational policies aim to facilitate and entice young people to colleges. As the number of scholars grows, more university providers emerge, and higher education quality improves (Altbach & Peterson, 2007). To strengthen the higher education sector, these new policies will require enough funding. Each MENA area country took a different path to adopt these policies:

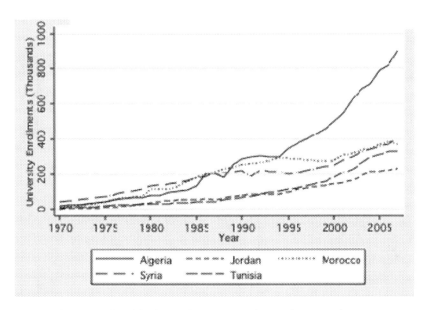

Fig. 2.2 The growth of higher education in the Arab states (*Source* UNESCO UIS, 1970–2010)

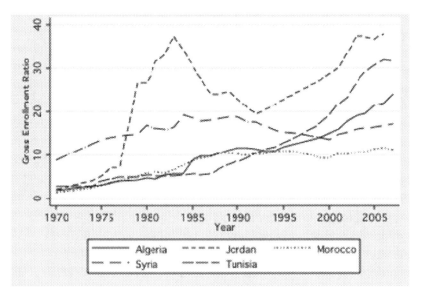

Fig. 2.3 Gross enrollment rates in higher education in the Arab states (*Source* UNESCO UIS, 1970–2010)

1. Egypt is the Arab country with the largest population (96.5 million in 2018). It served as a reform model throughout the twentieth century. Al Azhar University was nationalized in 1961, while Cairo University (established in 1908) and the American University in Cairo were also notable institutions during this period (founded by Protestant missionaries in 1919). New legislation 101/1992 was passed in 1992, permitting profit for private colleges, while amendments in 2006 allowed cost-sharing in the public higher education system (Fahim & Sami, 2011). Egypt's higher education system enrolls around 2.9 million students (Mohamed et al., 2019). The sector is governed by the Ministry of Higher Education, and the National Authority for Quality Assurance and Accreditation in Education (NAQAAE), formed in 2007, assures quality assurance. They announced a sustainable growth strategy in 2016, taking into account many factors such as improving Egyptian universities' worldwide rankings, attracting international students, lowering graduate student unemployment, and increasing public finances by 8% in 2019 (Mohamed et al., 2019). Since the 2011 revolution, security personnel have been deployed to universities to quell student protests.

2. Jordan is a monarchy with a population of 10 million people. Jordan University was created in 1962, and to enhance local capability, a public university was established in each governorate. The higher education system is being restructured in order to incorporate the information economy, and the sector is being opened up to private institutions. In 2018, 19 of the 29 institutions were private, enrolling around 27.5% of all scholars. The Council of Higher Education and the Ministry of Higher Education and Scientific Research handle the higher education sector's budget, admissions, and labor-force preparation. A body for accreditation and quality assurance was created in 2007. Two laws were passed in 2018 to promote competitiveness, research funding, and the provision of technical learning and institutional certification.

3. Lebanon is a country of 6.8 million people with a multi-confessional population. Religious missionaries established private universities (El-Ghali, 2010), while the Lebanese University was formed in 1951. The civil war that erupted in 1975 had an impact on the higher education

sector. The 1977 law's decree 122 permitted higher education institutions to construct outposts outside of their main campuses in order to enhance scholars' access to universities during the conflict (Bashshur, 2006). The Lebanese university had 47 branches by the end of the war, and according to the Taef constitution, prominent jobs within the public university were distributed to certain confessions (Waterbury, 2020), while there were nine private institutions. Because of decentralization and the high proportion of private colleges (Nahas, 2011), Lebanon has one of the highest gross enrollment rates (46%), enrolling 60% of scholars. The country's only public university comprises 17 faculties and 50 branches. The Ministry of Education and Higher Education oversees the higher education system, with the Council of Higher Education serving only as a consultative body. Recent improvements include the implementation of the French license—master—doctorate in 2005 (LMD). Legislation 285 was introduced in 2014 to connect private university certificates with those given in Europe. A statute was prepared to establish an independent quality certification body (Scholz & Maroun, 2015), but it was never passed, which is why private colleges seek international accreditation.

4. Prior to the civil conflict, Syria had a population of 21 million people. The Ottoman Medical School, which is now known as Damascus University, was the first university to be established in 1901. The Institution of Aleppo was founded in 1958 as a second university. Syria, being a communist state, followed the Soviet model, prioritizing technical and national education above higher education, which explains why just 15% of the university-age population is enrolled. Syria has steadily turned toward a market economy since the late 1990s. The expansion of the higher education system coincided with the liberalization of the economy and the implementation of reforms in 2001: the establishment in 2006 of a new public university, Al-Furat, and the launch of the open learning program, which doubled the number of students from 1997 to 2007, paving the way for the establishment of private universities. In 2010, 147.575 pupils were enrolled in the opening learning programs as a result of these revisions (Buckner, 2013). There were seven public universities in

2016 (Immerstein & Al-Shaikhly, 2016). Allowing private universities to function in 2001 resulted in the establishment of 15 private universities by 2010 (Waterbury, 2020), with a total of 21 by 2019. Despite a rise in the number of private institutions, just 33% of all scholars attended one in 2018. The Syrian higher education system is overseen and administered by the Ministry of Higher Education and the Council for Higher Education. Despite certain autonomy granted to colleges on a faculty level, curricular choices should be made on a national level. Prior to the civil conflict, Syria had a population of 21 million people. The Ottoman Medical School, which is now known as Damascus University, was the first university to be established in 1901. The Institution of Aleppo was founded in 1958 as a second university. Syria, being a communist state, followed the Soviet model, prioritizing technical and national education above higher education, which explains why just 15% of the university-age population is enrolled. Syria has steadily turned toward a market economy since the late 1990s. The expansion of the higher education system coincided with the liberalization of the economy and the implementation of reforms in 2001: the establishment in 2006 of a new public university, Al-Furat, and the launch of the opening learning program, which doubled the number of students from 1997 to 2007, paving the way for the establishment of private universities. In 2010, 147.575 pupils were enrolled in the opening learning programs as a result of these revisions (Buckner, 2013). There were seven public universities in 2016 (Immerstein & Al-Shaikhly, 2016). Allowing private universities to function in 2001 resulted in the establishment of 15 private universities by 2010 (Waterbury, 2020), with a total of 21 by 2019. Despite a rise in the number of private institutions, just 33% of all scholars attended one in 2018. The Syrian higher education system is overseen and administered by the Ministry of Higher Education and the Council for Higher Education. Despite certain autonomy granted to colleges on a faculty level, curricular choices should be made on a national level.

5. Morocco is a 37-million-individual state that was colonized by France between 1912 and 1956; its higher education system is similar to that of France. The public University of Mohammed V was established in 1957 and currently enrolls over one million students. There were five private universities, one public, five non-profit partnerships, a public university run by a private administration, and 150 private institutions providing specific programs in 2019. From 2008 to 2018, the proportion of the appropriate age cohort enrolling in universities climbed from 13% to 36%. The process of obtaining permission to create private institutions began officially in 2005 and practically in 2011. Since the implementation of accrediting standards with Decree 3061 in 2012, the number of scholars at private institutions has grown but remains below 7.5% of all scholars. The Ministry of National Education oversees the higher education system, which has been adapting the LMD system since 2004, matching its credentials with European ones, and will transition from the license degree used in Europe to the bachelor's degree used in North America in 2020.

6. Tunisia has one of the highest human development metrics in the area. From the first Islamic religious institutions formed in 737 to the greatest theological institution in 1956. Tunisia's higher education system is comparable to that of France. The École Normale Supérieure was formed in 1956 and was absorbed into Tunis's public university in 1960 (Fryer & Jules, 2013). There are 203 public faculties offering specialty programs in addition to the 13 public universities. Then, in the early 1990s, 24 technological studies institutes were established to strengthen the relationship between education and the job market. Despite the legislative authority to establish private institutions since 2000, and despite the rise in the number of these institutions (76 private institutions in 2016), the percentage of scholars enrolled in private institutions is approximately 11.5%. The Tunisian higher education system is governed by the Ministry of Higher Education and Scientific Research. Since 2008, changes have given universities significant autonomy in governance, and in 2015, an effort for the construction of an education plan to execute national evaluation and the alignment of quality services to worldwide

standards was initiated. The Arab Gulf States have many similarities, including a history of British domination, petrodollar riches, and a monarchical political structure. National residents are considered minorities in Qatar and the United Arab Emirates (UAE), and they have advantages over foreign employees in the job market. Governments are spending extensively on education because they want to nationalize their labor force and train it to be highly skilled (Ridge, 2014), while their economy shifts toward high-skilled service and technology. They are also receptive to outside knowledge and have asked international institutions to establish branch campuses as part of their national development ambitions. The emphasis here is on Qatar, the United Arab Emirates (UAE), and the Kingdom of Saudi Arabia (KSA) and their high-profile education programs.

7. Qatar is a small and wealthy nation. It has one of the highest incomes per capita in the world (GDP per capita of USD 65,600). It gained its independence in 1971. In 1973, the College of Education was founded. It is the first public university aiming to train teachers. In 1977 the College became Qatar University and overall, enrollments highly increased (20,000 students).

   The Ministry for Education and Higher Education and the Supreme Education Council regulate the Higher Education System in Qatar. They launched 2018 the National Development Strategy, aiming to increase enrollments, specifically of male students, and the diversification of higher education by attracting branches of foreign universities to operate in Qatar.

   The United Arab Emirates is a federal state made up of seven emirates, each with its ruler. Since 1971, the UAE has developed around one hundred universities and attracted major institutions such as Sorbonne and New York University. The emphasis is on vocational training to implement the knowledge economy and "Emiratize" the workforce (Kirk & Napier, 2009).

   The UAE has three federal universities: United Arab Emirates University, founded in 1976, which offers various programs; The Higher College of Technology, founded in 1988, which provides vocational education and has 17 branches throughout the country; and Zayed University, founded in 1998, which used to serve only female students but now serves both genders and international students.

Each emirate has its own private university rules, and the UAE has free trade zones that host several private institutions. The Ministry of Higher Education and Scientific Research licenses and accredits higher education institutions and programs in the country, while the Commission for Academic Accreditation accredits all degree programs offered by private universities located outside of free trade zones. As of 2018, the Certification Authority Authorization had recognized over 950 programs in the UAE (CAA).

The Kingdom of Saudi Arabia was a poor kingdom with only 12 schools and 700 students. This was the situation before the discovery of oil in 1938. The founding of the Ministry of Education in 1954 resulted in the development of 365 schools that educate 42,000 pupils (Simmons et al., 1994). Despite this, education was solely available to boys until the introduction of a school for girls in 1960 (Al-Rawaf & Simmons, 1991).

Seven universities have been established in the last 20 years, leading to the foundation of the Ministry of Higher Education. Its duties led to the development of new institutions and collaboration with other government ministries (Alamri, 2011). KSA's economy benefited from having the world's biggest subsurface oil resource.

As a result, the budget of the Ministry of Higher Education expanded in tandem with the rise in oil prices, resulting in the development of the King Abdullah Scholarship Program.

As a result of this initiative, KSA could send around 70,000 students to study abroad, placing the country fourth in the world in terms of students desiring to learn abroad.

The Ministry of Higher Education also supported private universities in Saudi Arabia. The KSA education system was altered instantly at all levels as a result of the KSA Vision 2030. In comparison with other GCC nations, the student population is greater.

This gives a viable opportunity to invest in the education industry.

In the future, this big student population will demand higher education opportunities (Saudi Arabia Education Report, 2021).

Regardless of the fact that many deans of universities in Saudi Arabia were educated abroad, many challenges exist in the country's higher education system, including the centralization of the Ministry of Higher Education and the discrimination of expatriate faculty in terms of salaries and incentives in comparison to their Saudi colleagues.

Some critical components are missing, such as online education and research money, not to mention the limiting of academic freedom owing to political considerations (Saudi Arabia Education Report, 2021).

KSA has 60 universities, the bulk of which are public.

Riyadh, Jeddah, Buraydah, and Madinah have the most colleges and universities, with Riyadh having the most private universities. The number of students enrolled in higher education has climbed in recent years but has declined from its peak in 2017.

To develop education and motivate scholars in various disciplines, scientific conferences, research seminars, journals, and professional organizations should be secured and enhanced. The education system must move from a teacher-centered to a student-centered approach, employing a variety of methods to engage pupils. Discrepancy in the curriculum needs to be addressed, as it wastes resources including time, and affects the level and objectives of the programs (Journal of Higher Education, 2011).

Higher Education System and Governance in MENA

Governance is characterized by the ability of the public and private sectors to work together to improve the well-being of individuals in a decided society by seeking out the best chances to face and overcome social difficulties. In our case, it includes the role of all stakeholders within the university, in their interaction to take decisions needed to solve struggles or to overcome challenges. It defines the struggle over power, the designing of structure in HEIs, as much as the means needed to ensure accountability (Corcoran, 2004).

There are two types of governance related to HEIs:

- Internal governance defines processes, procedures, and policies within the institution. Those elements reflect and determine the authority relations and the distribution of power (Rowlands, 2013).
- External governance is related to national law, quality assurance, and rules.

The dynamic between internal and external governance in educational institutions defines higher education governance (Boer & File, 2009). The global context has given an important meaning to the interaction between internal and external governance because factors in the context, such as government decisions related to higher education systems, or, as has been the case in recent decades, the orientation of market forces inviting universities to be part of the knowledge economy, can have a significant impact on internal governance (Neave, 2003). This describes higher education governance as a reaction to government pressure and socioeconomic developments in the management of HEIs.

In the MENA region, governance of higher education institutions seems an essential need due to the complexity of the context: conflicts and wars in some countries, and pluralism on different levels: culture, religion, interests, and political system. Following the Arab Spring, a gap was shown between conventional society and young concerns, as well as the necessity to reform society to transition from consumer societies to productive ones, mostly through adaptation and alignment with the global market. Faced with these issues, higher education becomes more aware of its position as a source for forming future leaders and drawing the society's future well-being (Altman, 1996). For all of these reasons, the MENA area needs to enhance and change its higher education governance more than ever before to tackle problems and seek possibilities. This is the primary approach for colleges to increase their value and provide the appropriate context (Al-Haddad & Yassin, 2018).

The major developments in the global market caused changes in communities and educational systems, placing pressure on the implementation of good governance. Among these modifications are the following:

– The growing population and aspirations of the young are driving up demand for higher education as a means of social mobilization.
– Educational evolution globally that results in a continuous offer of new educational programs.
– The necessity to improve scientific research to better equip universities to adapt to a knowledge economy (Hénard and Ahrashaw, 2007; Mitterle, 2008).
– The adoption of a world ranking among higher education institutions. Governance is an essential criterion.

These modifications necessitate the introduction of governance at universities, as well as adherence to three principles: transparency, participation, and accountability (Al-Haddad & Yasin, 2018).

Transparency refers to the clarity and simplicity with which information flows through the institution, allowing students to connect easily with their leaders and avoid leaving unresolved problems, giving up a huge area for participation, thinking, and management. Participation is about allowing students to be a part of policy-making and decision-making within the university. As a stakeholder, students should be involved in the functioning and reforming of the system which turns out to be an indicator of governance.

Accountability allows us to monitor the work so the institution can reach its objectives. It reflects the democratic nature of the institution by the fact that all stakeholders are accountable for their tasks and respect the rules and regulations of the university. It enhances democratic leadership and increases external trust.

The implementation of these principles within the university affects all the dimensions of the institution, creating a chain effect where every area can affect the rest (Muasher, 2016; Saleem, 2014):

- Governance should be conducted by company culture, with a defined philosophy in place (Nufil, 1990).
- Posting credible data and information about the university, allowing the public easy access to university functioning.
- Reducing uncertainty through transparency and clarity.
- The ability to attract local or international investments to secure the financial resources required to achieve the university plan.
- Implementing equity and equality to achieve justice and create equal opportunities and reduce the possibility of corruption and favoritism.
- Managing the university efficiently and effectively. It helps to use the resources the right way to implement an action plan and reach goals.
- Improving the efficiency of the university through quality assurance, which gives the scholars a highly competitive advantage in the market.

Different models are used to practice good governance in a higher education institution (Saleem, 2014):

- The academic model assures that a university has to deal with academic material. This model enhances the power of an academic board, capable of decision-making affecting the whole institution (Aal Abbas, 2009).
- The trustee model empowers members of the board of trustees who are not necessarily involved in the university. They act as guardians and prevent any conflicts of interest (Al-Farra, 2013).
- The stakeholder model implicates all the stakeholders in the management of the university such as students and alumni, the local community, supporting firms in the market, employers, and faculty members.

Implementing any model of governance should be preceded by ensuring several elements needed for good governance:

- Clear institutional structure with its workflow, laws, regulations, bodies of management, and administrative leadership.
- Participative management involving among others local communities, students, and employers.

- Accountability, ensuring that all staff are assuming their responsibilities.
- Allowing the governance board to supervise all the committees.
- Implementation of local, regional, and international quality assurance.

Once these standards are respected, governance application can follow a process of five stages:

- **Stage 1:** democratizing the governance culture within the university and with the external environment.
- **Stage 2:** implementing governance through a strengthened structure capable of adapting to the changes, maintaining an equilibrium between the drive to change (the dynamic dimension) and the protection of the institutional identity (the static dimension). During this stage, a complex process is implemented involving all the bodies of the university without neglecting the ethical and moral foundations.
- **Stage 3:** an action plan should be developed determining the goals, tasks, and duties of governance.
- **Stage 4:** monitoring the implementation step by step. This stage reflects the goodwill or the resistance of the stakeholders to the change.
- **Stage 5:** developing the governance through controlling and adjusting all the previous steps, through an evaluation consolidating the good implementation and looking for remedies where difficulties emerge.

Despite the reforms applied in different countries of the MENA region, the quality of higher education remains one of the lowest in the world. None of the MENA universities are in the top 200, while only two are ranked within the top 500 (Devarajan, 2016). Different problems affect the MENA higher education system (Al-Rashdan, 2009):

- Lack of practical educational policy as a result of a lack of philosophy and vision. It has a detrimental impact on higher education because it prevents the development of a defined strategy (Nufil, 1990).
- The absence of participative management in the public sector. Personnel in charge of public colleges are government officials whose ultimate goal is to serve and please the political system, which is

their employer. As a result, there are no criteria or responsibilities for scientific and educational activities (Abdullah, 2003).

- MENA universities have little influence over their surroundings. It is more regulated by the government, as seen by police presence in Egyptian universities to control students and prevent them from engaging in the protest movement.
- The lack of interaction among MENA institutions and their preference to communicate with international universities to address difficulties. Some of the challenges are cultural in nature, and collaboration among local and regional colleges may be the quickest approach to discovering a solution.
- Adoption of traditional forms of education creates a handicap because students won't be able to discover their innovative capacity nor develop their analytical skills (Barq'an & Al-Qurashi, 2012). By extension, students won't face social problems through an analytical approach (Al-Yusuf, 2000), which explains, the tendency of youth in the MENA societies to be reactional and to shift toward extremism.
- Absence of unified programs that aid in tailoring programs capable of integrating global economic change.
- Frameworks are lacking at several legal, technological, scholarly, and institutional levels. This is why solutions to issues are frequently improvised.
- Discontinuity between school education and university curriculum since university material is inadequately related to the high school program. As a result, during their first year of university, students are entirely exposed to fresh knowledge that is unrelated to what they studied in high school.
- The use of traditional methods to manage the HEIs. These methods reduce the effectiveness and efficiency of these institutions and induce low output caused by poor quality management (Barq'an & Al-Qurashi, 2012).

The implementation of good governance is a crucial part to solve the previously mentioned problems and to allow HEIs to deal with the complexity of the environment. Good governance enables HEIs in the MENA to face challenges and create opportunities.

Challenges and Opportunities of Higher Education Institutions

- Independent of the global socio-political context, which is the main challenge for reforms and improvement in the MENA, there are several challenges in urgent need of resolution through the main opportunity of implementing reforms, because societies in the MENA are experiencing ongoing crises on various levels. Aiming for a stronger higher education system necessitates a reform strategy that can overcome the following challenges:
- Governance is a major problem since it offers autonomy and promotes transformation at both the national and institutional levels (Waterbury, 2019). While some analysts estimated that the Arab uprising had a positive impact on the independence of higher education institutions (Hamdan, 2011), it also resulted in the reassertion of authoritarian control and the destruction of educational infrastructure in some countries, and in Turkey after the 2016 coup, there was a kind of "sweeping purge" of academic cadres.
- The mismatch between education and the labor market is a significant impediment to the MENA higher education system. It is mostly due to inadequate training in the information economy. In the MENA region, general unemployment is approximately 10%, but young unemployment is around 25% on average (ADHR, 2016). Because the product of the school system is unsuitable for the demands of the private sector, educated people who are unable to find work turn to the gray economy of the informal sector, where they are underpaid. This mismatch increases the unemployment of educated young, resulting in brain drain and the hunt for a competent job overseas (Hanafi & Arvanitis, 2016). This mismatch leaves a big portion of the kids despondent and ready to criticize the system (Elbadawi & Makdisi, 2017). According to some studies, the low return on education is the primary reason or cause for political protests, which is what sparked the Arab upheavals (Campante & Chor, 2012). To overcome the problems, some governments, such as the Kingdom of Saudi Arabia, develop a vision. KSA adopted Vision 2030, with the goal of privatization, strengthening the private sector, reforming education,

connecting it to the labor market, and lowering general unemployment. This is their road to a post-petroleum economy in KSA (QS World News, 2017).

- Quality Assurance (QA) entails developing a set of standards to assure the quality of higher education services. The goal of QA is to promote autonomy and quality in higher education through implementing standards, accreditation, KPIs, strategic planning, and benchmarking (Faek, 2017; Hajji, 2008). The Arab Organization for Quality Assurance in Education (ARQA) was established in 2007. By 2012, around 14 MENA nations were involved in quality assurance, however strategic planning and KPIs remain unpopular in MENA HEIs today, making meaningful change difficult to achieve.

- R&D capability is still undervalued in the Middle East and North Africa (MENA). There are excellent scientists and researchers outside their nations, yet institutions in their home countries are resistant to unlocking scientific research and innovation. The private sector contributes roughly 10% to R&D, with the remainder provided by the government and public universities.

Conclusion

The Higher Education System in the MENA is a sub-system, directly related to the system in which it functions. By system, we mean the societies of the different countries in which are implemented the HRIs. As much as these HESs can affect their environment, they are also affected by this environment as well as the social complexity, the political system, the local laws, and the local culture. HEIs are continuously dealing with crises: modernism versus fundamentalism, socioeconomic crisis, war, the Arab uprising, etc. Does this context explain the deficit in the higher education system output? In 2019, 91% of Arab researchers stated a desire to leave their nations, despite their individual governments requiring their expertise to establish "knowledge economies" and connect with the global market.

The challenges are many, producing a barrier that prevents higher education institutions from evolving. The lack of strong governance prevents the formation of a relationship between education and the labor market. The mismatch between education and the labor market raises the rate of unemployment among young graduates, leaving many despondent and looking for chances outside of their nations. The absence of funds for research and development contributes to brain drain since highly skilled individuals seek better career prospects abroad.

Quality assurance is still inadequately implemented in the MENA HES, even though it is required to fulfill the norms and needs of the private sector. 52% of Arab researchers are unable to subscribe to academic journals, 47% lack adequate internet access, and more than 71% are unable to attend global conferences for a variety of reasons, including the inability to obtain a visa, insufficient financial means, and so on, limiting their capacity to build communication and enhance partnerships and cooperation.

The MENA higher education system is grappling with these issues, but the global education system has incorporated information technology and is anticipating the use of artificial intelligence, constantly eager to match and link to the growing global economy. Government involvement in the higher education system is beneficial on one hand but inhibits evolution on the other, primarily because an excess of control hinders institutions' autonomy, productivity, and ability to change. The biggest issue in revamping the higher education system is the political establishment's desire to complete such a task. Indeed, the political authorities are eager to overcome the socioeconomic crisis, reform the higher education system, and enable it to link education services to the labor market; however, these HES reforms will expose the system to the global world, to greater independence, which the same political authorities regard as a threat. It's becoming a terrible loop.

References

Aal Abbas, M. (2009). *Hawkamat al-jamaat: Diraasah Tahleeliya'* [Governance of universities: An analytical study]. A paper presented at the Symposium on Governance of Corporates and the Current Practices and Future Horizons. Abha King Khaled University, KSA.

Abdesallem, T. (2009). *Financing higher education in Tunisia.* Economic Research Forum.

Abdullah, M. (2003). Azmat al-ta'lim al-'ali fi al-watan al-'arabi wal-tahaddiyat al-mu'asira – waqi' wa-bada'il [Higher education crisis in the Arab nation and contemporary challenges—Reality and alternatives]. *Shu'un Arabia* (113), 129.

Ahrashaw, A.-G. (2007). Al-siyasa al-ta'limiya wa-khutat al-tanmiya al-'arabia – hasila wa afaq [Educational policy and Arab development plans—results and prospects]. *Shu'un Aarabiya, 107,* 141.

Alamri, M. (2011). Higher education in Saudi Arabia. *Journal of Higher Education Theory and Practice, 11*(4), 88–91.

Al-Farra, M. (2013). Al hawkama fi mu'assasat al-ta'leem al'ali fi filisteen – hala dirasiya li kulliyat al'ulum al-iqtisadiya fi Ghaza [Governance in higher education institutions in Palestine—A case study of the administration and economics faculties in Gaza]. In *Zaytounah University, the third Arab international conference for quality of higher education.* Al- Zaytoonah University.

Al-Haddad, S., & Yasin, A. (2018). Higher education governance in the Arab world, exploring the challenges of the education and social realities. In *Governance reform in higher education institutions in the Arab world: An institutional initiative* (Chapter 4, pp. 83–104). Springer.

Al-Rashdan, A.-F. (2009). *Al- ta'leem al-'ali fi al'alam al'arabi: aamaal wa tahadiyat* [Higher education in the Arab world: Hopes and challenges] (pp. 77–90). Department of Political Science. Mu'tah University, Jordan.

Al-Rawaf, H., & Simmons, C. (1991). The education of women in Saudi Arabia. *Comparative Education, 77,* 187–295.

Altbach, P. G., & Peterson, P. M. (2007). *Higher education in the new century: Global challenges and innovative ideas* (Vol. 10). Sense Publishers.

Altman, I. (1996). Higher education and the psychology in the millennium. *American Psychologist, 51*(4), 371.

Al-Yusuf, A. (2000). 'ilaaqat al-tarbiya bil-mujtama' wa-tahdid malamihha al-naw'iya [Education's relationship with society and determining its quantitative features]. *Alim Al-Fikr, 1,* 18–23.

Anderson, L. (1987). The state in the Middle East and North Africa. *Comparative Politics, 20,* 1–18.

Arab Human Development Repot (ADHR). (2016). *Youth and the prospects for human development in a changing reality.* UNDP. http://www.arabsatstes.undp.org/content/dam/rbas/report/ADHR%20Reports/ADHR%202016/ADHR%20Final%202016/ADHR2016En.pdf

Barq'an, A., & Al-Qurashi, A. (2012). *Hawkamat al-jaami'aat wa dawriha fi muwaajahat altahadiyat* [Governance of universities and its role in facing the challenges]. Paper presented at the International conference of globalization of administration in the globalization era. Al-Jinan University, Lebanon.

Bashshur, M. (2006). Standard of quality of higher education in Lebanon. In M. Bashshur, Y. Courbage, & B. Labaki (Eds.), *L'enseignement supérieur dans le monde arabe: une question de niveau?* [Higher education in the Arab world: a question of level?]. Institution Français du Proche-Orient (French Institute of the Near-East).

Boer, H., & File, J. (2009). *Higher education governance reforms across Europe.* Center for Higher Education Policy Studies (CHEPS).

Bowman, H. J. (1962). The land grant colleges and universities in human resource development. *Journal of Economic History, 22*(04), 523–546.

Buckner, E. (2011). The role of higher education in the Arab state and society: Historical legacies and recent reform patterns. *Comparative & International Higher Education., 3*(1), 21–26.

Buckner, E. (2013). The seeds of discontent: Examining youth perceptions of higher education in Syria. *Comparative Education, 49*(4), 440–463. https://doi.org/10.1080/03050068.2013.765643

Buckner, E. (2022). *Degrees of dignity: Arab higher education in the global era.* University of Toronto Press.

Buckner, E., & Saba, K. (2010). Syria's next generation: Youth unemployment, education, and exclusion. *Education, Business and Society: Contemporary Middle Eastern Issues, 3,* 86–98.

Campante, F., & Chor, D. (2012, Spring). Why was the Arab world poised for revolution? Schooling, economic opportunities, and the Arab Spring. *Journal of Economic Perspectives, 26*(2), 167–188. https://ink.library.smu.edu.sg/cgi/viewcontent.cgi?article=2428&context=soe_research

Cohen, S. (2004). *Searching for a global middle class in Morocco.* Duke University Press.

Corcoran, S. (2004). Duty, discretion and conflict: University governance and the legal obligations of university boards. *Australian Universities Review, 46*(2), 30.

Devarajan, S. (2016). https://blogs.worldbank.org/arabvoices/paradox-higher-education-mena. An English version of a keynote speech given at the recent MENA conference on "Paradigm Shifts in Tertiary Education" in Algiers on May 30–June 2.

Elbadawi, I., & Makdisi, S. (Eds.). (2017). *Democratic transitions in the Arab world*. Cambridge University Press. https://www.cambridge.org/core/books/democratic-transitions-in-the-arab-world/ABD52D28BF5F18952794C7223FB73590

El-Ghali, H. (2010). Higher education and youth unemployment in Lebanon. *Comparative and International Higher Education, 2*(1), 12–13.

Faek, R. (2017, September 12). A regional survey: How Arab countries regulate quality in higher education. *Al Fanar Media*. https://www.al-fanarmedia.org/2017/09/higher-ed-survey-when-quality-assurance-isnt-reassuring/

Fahim, Y., & Sami, N. (2011). Adequacy, efficiency and equity of higher education financing: The case of Egypt. *Prospects, 41*(1), 47–67. https://doi.org/10.1007/s11125-011-9182-x

Fryer, L. G., & Jules, T. D. (2013). Policy spaces and educational development in the Islamic Maghreb region: Higher education in Tunisia. *International Perspectives on Education and Society, 21*, 401–425. https://doi.org/10.1108/S1479-3679(2013)0000021017

Guazzone, L., & Pioppi, D. (2009). *The Arab state and neo-liberal globalization: The restructuring of state power in the Middle East*. Ithaca Press.

Hajji, S. (2008). Management universitaire à l'épreuve de la réforme. *Prospectives Universitaires, 1*(2008), 127–136.

Hamdan, S. (2011, November 6). Arab spring spawns interest in improving quality of higher education. *New York Times*. https://www.nytimes.com/2011/11/07/world/middleeast/arab-spring-spawns-interest-in-improving-quality-of-higher-educatin.html

Hanafi, S., & Arvanitis, R. (2016). *Knowledge production in the Arab world: The impossible promise* (p. 145). Routledge. https://www.google.com/url?sa=t&rct=j&q=&esrc=s&source=web&cd=2&ved=2ahUKEwi01K3nvJbdAhXsxoUKHUiyA8YQFjABegQICRAC&url=meta-journal.net%2Farticle%2Fdownload%2F7341%2F7563%2F&usg=AOvVaw1YYzaLNZpClpAeE43CKiHu

Hénard, F., & Mitterle, A. (2008). *Governance and quality in higher education* (Paper Series 9). The World Bank.

Heyneman. (1997). Education and social stability in Russia: An essay. *Compare, 27*(1).

Immerstein, S., & Al-Shaikhly, S. (2016, April 4). Education in Syria. *World Education News & Reviews*. https://wenr.wes.org/

Kabbani, N., & Salloum, S. (2009). Financing higher education in Syria. In *Regional conference on financing higher education in Arab countries*. Economic Research Forum (ERF).

Kabbani, N., & Salloum, S. (2011). Implications of financing higher education for access and equity: The case of Syria. *Prospects, 41*(1), 97–113. https://doi.org/10.1007/s11125-011-9178-6

Kirk, D., & Napier, D. (2009). The transformation of higher education in the United Arab Emirates: Issues, implications, and intercultural dimensions. In J. Zajda, H. Daun, & L. Saha (Eds.), *Nation-building, identity and citizenship education: Cross-cultural perspectives* (pp. 131–142). Springer.

Mazawi, A. E. (2007). "Knowledge society" or work as "spectacle"? Education for work and the prospects of social transformation in Arab societies. In L. Farrell & T. Fenwick (Eds.), *World Yearbook of Education 2007* (pp. 269–285). Routledge.

Mazawi, A. E. (2005). Contrasting perspectives on higher education in the Arab states. In J. Smart (Ed.), *Higher education: Handbook of theory and researches* (Vol. XX, pp. 133–189). Springer.

Mohamed, R., Skinner, M., & Trines, S. (2019). Education in Egypt. *World Education News and Reviews*. https://wenr.wes.org

Muasher, M. (2016). *Tahseen al-haakimiya fi al-alam al-arabi* [Improving governance in the Arab world]. The second Arab awakening and the battle for pluralism.

Nahas, C. (2011). Financing and political economy of higher education: The case of Lebanon. *Prospects, 41*(1), 69–95. https://doi.org/10.1007/s11125-011-9183-9

Nahas, C. (2009). *Financing higher education in Lebanon*. ERF.

Nakhle, K. (2006). Palestinian tertiary educational system: Overview, challenges and possible responses. In M. Bashshur, Y. Courbage, & B. Labaki (Eds.), *L'enseignement supérieur dans le monde arabe: une question de niveau?* [Higher education in the Arab world: A question of level?]. Institution Français du Proche-Orient (French Institute of the Near-East).

Neave, G. (2003). The Bologna declaration: Some of the historic dilemmas posed by the reconstruction of the community in Europe's systems of higher education. *Educational Policy, 17*(1), 141–164.

Nufil, M. N. (1990). Ta'ammulat fi falsafat al-ta'lim al-jami'I al-'arabi [Reflections on Arab university education philosophy]. *Majallat al-tarbiya al-jadida, 151,* 7.

QS World News. (2017). https://www.topuniversities.com/subject-rankings/2017

Ridge, N. (2014). *Education and the reverse gender divide in the Gulf States: Embracing the global, ignoring the local.* Teachers College Press.

Rowlands, J. (2013). Academic Board: Less intellectual and more academic capital in higher education governance? *Studies in Higher Education, 38*(9), 1274–1289.

Saleem, M. (2014). Intishar thaqafat al-hakimia yusa'id ala ta'zeez ada' al-jaami'aat [*The spread of governance culture helps to promote the performance of universities*]. The University of Jordan.

Saudi Arabia Education Report. (2021). *Opportunities in the sector.* Knight Frank.

Schofer, E., & Meyer, J. (2005). The worldwide expansion of the higher education in the twentieth century. *American Sociological Review, 70,* 898–920.

Scholz, C., & Maroun, M. (2015). The Bologna process and higher education reform in the eastern and southern Mediterranean: The case of Israel, Egypt and Lebanon. In *IEMed Mediterranean Yearbook 2015* (pp. 297–302). European Institute of the Mediterranean.

Shanta, D. (2016, June). *The paradox of higher education in MENA.* www.alfanarmedia.org

Simmons, C., Simmons, C., & Allah, M. H. (1994). English, Israeli-Arab and Saudi Arabian adolescent values. *Educational Studies, 20*(1), 69–86. https://doi.org/10.1080/0305569940200106

Stromquist, N. P. (2002). *Education in a globalized world: The connectivity of economic power, technology, and knowledge.* Rowman & Littlefield.

Teixeira, P. (2009). Mass higher education and private institute. In *Higher education to 2030: Globalization* (Vol. 2, pp. 231–258). Center for Educational Research and Innovation, OECD.

Waterbury, J. (2019). Chapter 6: Reform of higher education in the Arab world. In *Major challenges facing higher education in the Arab world: Quality assurance and relevance* (pp. 133–166). Springer.

Waterbury, J. (2020). *Missions impossible: Higher education policymaking in the Arab world.* American University in Cairo Press.

World Bank. (2008). *The road not traveled: Education reform in the Middle East and North Africa.* World Bank.

3

Inclusion and Diversity

Georges Yahchouchi and Sareh Rotabi

Introduction

In the recent past, there have been numerous research papers discussing the difficulties that underrepresented groups tend to face, while also focusing on the importance of promoting equality, diversity, and inclusion (EDI) within universities. Yet, in spite of various initiatives, many research-based universities still have difficulty to build comprehensive processes that deliver equal opportunities to individuals from diverse backgrounds. Improving equality, diversity, and inclusion in academia provides several benefits. It fosters a sense of belonging and improves dedication and proficiency. Furthermore, it also allows academic institutions to sustain their continuing importance in this dynamic world. Through ensuring equal access for individuals with different talent and

G. Yahchouchi (✉) · S. Rotabi
American University of the Middle East (AUM), Egaila, Kuwait
e-mail: Georges.yahchouchi@aum.edu.kw

S. Rotabi
e-mail: Sareh-rotabi@aum.edu.kw

N. Azoury and G. Yahchouchi (eds.), *Governance in Higher Education*, https://doi.org/10.1007/978-3-031-40586-0_3

capabilities, academic institutions are capable of supporting social unity, which contributes to enhancing their potential for innovative research and teaching. Considering inclusive research and innovation programs into the curriculum attracts a wider range of students and scholars. This inclusive approach to EDI empowers underrepresented groups, improves the success of the academic institutions, and strengthens the academic innovativeness as a whole. This also guarantees the long-term relevance and sustainability of research-based academic institutions. In order to attain EDI, it is vital for the leaders and managers at the university to become fully aware of the difficulties encountered by underrepresented groups which impact both these groups as well as the academic community at a broader perspective. Hence, identifying any biases in the education system is important for a cultural transformation at an institutional level (LERU, 2019).

As per UNESCO (2019b), inclusion is a transformative process that targets having an equal access to quality learning for individuals at any ages, valuing diversity and reducing discrimination in education. This definition focuses on the significance of building inclusive environments in various educational settings, where diversity is seen as an enriching factor. Inclusion and equity in education are essential in achieving Sustainable Development Goal 4 (Quality Education) that targets ensuring an inclusive and equitable quality education for all. As the world approaches the Sustainable Development 2030 agenda, there is a strong demand for learning, which is evident in the existing inequalities in education sector at a global level. Around two hundred sixty million children who are anticipated to be at the school are currently not enrolled (UNESCO Institute for Statistics (UIS), 2019a). Several complications namely physical disabilities, gender inequalities, and economic circumstances contribute to this concern. According to the 2019 Human Development Report, enhancement of technology enables creating a societal divide similar to the one caused by the Industrial Revolution (UNDP, 2019). It is widely agreed upon that a serious action is needed to decrease the obstacles toward inclusion and equity, while embracing transformative lifelong learning pathways driven by digital innovations.

The emergence of the COVID-19 pandemic in late 2019 has stressed the significance of cultivating a diverse workforce capable of working effectively in different circumstances. This diversity is instrumental in enriching the learning experiences of the students, especially given the unforeseen shift to fully online education as well as the implementation of distance learning approaches. In general, when discussing diversity and inclusion in the Higher Education sector, the main focus is usually on the diversity of the students with regard to the demographics, backgrounds, ethnicities, and aptitudes. However, there exists a wider perception referred to as "campus diversity," which includes all internal stakeholders in the campus community. This includes faculty members, administrative and technical personnel, students, along with university leadership. Each individual on campus plays a vital role in the overall enhancement of campus diversity (Yahchouchi, 2022).

This chapter will focus on the significance of inclusion and diversity in higher education. We will examine the existing state of efforts to promote diversity and inclusion in academic institutions and evaluate the effectiveness of strategies such as affirmative action policies, diversity training programs, and targeted recruitment efforts. We will also explore the challenges faced by institutions in fostering diversity and inclusion. Furthermore, we will investigate the role of technology and digital tools in supporting the goals of inclusion and diversity in education. By undertaking this, we aim to contribute to the ongoing discussion on creating diversity and inclusion in higher education.

Importance of Inclusion and Diversity in Higher Education

The terms equality, equity, diversity, and inclusion are often used reciprocally, even though they have different meanings. Equality is associated with the notion that each person should have the same privileges and be treated equally without discrimination. Equity goes beyond equality by addressing relative disadvantages and providing support based on individual needs. Equity also recognizes that structural obstacles can hinder participation, making individualized support necessary when those obstacles cannot be excluded. On the other hand, Diversity is a multidimensional notion influenced by cultural framework and awareness of variances. Inclusion commonly refers to social inclusion, aiming to reach students that reflect the diversity of culture, as a whole (Claeys-Kulik et al., 2019). There are numerous discussions and studies addressing the significance of inclusion and diversity in higher education. According to UNESCO, an educational environment that is inclusive, positively contributes in the achievement of all students, when the excluded ones are also considered (UNESCO, 2009a, 2009b, as cited in Varga et al., 2021). Moreover, diversity among students includes personal characteristics, inherited advantages or disadvantages, socioeconomic backgrounds, and their impact on the cultural environment (Dezső, 2015, as cited in Varga et al., 2021). These characteristics are impacted by the environment, both socially and culturally. Moreover, society's norms that may either emphasize or ignore certain diversity attributes, lead to advantageous or disadvantageous conditions (Varga et al., 2021).

Current researchers highlight the significance of accepting the needs to build an environment that validates equity. Accomplishing an inclusive environment and effectively addressing diversity requires responsive actions tailored to individuals' needs. This necessitates a positive attitude, open-mindedness, and an appreciation for the value of diversity. Pedagogical professionalism is crucial for understanding students' diverse backgrounds and providing personalized support (Varga et al., 2021). The Diverse Learning Environment Model (DLE) recognizes the internal and external factors that affect institutions' decision in forming educational outcomes that are equitable (Hurtado et al., 2012). Furthermore, researchers agree that supporting equity in education is aligned with an enhancement in academic excellence and quality of education (Hurtado & Ruiz, 2015). Building upon these findings, the Inclusive Excellence movement, which has been ongoing in the United States for almost twenty years, is grounded in the belief that inclusive practices lead to improve the resulting outcomes (Milem et al., 2005; Williams et al., 2005).

Global studies have confirmed the value of inclusive models, with the United States employing the term "inclusive excellence" to nurture an inclusive environment in higher education (Milem et al., 2005). From university leaders' perspective, diversity supports student success as well as the university competitiveness at institutional level (O'Donnel et al., 2011; Danowitz & Tuitt, 2011). The meaning of diversity differs among global studies, with the term applied to underrepresented groups in higher education sector, namely African American, Latin-American, and disabled students in the United States (Harris-Lee, 2019; Lombardi et al., 2013; Burgstahler, 2015), and immigrant families in Canada and Western Europe (Guo & Jamal, 2007; Cooper, 2010). Equitable support for academic performance among learner groups is essential for enhancing institutional reputation and student well-being (Bailey & Dynarski, 2011; Myers, 2016). Researches indicate that interventions supporting inclusivity contribute to the development of academic excellence, making inclusion an essential aspect of university innovations (Brusoni et al., 2014; May & Bridger, 2010; Solomon et al., 2017). It is crucial to make ongoing interventions to ensure that the development of inclusivity at higher education is sustainable and successful (Arató & Varga ed., 2015; Nolan & Targett, 2017).

The Current State of Efforts in Promoting Diversity and Inclusion in Academic Institution

The promotion of equity, diversity, and inclusion (EDI) is a vital strategic concern in the higher education sector. EDI influences several factors at the higher education namely institutional culture, teaching as well as research. Universities are vigorously working to build comprehensive processes and cultures that offer equal chances for individuals from diverse backgrounds. In year 2015, the commitment toward inclusivity was covered by higher education ministers at the Ministerial Meeting of the Bologna Process and was restated by the European Commission in its 2017 agenda for higher education. Efforts to promote EDI in academia spread beyond gender equality, with initiatives addressing other causes of inequality and discrimination, namely the Horizon Europe request for public bodies to have an inclusive plan related to the Gender Equality that includes intersectional indicators. Reports and position papers by

Claeys-Kulik, Jørgensen, and Stöber (2019) and Buitendijk, Curry, and Maes (2019) provide guidance on best practices and approaches for fostering inclusivity in academia. The Council of Europe emphasizes the need for academic institutional leaders to tailor their diversity and inclusion arguments to different groups and backgrounds (Bergan & Harkavy, 2018). The concept of diversity has expanded over time to include gender diversity, age, and other potential contexts for discrimination. EU legislation recognizes various grounds for discrimination, including race, ethnicity, religion, disability, and age.

The European Commission's focus on addressing EDI from an intersectional perspective encourages the adoption of inclusive organizational practices that promote equity across multiple intersecting identities. Approaching EDI from a political viewpoint in the higher education sector provides new insights and possibilities (Weimer & Nokkala, 2020). However, initiatives aimed at promoting EDI at universities have failed to address common obstacles faced by underrepresented groups and overlooked the broader needs of the university community. Inclusivity in teaching curricula and research programs has not received sufficient attention.

During the year 2019, the European Commission funded European Universities, with a target of creating internationally competitive degree programs that offer quality education opportunities across several European countries. Currently, more than three hundred academic institutions within forty-four European University Alliances (EUAs) are supporting the values of the European and simultaneously developing their level of competitiveness and the quality education. Several universities in Spain, Slovakia, Finland, Italy, France, and Austin followed an inclusive method to promote EDI in EUA. They focused on promoting the principles of EDI across projects by considering micro level actions. It was observed that in the midrange, the experience that the students in the EUA experience can aid in their transition from university to the workforce, accordingly enabling them to implement the knowledge gained from EDI in their lives whether as employees or as citizens (Siri et al., 2022).

The recent COVID-19 pandemic caused a disruption in the higher education sector and necessitated the execution of new policies and strategies in the academic models. Several researches have observed the reactions of academic institutions and corporates with regard to the impacts of the latest COVID-19 (Donald, Ashleigh, & Baruch, 2021). Concerns have risen regarding the potential inequalities faced by different categories of the students along with implications for their learning paths as well as future job views. These categories are namely those students who are working, the ones that are parents as well as those who are studying remotely (Farhadi, 2022; Murphy, 2020). Challenges and lessons related to accessibility and adaptation have been examined for students with special needs or disabilities (Fondazione Agnelli, 2020) and female academics' work–life balance (Malisch et al., 2020). Moreover, the notion of ethics of care in academia has also been explored (Corbera et al., 2020). Initiatives addressing the link between COVID-19 and EDI have been implemented at the department level, with a focus on committees and pledges (Gordon Perue et al., 2021; Harpe et al., 2021). Recommendations and best practices for promoting inclusive academia have been provided in reports and position papers (Buitendijk et al., 2019; Claeys-Kulik & Ekman Jørgensen, 2018). The leaders at the academic institutions are encouraged to shape their opinions for diversity and inclusion to diverse audiences and backgrounds (Bergan & Harkavy, 2018). The involvement of the students is essential in promoting diversity and inclusion on campus. The organizations led by the students play a crucial role in assisting the negotiation among dissimilarities since top-down approaches tend to be unsuccessful in the long term (Alger, 2018). Researches in the field of EDI and students with disabilities reveal that there has been a limited engagement from academic and non-academic staff, and student in this regard (Wolbring & Lillywhite, 2021).

It is imperative to closely monitor and highlight these challenges to promote EDI in higher education effectively. By adopting comprehensive strategies, namely fostering student participation, and leveraging online platforms, higher education institutions can work toward creating a more inclusive environment.

Growing Recognition of the Need to Address Issues of Diversity and Inclusion in the Education System

Based on the United Nations Educational, Scientific and Cultural Organization (UNESCO), education has a vital role in attaining the Sustainable Development Goal (SDG 4), which aims to ensure inclusive and equitable quality education for all. The SDG agenda for the year 2030 offers guidance for the execution of this goal (UNESCO, 2020c).

In 2019, the International Forum on Inclusion and Equity in Education, arranged by UNESCO and the Ministry of Education of Colombia, restated the commitment to inclusion in education. The occasion marked the 25th anniversary of the Salamanca Declaration and emphasized the significance of having an equal access for all learners to quality learning opportunities. The outcome declaration, known as the Cali Commitment to equity and inclusion in education, addressed the transformative nature of inclusion and its goal of eliminating discrimination and appreciating diversity (UNESCO, 2019).

Among provinces in Canada, New Brunswick has been a pioneer in providing an inclusive education via embedding it in its legislative processes, local authority plans, and specialized guidelines (Porter & Aucoin, 2012). Policy 322 on Inclusive Education, mandated by the Minister of Education, sets out the key components of an inclusive education system, including personalized learning plans, inclusive graduation, and guidelines for common learning environments (UNESCO, 2020c). In year 1977, Italy passed a law to close special schools and promote inclusive education. Recent adjustments have further supported the inclusivity of the education system, eliminating the likelihood of prohibiting from school as a corrective agreement (Ianes et al., 2019).

It is important to take into account the background when repeating successful inclusion practices from one country to another, as various factors such as social, political, cultural, economic, and institutional impacts can contribute to educational inequities (UNESCO, 2020c). Global trends that prioritize competition, school autonomy, and parental choice can create obstacles to inclusion and equity in education. The development of independent state-funded schools based on autonomy may not benefit learners from low-income and minority backgrounds (Meyland-Smith & Evans, 2009; Salokangas & Ainscow, 2017). Despite debates surrounding these trends, some education systems have managed to achieve high rankings in both quality and equity (OECD, 2012).

In summary, UNESCO and various countries have recognized the significance of inclusive education in attaining sustainable development goals. Efforts to promote inclusion and equity in education have been made through global forums, legislative processes, and policy frameworks. While effective inclusion practices exist, they should be adapted to specific backgrounds. Global trends emphasizing school autonomy and competition pose challenges to inclusivity and equity in education, demanding vigilant attention of their impact on underrepresented group of learners.

The Challenges that Institutions Face in Promoting Diversity and Inclusion

Since 1990s, numerous efforts have been implemented to endorse quality education for all without any discrimination. Yet, the existing education systems across countries show the ineffectiveness of these efforts as no tangible transformation have been spotted. More effective ways are needed to be identified in order to address the obstacles and then plan for progress (UNESCO, 2020c).

Simultaneously, new challenges are being emerged at a global level which makes it even more critical to foster inclusion and equity in the education system. Some of these challenges are being generated via change in the climate, migration, and increase in the overall numbers of refugees, pandemics, as well as demand for new skills mainly due to the digital innovations and fundamental changes across economies. It is also essential to consider that the education driven by the Artificial Intelligence needs to be reachable for all irrespective of their backgrounds (UNESCO, 2019c). In spite of the prospects that Artificial Intelligence would bring, there exists a concern that unless a thorough intervention happens, they may contribute in worsening the economic, social, and political structures and add more into the inequalities across different demographics (Ashar & Cortesi, 2018).

Strategies Implemented by Educators and Policymakers Aiming to Create an Inclusive and Supportive Learning Environment

As per LERU position paper (2019), creating an equal, diverse, and inclusive university requires taking four critical steps. First, leaders are required to familiarize themselves with the main lessons from the broad research on opportunity and bias, which recognizes the challenges that underrepresented faculty, staff, and students tend to face. Second, it is important to observe and track the current condition and the influence of any programs that targets bringing the change. This includes using both quantitative and qualitative data to understand the particular issues at each institution as well as monitoring data with human experiences. Third, institutions must build an official strategy that considers customized solutions for different groups and issues while ensuring a holistic, synergistic, and sustainable approach. Fourth, leaders should communicate the need for transformation from top leadership level and lead by example. Through this, academic leaders can build a widespread change that is nurtured through existing strengths while concentrating on the specific needs of their community.

Based on the report on Diversity, Equity, and Inclusion in European Higher Education Institutions (Claeys-Kulik et al., 2019), there have been several policy responses at different levels to boost diversity and inclusiveness in higher education. At the European level, political commitments have been made, such as the Paris Declaration of EU member states in 2015, which emphasize on endorsing citizenship, freedom, tolerance, and non-discrimination via education. Furthermore, the Yerevan Communiqué in 2015 and the Paris Communiqué in 2018, within the Bologna Process, targeted to reinforce the social aspect of higher education. In the framework of EU policies, social inclusion gained prominence in 2017 when the European Commission incorporated it in its agenda for higher education and covered the European Social Pillar. Gender equality has been a priority in the context of the European Research Area for the past twenty years. At the global level, the UN Sustainable Development Goals (SDGs), implemented in 2015, emphasized the role of education in decreasing inequalities, encouraging gender equality, and offering quality education for all. In spite of these commitments, only a few European countries, namely Austria, Sweden, Ireland, Netherlands, and Croatia have taken solid movements to nurture social inclusion in higher education at their educational systems.

In the meantime, several universities and institutions at the higher education sector have acknowledged inclusiveness as a strategic question, impacting research, teaching and learning as well as institutional cultures. They have taken proactive actions to ensure individuals from underrepresented backgrounds can enroll and succeed in higher education. The report provides a complete overview of these efforts, based on quantitative data collected from one hundred fifty-nine higher education institutions across thirty-six European systems. It targets to raise awareness among university leaders, managers, staff, scholars, students, and policymakers at the European and national levels as they build strategies and policies to promote diversity, equity, and inclusion in higher education and research (Claeys-Kulik et al., 2019). As per UNESCO's report on education inclusion (2020c), the author suggested six recommended strategies with an objective to foster equity and inclusion across educational systems. It is worth mentioning that these recommendations do not necessarily need an extensive support of additional resources. Instead, their drive is to boost the more efficient utilization of existing resources, particularly human resources. Hence, these recommendations have consequences for several stakeholders, namely policymakers, administrators, teachers, scholars, students, and their families.

Clearly Define Inclusion and Equity in Education

Create a clear definition of inclusion and equity in the education (UNESCO, 2020c). Across several countries, the meaning of inclusive education is primarily about providing a service for children with disabilities within the framework of educational backroads. Yet, on a global scale, the meaning of inclusive education has evolved to encompass a broader perspective that values diversity across all learners. The objective is to highlight and reduce the social elimination that is caused by behaviors and reactions to different form of diversity, namely gender, religion ethnicity, and so on. According to inclusive education, education is considered a key human right that contributes in building an equitable society. Moreover, policy development should occur at all levels of the education system, as fostering inclusion and equity is not just a technical change, however, it reflects a rational shift that needs building an inclusive culture across the education system. This requires a commitment from various stakeholders involved in the system. Hence, it is important to create a clear meaning of the objective to all involved stakeholders. UNESCO has defined inclusion as "a process that helps overcome barriers limiting the presence, participation, and achievement of learners," and equity as "ensuring fairness, where the education of all learners is seen as having equal importance" (UNESCO, 2017).

Use Evidence to Identify Barriers that Hinder Learners' Participation and Progress

On average, individuals are subject to experience exclusion across different scopes, including social, physical, psychological, and systemic barriers (UNESCO, 2020c). Physical exclusion may occur due to the geographic factors or limited access to facilities, whereas social exclusion tends to occur when certain individuals within a group are underrepresented or not encouraged to participate. Psychological exclusion refers to individuals' self-perception of being included, underrepresented, or excluded, regardless of the external environment. Systemic exclusion can rise from requirements that eliminate certain groups, such as the poor, migrants, and refugees (UNESCO, 2019d).

To ensure accountability and highlight equal access and equity concerns in the education systems, it is imperative to recognize the groups that are being included, separated, or omitted from schooling.

Collecting a comprehensive evidence is essential, incorporating all types of exclusion. (UNESCO, 2020c). Involving with this evidence can aid in building effective strategies in fostering the participation and progress of all types of learners. It is important to collect related data, namely policy analysis, facility valuations, and inspection of practices (UNESCO, 2019d).

Considering the opinions of young generation along with those that are usually counted as underrepresented group is essential as their perspectives can create a challenge for the practitioners as well as policymakers in building process that is effectively inclusive (Ainscow & Messiou, 2017). Any action plan that is generated by the concerned bodies should take into consideration the needs of these underrepresented group while reducing obstacles in their learning and participation path.

The development in technology enables the generation of data on various context affecting inclusion, separation, and exclusion in education systems. Analyzing these factors can build conditions that nurture inclusion and equity. Indeed, evidence serves as a catalyst for educational transformation as well as decision-making (UNESCO, 2020c).

These considerations have significant implications for creating national systems of education accountability. Absence of accountability hinders growth, resulting in harmful practices. Hence, accountability processes should comprise policy interventions, law, and mechanisms to protect citizens' rights. Strengthening mechanisms is vital to uphold and impose the right to education and hold governments responsible for their promises (UNESCO, 2017/8).

Provide Support to Teachers in Promoting Inclusion and Equity

In general, schools that are known to be inclusive schools have certain characteristics in common, namely a welcoming environment for all types of students, including underrepresented groups (UNESCO, 2020c). According to the research papers, it is imperative to build classroom environment that encourages ultimate participation from all learners as well as high learning levels for all (Dyson & Roberts, 2004; Johnson et al., 1998).

According to data from OECD, in countries where teachers recognize that their career is being appreciated, they are more likely to exhibit higher level of equity in their learning results (Schleicher, 2015). Furthermore, to restructure schools and enhance processes, teachers need to feel that they are being supported while responding positively to student diversity and viewing differences among students as opportunities for elevating learning instead of observing it as a problem to be resolved. This requires reflecting on the challenges students face in order to drive change and provide understandings about how these changes can be accomplished. In order to ensure a successful execution, cultivating a culture of collaboration and problem-solving is essential (UNESCO, 2020c). The development of inclusive practices necessitates collaboration among stakeholders within specific contexts to address the educational challenges faced by specific learners. Following UNESCO's 48th International Conference on Education, the interest to improve teacher's education by providing support to meet students' needs has emerged (Florian & Pantic, 2017). These improvements are necessary to start from early stage of teacher's education and to continue during their careers.

As the education systems are becoming more inclusive, it is expected from teachers to be ready in responding toward increased diversity level among students. As a result, continuous professional development opportunity for teachers is vital. Additionally, it is important to take into consideration the regional differences in the teachers' qualifications and in measuring teacher preparedness for the inclusive education (UNESCO, 2020c). Furthermore, the senior staff in the school contribute significantly in offering an effective leadership that highlights such challenges and promotes an encouraging environment for teacher's professional learning. It is worth noting that teachers' qualifications may vary, hence SDG 4 covers an agenda that focuses on teacher's development at all levels of education (UNESCO, 2020c).

Design Curriculum and Assessments Carefully to Reflect the Needs of All Learners

In an education system that incorporates inclusivity and equity, continuous assessment of students' progress through the curriculum is important. Teachers are expected to have an understanding of students' unique characteristics, cultural backgrounds, and linguistic diversity to be able to provide safe and inclusive learning environments in their classrooms. Assessments should go beyond evaluating performance levels and focus on the effectiveness of teaching for all students. Personalized approaches, taking into account the interrelationship between curriculum, learner, pedagogy, and the learning community, can improve learning outcomes. It is crucial to provide professional development opportunities for teachers, along with collaboration with other professionals as well as engagement with colleagues, parents, and students. Identifying linguistic and cultural diversity encourages inclusion (UNESCO, 2020c).

Structure and Manage Education Systems in Ways that Engage All Learners

Undertaking the process of restructuring education provision is critical step to move toward inclusive and equitable education system, however, this approach may face resistance from stakeholders, namely parents who expressed concerns about the potential disappearance of support services (UNESCO, 2020b). To address these problems, a joint commitment among leaders at national and school levels is vital, to assess the differences, participate in collaborations, and ensure equal educational opportunities. Collaboration between schools strengthens their capability to react to learner diversity and reduces polarization, leading to teachers re-examining their practices to better support underachieving students (Muijs et al., 2011). Effective leadership at all levels plays a vital role in promoting inclusion by prioritizing, focusing on teaching and learning, fostering supportive communities, engaging families, and providing multi-agency support (Riehl, 2000).

The distribution of financial support within education is another critical element, and there is no ultimate approach to fund inclusion. Funding mechanisms should aim in preventing any form of exclusionary strategies, providing an incentive toward a school development approach. This will support social responsibility, which will contribute to having an inclusive education, ensuring innovative and flexible learning environments; hence, resulting in the development of transparent and responsible systems (European Agency for Special Needs and Inclusive Education, 2020).

Involve Communities in the Development and Implementation of Inclusive and Equitable Education Policies

To promote inclusion and equity in education, it is imperative for governments to activate human and financial resources and form partnerships among key stakeholders (UNESCO, 2020c). These stakeholders include parents, teachers, administrators, policymakers, community civic groups, and members of underrepresented groups. Involving families is particularly crucial, as they can support the development of inclusive practices in schools. Schools should collaborate with families and communities to disassociate the link between underrepresented groups and poor educational results. Establishing partnerships with employers, community groups, and universities ensures an effective support for all children. It is important to identify that all results are interconnected, and the elements that encourage or inhibit one result are likely to affect overall results (UNESCO, 2020c). This understanding emphasizes the holistic nature of youth development and the need for inclusive support.

In addition to the above-mentioned recommended strategies, it is crucial to take into consideration the targeted recruitment efforts in attracting and retaining diverse faculty. According to Williams and Wade-Golden (2013), even though it is a challenge to recruit and retain more diverse faculty, it is still possible. In order to accomplish this goal, it is critical to intervene in the traditional approach of hiring practices and going beyond the usual opinions about difficulty in term of hiring the underrepresented group (Smith et al., 2004). To have an effective recruitment practice, it needs a careful innovative approach that would include a commitment from all involved stakeholders. Institutions are expected to build international partnership that is on the basis of open and transparent communication as well as mutual accountability (Williams & Wade-Golden, 2013). According to researchers, most of the institutions tend to fail in intervening their common approaches in diversifying their faculty, as a result, they missed opportunities when it comes to diversity hires (Smith et al., 2004). Effective recruitment goes beyond job description. Academic institutions need to proactively recruit in order to achieve diversity. Common job advertisement and then waiting for applicants to apply or fill the form is not enough (Smith et al., 2004). The Successful recruitment for underrepresented faculty requires a multidimensional strategic plan (Moody, 2004; Smith et al., 2004).

It is worth noting that several academic institutions still lack a strategy that focuses on faculty diversity. They also do not have formal practices, including committee involved in searching, able to understand the diverse talent that exists; developing networks with diverse candidates and so on (Moody, 2004; Smith et al., 2004). Instead, they adopt a laissez-faire approach to faculty recruitment. This approach, which includes posting jobs in traditional platforms and following a common hiring process, often fails to bring in diverse applicant pools or hires (Smith et al., 2004; Turner, 2002). Smith et al. (2004) observed around 700 searches and discovered that using precise interventions, namely engaging diversity in the job description, applying a special hire strategy, or that have diverse search committee, often led to diverse hires. The result of their study revealed that 86% of African American, 100% of Native American, and 57% of Latino faculty hires resulted from searches using diversity-enriched search practices (Smith et al., 2004).

Hence, in order to achieve successful faculty diversity, it remains important for academic institutions to invest in the recruitment as well as retention-related activities that would include diversity-related training programs (Moreno et al., 2006; Turner & Myers, 2000).

Examining the Effectiveness of These Strategies

Executing the above-mentioned recommended strategies conveys substantial consequences for leadership practices in the education system. It necessitates organized and continued efforts, identifying the need for behavioral changes among adults in order to generate positive results for underrepresented students. Key contributors in the society, namely parents and representatives of underrepresented groups, must involve in the long-run advocacy to drive these changes (UNESCO, 2020c). Policymakers and practitioners are expected to expand their capacity for foreseeing attainable results and improving their sense of account-ability in driving inclusive education. Challenging negative assumptions, particularly related to expectations about students from specific groups based on their capabilities and behaviors, is also essential. An inclusive approach to inclusion and equity must start from early childhood care and education, both primary and secondary education, technical and vocational training, as well as tertiary education (UNESCO, 2019e).

Understanding such an approach necessitates governments and civil society to identify that talents are equally disseminated through socioe-conomic backgrounds, cultures, genders, and nationalities (UNESCO, 2019e). It requires a genuine commitment to inclusion and equity, highlighting the advantages for parents, their children, and the larger community. Identifying the interdependence of social inclusion and inclusive education is vital. As learners have diverse needs, they also have the right to fully contribute in a public social institution, namely a local school, which provides a wide-ranging scope of opportunities. The objec-tive should be to reduce the need for parents to select between meeting their child's needs and ensuring their rights and opportunities.

The ideal objective is to build education systems where such choices would be unnecessary. These systems must proactively aid local schools as well as educators by enabling them to improve their abilities to foster diversity as well as collaborations among sectors. By doing this, they align with the statement of the Salamanca, focusing on the value of inclu-sive schools in eliminating discrimination behaviors and hence encourage building more inclusive communities.

The above-mentioned strategic recommendations are based on the notion that equity and inclusion-related policies should not be separated from each other. Instead, they need to be perceived as values that notify all policies at the national level, and mainly the ones that are responsible of education-related areas (e.g. curriculum, budgets, etc.) (UNESCO, 2020c). These recommended strategies are critical in the development of educational systems toward being more inclusive and diverse. They suggest that improving inclusion and equity is the pathway to accomplishing excellence in the education systems. Through taking actions based on these recommendations, it will be possible to contribute in the SDG 4. It is worth mentioning that while the development of the education system may appear to be technically feasible, it also encompasses complexities from political and social viewpoints.

Explore the Ways in Which technology and Digital Tools can be Leveraged to Support the Goals of Inclusion and Diversity in Education

As per the 2030 Agenda for Sustainable Development, there exists a significant potential of digital technologies, including AI, in accelerating development, connecting the digital divide, and promoting inclusive knowledge societies built on the basis of gender equality, human rights, and empowerment (UNESCO, 2020a). Innovations in AI technologies, for instance, the use of educational data in crisis conditions, the use of machine translation and image recognition for international learning resources, have displayed potential in promoting inclusive and equitable access to education (UNESCO, 2020a). Furthermore, AI tools have been developed to overcome language barriers, promote inclusive education for refugees, bridge gender divides, and address the needs of people with disabilities (UNESCO, 2020a; Villasenor, 2019). However, to realize the potential of AI for sustainable development in quality education, it is important to steer its development and use it considering the human values while emphasizing on inclusion, equity, and gender equality (Villasenor, 2019). Regulatory frameworks are essential to ensure ethical and non-discriminatory utilization of AI algorithms and tools, and transparent management of learners' data (UNESCO, 2020a). Multi-stakeholder partnerships and global cooperation are vital to highlight the challenges of AI and to promote inclusive education (Hu et al., 2019; UNESCO, 2020a).

Diversity and Inclusion in the Higher Education at MENA Region

In order for academic institutions to remain relevant, it is critical that they remain conscious and proactive in adopting international best practices, including integrating diversity and inclusion into their curriculum and other strategic decisions. Considering that academic institutions in the MENA region encompass individuals from diverse backgrounds, it is crucial for students to embrace cultural diversity and acquire the communication skills needed to engage with individuals from different backgrounds. Furthermore, the increasing number of female leaders in higher education can also contribute positively to the diverse community. In recent years, several academic institutions have taken initiatives toward achieving the Sustainable Development Goals (SDGs), particularly Goal 10, which aims to decrease inequality across countries by promoting social, political, and economic inclusion for all, including individuals with disabilities. As diversity is also considered in university rankings, it remains important to further discuss and measure the integration of diversity and inclusion within the higher education sector in the MENA region.

References

Ainscow, M., & Messiou, K. (2017). Engaging with the views of students to promote inclusion in education. *Journal of Educational Change, 19*(1), 1–17.

Alger, R. J. (2018). Access to success—Making campuses both diverse and inclusive. In S. Bergan & I. Harkavy (Eds.), *Higher education for diversity, social inclusion and community: A democratic imperative* (pp. 63–73). Council of Europe.

Arató, F., & Varga, A. (Eds.). (2015). Inclusive University: How to increase academic excellence focusing on the aspects of inclusion. University of Pécs, Faculty of Humanities, Institute of Education, Pécs. Autonomy and Responsibility Study Volume IV. http://kompetenspedagogus.hu/sites/default/files/arato-f-varga-a-inclusive-universityuniv-pecs-2015.pdf

Ashar, A., & Cortesi, S. (2018). *Why inclusion matters for the future of artificial intelligence.* United Kingdom.

Bailey, M., & Dynarski, S. (2011). *Gains and gaps: Changing inequality in U.S. College entry and completion.* National Bureau of Economic Research. https://doi.org/10.3386/w17633

Bauman, G., Bustillos, L., Bensimon, E., Ch., Brown, & Bartee, R. (2005). *Achieving equitable educational outcomes with all students: The institution's roles and responsibilities.* Association of American Colleges and Universities.

Bergan, S., & Harkavy, I. (Eds.). (2018). *Higher education for diversity, social inclusion and community (Issue 22).* Council of Europe Higher Education Series. Council of Europe Publishing.

Brusoni, M., et al. (2014). *The concept of excellence in higher education.* European Association for Quality Assurance in Higher Education AISBL.

Buitendijk, S., Curry, S., & Maes, K. (2019). Equality, diversity and inclusion at Universities: The power of a systemic approach. LERU Position Paper. https://www.leru.org/publications/equality-diversity-and-inclusion-atuniversities

Burgstahler, S. (2015). *Universal design of higher education: From principles to practice* (2nd ed.). Harvard Education Press.

Claeys-Kulik, A.-L., & Ekman Jørgensen, T. (2018). Universities' strategies and approaches towards diversity, equity and inclusion. Examples from across Europe. http://hdl.voced.edu.au/10707/468508

Claeys-Kulik, A.-L., Jørgensen, T. E., & Stöber, H. (Eds.). (2019). *Diversity, equity and inclusion in european higher education institutions: Results from the invited project.* Carme Royo & Hélène Mariaud (Editorial board). https://eua.eu/downloads/publications/web_diversity%20equity%20and%20inclusion%20in%20european%20higher%20education%20institutions.pdf

Cooper, M. (Ed.). (2010). *Changing the culture of the campus: Towards an inclusive higher education—Ten Years on.* European Access Network.

Corbera, E., Anguelovski, I., Honey-Rosés, J., & Ruiz-Mallén, I. (2020). Academia in the time of COVID-19: Towards an ethics of care. *Planning Theory & Practice, 21*, 191–199.

Danowitz, M. A., & Tuitt, F. (2011). Enacting inclusivity through engaged pedagogy: A higher education perspective. *Equity & Excellence in Education, 44*(1), 40–56. https://doi.org/10.1080/10665684.2011.539474

Dezső, R. (2015). Plurális intelligencia-koncepciók, tanulásközpontú pedagógiai megközelítések és az inkluzivitás összefüggései [Concepts of plural intelligence, learning-centered pedagogical approaches, and the correlations with inclusivity]. In F. Arató & A. Varga (Eds.), *Befogadó Egyetem, Az akadémiai kiválóság fejlesztése az inklúzió szempontjainak érvényesítésével* [Inclusive University: Developing academic excellence by implementing the perspectives of inclusion] (pp. 75–88).

Donald, W. E., Ashleigh, M. J., & Baruch, Y. (2021). *The university-to-work transition: Responses of universities and organizations to the COVID-19 pandemic*. Personnel Review. Advance online publication. https://www.emerald.com/insight/content/doi/10.1108/PR-03-2021-0170/full/html

Dyson, A., Howes, A., & Roberts, B. (2004). What do we really know about inclusive schools? A systematic review of the research evidence. In D. Mitchell (Ed.), *Special educational needs and inclusive education: Major themes in education*. Routledge.

European Agency for Special Needs and Inclusive Education and UNESCO. (2020). Inclusive education in action. https://inclusive-education-in-action.org/

Farhadi, B. (2022). *"The sky's the limit": On the impossible promise of e-Learning in the Toronto District School Board* (Ph.D. Thesis), University of Toronto. http://hdl.handle.net/1807/97442

Florian, L., & Pantic, N. (2017). Teacher education for the changing demographics of schooling: Policy, practice, and research. In Teacher Education for the Changing Demographics of Schooling: Inclusive Learning and Educational Equity (Vol. 2, pp. 1–5). Springer.

Fondazione Agnelli. (2020). *Oltre le Distanze. Indagine Preliminare.* https://www.fondazioneagnelli.it/wp-content/uploads/2020/05/OLTRE-LE-DISTANZE-SINTESI-RISULTATI-QUESTIONARIO-1.pdf

Global Education Monitoring Report (GEM). (2019). *Migration, displacement and education: Building Bridges, Not Walls.* UNESCO. [Online]. https://unesdoc.unesco.org/ark:/48223/pf0000265866

Gordon Perue, G. L., Fox-Rosellini, S. E., Sur, N. B., Marulanda-Londono, E., Margolesky, J., Tornes, L., Bure, A., Kalika, P. M., Chileuitt, A. A.,

Allespach, H., et al. (2021). Development of an equity, diversity, inclusion, and Anti-racism Pledge as the foundation for action in an academic department of neurology. *Neurology, 97*, 729–736. https://doi.org/10.1212/WNL.0000000000012626

Guo, S., & Jamal, Z. (2007). Nurturing cultural diversity in higher education: A critical review of selected models. *Canadian Journal of Higher Education, 37*, 27–49. https://doi.org/10.47678/cjhe.v37i3.529

Harpe, J. M., Safdieh, J., Broner, S., Strong, G., & Robbins, M. (2021). Creating a neurology department diversity, equity and inclusion committee (1302). *Neurology, 96* (Suppl. 15), 1302. http://n.neurology.org/content/96/15_Supplement/1302.abstract

Harris, T. N., & Lee, C. N. (2019). Advocate-mentoring: A communicative response to diversity in higher education. *Communication Education, 68*(1), 103–113. https://doi.org/10.1080/03634523.2018.1536272

Hurtado, S., Alvarez, C. L., Guillermo, W. Ch., Cuellar, M., & Arellano, L. (2012). A model for diverse learning environments: The scholarship on creating and assessing conditions for student success. In J. C. Smart & M. B. Paulsen (Eds.), *Higher education: Handbook of theory and research, higher education: Handbook of theory and research 27* (pp. 41–122). Springer Science and Business Media B.V. https://doi.org/10.1007/978-94-007-2950-6_2

Hurtado, S., & Ruiz, A. A. (2015). Thinking about race: The salience of racial identity at two- and four-year colleges and the climate for diversity. *Journal of Higher Education, 86*(1), 127–155. https://doi.org/10.1353/jhe.2015.0000

Hu, X., Neupane, B., Echaiz, L. F., Sibal, P., & Rivera Lam, M. (2019). *Steering AI and Advanced ICTs for Knowledge Societies: A Rights, Openness, Access, and Multi-stakeholder Perspective.* UNESCO. https://unesdoc.unesco.org/ark:/48223/pf0000372132

Ianes, D., Demo, H., & Dell'Anna, S. (2019). Historical steps and current challenges for the Italian inclusive education system. In J. Donlic, E. Jaksche-Hoffman, & H. K., Peterlini (Eds.), *Ist inklusive Schule möglich?* (pp. 77–90). Nationale und internationale Perspektiven.

Johnson, D. W., Johnson, R. T., & Holubec, E. (1998). *Cooperation in the classroom.* Interaction Book Company.

LERU. (2019). *Equality, diversity and inclusion at universities: The power of a systematic approach.* https://www.leru.org/files/LERU-EDI-paper_final.pdf

LERU position paper. (2019). Equality, diversity and inclusion at universities: The power of a systematic approach. Lead authors: Prof. Simone Buitendijk,

Vice-Provost (Education), Imperial College London; Prof. Stephen Curry, Assistant Provost EDI, Imperial College London; Dr. Katrien Maes, Deputy Secretary-General LERU.

Lombardi, A., Murray, C., & Dallas, B. (2013). University faculty attitudes toward disability and inclusive instruction: Comparing two institutions. *Journal of Postsecondary Education and Disability, 26*(3), 221–232.

Malisch, J. L., Harris, B. N., Sherrer, S. M., Lewis, K. A., Shepherd, S. L., McCarthy, P. C., Spott, J. L., Karam, E. P., Moustaid-Moussa, N., Calarco, J. M., et al. (2020). Opinion: In the wake of COVID-19, academia needs new solutions to ensure gender equity. *Proceedings of the National Academy of Sciences of the United States of America, 117*, 15378–15381.

May, H., & Bridger, K. (2010). *Developing and embedding inclusive policy and practice in higher education.* The Higher Education Academy.

Meyland-Smith, D., & Evans, N. (2009). *A guide to school choice reforms.* Policy Exchange.

Milem, J., Chang, M., & Antonio, A. (2005). *Making diversity work: A researched-based perspective.* Association of American Colleges and Universities.

Moody, J. (2004). *Faculty diversity: Problems and solutions.* Routledge.

Moreno, J. F., Smith, D. G., Clayton-Pedersen, A. R., Parker, S., & Teraguchi, D. H. (2006). *The revolving door for underrepresented minority faculty in higher education: An analysis from the campus diversity initiative.* Association of American Colleges & Universities.

Muijs, D., Ainscow, M., Chapman, C., & West, M. (2011). *Collaboration and networking in education.* Springer.

Murphy, M. P. (2020). COVID-19 and emergency eLearning: Consequences of the securitization of higher education for post-pandemic pedagogy. *Contemporary Security Policy, 41*, 492–505.

Myers, B. (2016). *The flagship diversity divide.* The Chronicle of Higher Education.

Nolan, J., & Targett, N. (2017). Developing and sustaining inclusive excellence and a safe, Healthy, Equitable Campus Community at UNH. Interim Report Presidential Task Force on Campus Climate.

O'Donnell, K., et al. (2011). Putting high-impact practices and inclusive excellence at the center of GE Reform: Lessons from the California State University LEAP Initiative. *Peer Review, 13*(2).

OECD. (2012). *Equity and quality in education: Supporting disadvantaged students and schools.* OECD Publishing.

Porter, G., & Aucoin, A. (2012). *Strengthening inclusion, strengthening schools.*

Riehl, C. J. (2000). The principal's role in creating inclusive schools for diverse students: A review of normative, empirical, and critical literature on the practice of educational administration. *Review of Educational Research, 70*(1), 55–81.

Salokangas, M., & Ainscow, M. (2017). *Inside the autonomous school: Making sense of a global educational trend*. Routledge.

Schleicher, A. (2015). *Schools for 21st-Century learners: Strong leaders, confident teachers, innovative approaches*. OECD Publishing.

Siri, A., Leone, C., & Bencivenga, R. (2022). Equality, diversity, and inclusion strategies adopted in a European University Alliance to facilitate the higher education-to-work transition. *Societies, 12*(1), 140.

Smith, D. G., Turner, C. S. V., Osefi-Kofi, N., & Richards, S. (2004). Interrupting the usual: Successful strategies for hiring diverse faculty. *Journal of Higher Education, 75*, 133–160.

Solomon, A., et al. (2017). *Data-driven action plans for student success and inclusive excellence*. Association of American Colleges and Universities.

Turner, C. S. V. (2002). *Diversifying the faculty: A guidebook for search committees* (2nd ed.). As.

Turner, C. S. V., & Myers, S. L., Jr. (2000). *Faculty of color in academe: Bittersweet success*. Allyn & Bacon.

UNDP. (2019). Human development report 2019: Beyond income, beyond averages, beyond Today: Inequalities in Human Development in the 21st Century. UNDP. [Online]. http://hdr.undp.org/sites/default/files/hdr2019.pdf

UNESCO. (2009a). *Policy guidelines on inclusion in education*.

UNESCO. (2009b). *Defining an inclusive education agenda: Reflections around the 48th Session of International Conference on Education*. UNESCO IBE.

UNESCO. (2017). *Ensuring inclusion and equity in education*. France.

UNESCO. (2017/8). *Accountability in education: Meeting our commitments*. Global Education Monitoring Report. Author.

UNESCO Institute for Statistics (UIS). (2019a). *Meeting Commitments: Are Countries on Track to Achieve SDG 4?* [Online]. https://unesdoc.unesco.org/ark:/48223/pf0000369009

UNESCO. (2019b). *Cali Commitment to equity and inclusion in education. Cali, Colombia, international forum on inclusion and equity in education*. [Online]. https://unesdoc.unesco.org/ark:/48223/pf0000370910

UNESCO. (2019c). *Artificial intelligence for sustainable development. Mobile learning week 2019*. Synthesis Report. UNESCO. https://iite.unesco.org/publications/ai-for-sustainable-development-synthesis-report/

UNESCO. (2019d). *Concept note for the 2020 Global education monitoring report on inclusion.* https://unesdoc.unesco.org/ark:/48223/pf0000265329

UNESCO. (2019e). *Educación Inclusiva e Interseccional a lo largo de la vida, para que nadie quede atrás.* UNESCO. https://unesdoc.unesco.org/ark:/48223/pf0000370418/PDF/370418spa.pdf.multi

UNESCO. (2020a). *Artificial intelligence and inclusion: Concept Note.* Mobile Learning Week 2020. Education 2030. UNESCO. https://en.unesco.org/sites/default/files/mlw-2020-concept-note-en.pdf

UNESCO. (2020b). *Inclusive education in action.* https://inclusive-education-in-action.org/

UNESCO. (2020c). *Towards inclusion in education: Status trends and challenges.* Education 2030.

Varga, A. (2015b). Hátrányos helyzet és iskolarendszer [Disadvantage and the education system]. In T. Kozma, V.Á. Kiss, Cs. Jancsák, & K. Kéri (Eds.), *Tanárképzés és oktatáskutatás* [Teacher training and educational research] (pp. 621–633). HERA, Debrecen.

Varga, A., Deli, K., & Fodor, B. (2019). A felsőoktatás befogadóvá válásának szemléleti kerete és gyakorlati megvalósítása a Pécsi Tudományegyetemen [The conceptual framework and practical implementation of inclusive higher education at the University of Pécs]. *Educatio, 28*(4), 755–766. https://doi.org/10.1556/2063.28.2019.4.7

Varga, A., Vitéz, K., Orsós, I., Fodor, B., & Horváth, G. (2021). Diversity and inclusion in higher education. *Képzés és gyakorlat, 19*, 70–81. https://doi.org/10.17165/TP.2021.1-2.7

Villasenor, J. (2019, January 3). *Artificial intelligence and bias: Four key challenges.* TechTank (blog). Brookings Institution. https://www.brookings.edu/blog/techtank/2019/01/03/artificial-intelligence-and-bias-four-key-challenges/

Weimer, L., & Nokkala, T. (Eds.). (2020). *Universities as political institutions— Higher education institutions in the middle of academic, economic, and social pressures.* Brill.

Williams, D. A., Joseph, B. B., & Shederick, A. Mc. (2005). *Toward a model of inclusive excellence and change in postsecondary institutions.* Association of American Colleges and Universities.

Williams, D. A., & Wade-Golden, K. C. (2013). Best practices for improving faculty diversity recruitment and retention. In D. A. Williams & K. C. Wade-Golden (Eds.), *The chief diversity officer [CDO]: Strategy, structure, and change management* (Chapter 7). Stylus Publishing.

Wolbring, G., & Lillywhite, A. (2021). The case of disabled people. *Societies, 11*, 49.

World Economic Forum. (2018). *The future of jobs report 2018.* World Economic Forum. [Online]. https://www.weforum.org/reports/the-future-of-jobs-report-2018

Yahchouchi, G. (2022). Rethinking diversity and inclusion in the wake of COVID19: Toward a more resilient institution. In C. Raj Kumar, M. Mukherjee, T. Belousova, N. Nair (Eds.), *Global Higher Education During and Beyond COVID-19* (pp. 73–101). Springer.

4

From In-Person to Hybrid Learning Mode

Marwan Azouri and Johnny Karam

Introduction

The COVID-19 pandemic has undeniably and drastically transformed the educational landscape on a global scale, prompting universities to pivot from traditional classroom settings to digital platforms for educational instruction (Wang et al., 2020). This unexpected shift, though necessitated by the imperative to safeguard the health and well-being of students and educators (Crawford et al., 2020), was accompanied by a plethora of challenges.

This abrupt perturbation of established pedagogical norms instigated complications both for students grappling with unfamiliar learning modalities and for faculty members striving to adapt to and effectively utilize these novel educational approaches (Bao, 2020). The adaptation

M. Azouri (✉)
Notre Dame University, Notre Dame, IN, USA
e-mail: mazouri@ndu.edu.lb

J. Karam
Tabarja Beach Resort, Tabarja, Lebanon

© The Author(s), under exclusive license to Springer Nature Switzerland AG 2023
N. Azoury and G. Yahchouchi (eds.), *Governance in Higher Education*, https://doi.org/10.1007/978-3-031-40586-0_4

required on the part of students pertained not only to the technological aspects of the transition but also to a range of soft skills like time management, self-motivation, and the ability to learn independently (Marinon et al., 2020). Similarly, faculty members were tasked with the responsibility of not only becoming technologically adept at these new platforms but also learning to engage students remotely and effectively translate in-person teaching methodologies to this new format (Johnson et al., 2020).

As the ramifications of the pandemic recede, universities find themselves at the threshold of a new era, cautiously resuming in-person learning while increasingly leveraging the advantages of digital platforms. Consequently, many institutions have been prompted to explore the potential benefits of hybrid learning models, integrating traditional and remote learning methods. This emergent model offers manifold advantages including increased flexibility, expanded access to education, and enhanced student engagement.

The Transition from Conventional to Hybrid Learning in Higher Education

Conventional, face-to-face pedagogy has stood as the cornerstone of higher education for a multitude of centuries, shaping the academic journey of countless scholars across generations (Kim & Bonk, 2006). Nevertheless, the emergence of the COVID-19 pandemic in 2020 triggered a swift and compulsory reconsideration of this enduring educational paradigm (Marinoni et al., 2020). As a response to the global health crisis and the attendant social distancing measures, universities from diverse geographical locales found themselves navigating the uncharted waters of online education. The constraints of the pandemic impelled these institutions to deviate from purely in-person pedagogical strategies, thereby endorsing a novel, hybrid learning model (Bao, 2020). This emergent model represents a dynamic confluence of traditional, in-person methodologies and innovative remote teaching techniques, designed to optimize learning outcomes in a rapidly evolving academic landscape (Raes et al., 2020). Through the adaptation and adoption of this hybrid model, universities worldwide have displayed remarkable resilience and ability to innovate under pressure, offering a template for the future of higher education that extends beyond the immediate crisis. In the face of unprecedented challenges, the turn toward hybrid learning stands as a testament to the flexibility and potential of contemporary pedagogical practices, laying the groundwork for more inclusive and adaptive learning environments in the years to come (Bates, 2020). Higher educational institutions are increasingly endorsing this pedagogical paradigm shift for a multitude of compelling reasons. Foremost among these is the flexibility that hybrid learning inherently provides to learners, according to a considerable degree of agency in their educational journey (Boelens et al., 2017). This flexibility is manifested in the choice to participate in in-person classes or engage in remote learning, an option that can be calibrated according to individual student's circumstances, commitments, and predilections (Bower et al., 2015). This enhanced adaptability intrinsic to the hybrid model is particularly beneficial to students grappling with rigorous schedules or those situated in geographically distant or rural areas, thus extending the reach of high-quality education beyond the physical boundaries of the campus (Lindsey, 2020). The capacity of hybrid learning to adapt to a diverse range of student needs and life situations underscores its potential to democratize education, promoting inclusive and equitable learning opportunities (Zawacki-Richter et al., 2019).

Secondly, the hybrid learning model substantially bolsters the accessibility of education. Traditional pedagogical models centered on physical attendance can pose insurmountable barriers for students located in rural or remote locations or for those confronting transportation challenges (Greenhow et al., 2019). The inability to participate in in-person classes due to these issues may prevent these students from accessing and engaging in quality education. In these instances, the role of the hybrid learning model becomes especially pivotal. It can facilitate the provision of quality education, essentially circumventing the geographical impediments that might otherwise thwart learning opportunities (Means et al., 2013). This aspect of hybrid learning leverages digital technology to democratize access to higher education, enabling learning to occur anytime, anywhere, and thus expanding educational opportunities for those traditionally marginalized by geographical or infrastructural constraints (Sun et al., 2008). Moreover, hybrid learning can also address the temporal constraints of traditional learning. Students can access learning materials at a time that suits them, allowing them to balance their studies with other personal or professional commitments (Bonk & Zhang, 2006). This capacity of hybrid learning to make education more flexible and accessible underlines its transformative potential in the landscape of higher education.

Finally, a hybrid learning model can contribute significantly to enhancing student engagement, a factor repeatedly identified as a crucial determinant of academic success (Kuh et al., 2008). So, we're talking about a blend of live and on-demand learning—kind of like mixing a live concert with Netflix. This hybrid style of education keeps things interesting and really hooks students in. Imagine being able to chat with your teachers and classmates in real-time sessions, kind of like being in class, but from anywhere. At the same time, you can revisit recorded lessons whenever you want, letting you really get to grips with the topics at your own rhythm. And it's not all just listening; you also get to dive into online activities like forums, quizzes, and group projects, which means you're continuously learning and interacting, even outside of normal school hours. In these ways, the diverse learning experiences offered by hybrid learning can foster a sustained interest and motivation among students, thereby potentially elevating their academic performance and overall learning outcomes.

Governance Challenges and Considerations

As we delve deeper into the intricate framework of hybrid learning, it becomes imperative to address the consequential ramifications this shift has on the governance of higher education institutions. The successful materialization of hybrid learning, as highlighted in this chapter, hinges upon an exhaustive reevaluation of the universities' organizational structures, policy frameworks, and decision-making protocols (Beaudoin, 2015).

– Revisiting Organizational Structures

In the annals of traditional academia, learning has primarily revolved around a centralized campus model. The bricks-and-mortar infrastructure, paired with a fixed staffing structure, offered an established system for in-person learning. Yet, as universities adapt to the demands of a global pandemic, the advent of hybrid learning has called for a more flexible, decentralized model. In the hybrid framework, physical and virtual learning environments coexist, requiring educational institutions to reassess their physical infrastructure. They must consider integrating digital technologies and platforms and modifying classroom designs to support both in-person and remote teaching. Moreover, staffing strategies need rethinking. Universities may need to employ more online moderators, instructional designers, and IT support to ensure smooth digital operations. Budget allocation will inevitably reflect these shifts, revealing a need for investment in digital infrastructure and professional development (Table 4.1).

– Institutional Policies and Regulations

As with any institutional change, the shift to hybrid learning requires careful reconsideration of existing policies and regulations. The regulatory frameworks that once upheld the quality standards of conventional in-person education may now fall short in catering to the realities of hybrid learning. In this new educational landscape, universities may find it necessary to develop innovative policies surrounding student attendance, performance evaluation, and academic integrity, all of which may take on new dimensions in a hybrid learning model (Jones, 2018). Policies must consider the flexibility and inclusivity inherent in hybrid learning and should accommodate the needs and preferences of a diverse student body.

– Decision-Making Processes

Finally, the evolution toward hybrid learning engenders a transformation in decision-making processes. Traditional in-person learning, with

Table 4.1 A comparative view of organizational structures for traditional in-person and hybrid learning models, encapsulating key areas of focus

Key area of focus	Traditional In-person learning	Hybrid learning
Learning Environment	Centralized campus model: Physical classrooms and facilities	Decentralized model: A combination of physical classrooms and digital platforms
Infrastructure	Physical buildings and spaces designed for in-person instruction	Physical spaces equipped with technology for in-person instruction and robust digital infrastructure for remote learning
Staffing	Traditional academic and administrative roles	Traditional roles plus online moderators, instructional designers, and IT support
Budget Allocation	Allocated based on physical infrastructure, academic, and administrative needs	Allocation additionally includes investment in digital platforms, online learning tools, and professional development for online teaching
Policy Framework	Policies and regulations cater to in-person learning and classroom management	Policies need to encompass online learning aspects such as attendance, evaluation, and academic integrity in a virtual space
Decision-Making Process	Typically top-down, centralized decision-making model	More collaborative, involving diverse stakeholders like students, faculty, and IT staff

its top-down decision-making structure, is being replaced by a more collaborative model in the context of hybrid learning (Bates, 2019).

The need to involve a wide array of stakeholders—students, faculty, and staff—means decision-making becomes more democratic, yet simultaneously more complex. Navigating the diverse perspectives of these stakeholders can be challenging but essential to creating an effective and inclusive hybrid learning environment.

Key Governance Challenges

The journey toward hybrid learning marks a pivotal step in the ever-evolving world of academia. Yet, like with any major transformation, it introduces its own unique set of management hurdles. These mainly involve reshaping organizational frameworks, adjusting institutional rules, and altering decision-making strategies, all of which need careful handling. Firstly, transitioning from the conventional face-to-face learning model to a hybrid one demands a restructuring of organizational systems. Traditional learning usually operates on a centralized campus model. In contrast, hybrid learning calls for a more dispersed model to accommodate both on-site and remote learning. This might mean that universities have to reconsider their physical facilities, along with their staffing and budgeting methods. Secondly, this move toward hybrid learning necessitates a reevaluation of institutional policies. Conventional in-person learning is usually guided by a set of policies and regulations aimed at maintaining educational standards. But these rules may need revising to fit the hybrid learning framework. For instance, universities may need to craft new policies concerning student attendance, grading, and academic honesty. Lastly, the switch to hybrid learning calls for a revamp in decision-making procedures. Traditional face-to-face learning typically operates under a top-down decision-making structure. But hybrid learning needs a more collective decision-making approach that includes input from students, teachers, and other staff members. This can be challenging, as it requires different stakeholders to come together and share their ideas. The governance challenges associated with the transition to hybrid learning are significant. However, by thoughtfully navigating these challenges, universities can create a learning environment that is flexible, accessible, and engaging for all students.

Reassessing Organizational Structures

As we traverse the transformative landscape of hybrid learning, it becomes imperative to pause and ponder over the seismic shift in organizational structures this new model necessitates. Traditional educational models have, for a long, revolved around a centralized campus model. The hallways of academia resonated with the lively discourse of knowledge exchange and the campuses stood as embodiments of scholastic camaraderie. Yet, the demands of the global pandemic and the resultant shift toward hybrid learning call for a more flexible, decentralized model. This transition, while paving the way for new learning modalities, warrants substantial modifications to not just physical infrastructure, but also to staffing strategies and budget allocation.

– Physical Infrastructure: Adapting to Dual Modalities

In the hybrid framework, physical and virtual learning environments coexist, necessitating a reevaluation of the traditional brick-and-mortar infrastructure. Universities are tasked with creating a seamless blend of physical classrooms and digital platforms. It involves modifying classroom designs to accommodate technology integration, equipping lecture halls with advanced tools to facilitate simultaneous in-person and remote teaching, and investing in robust digital infrastructure to support online learning. An example is the classroom design changes that encompass dual screens, one for the professor to interact with the students in class, and the other to engage with students attending remotely. The availability of high-speed internet and digital tools becomes crucial for the smooth running of hybrid learning. The advent of the hybrid learning paradigm, an amalgamation of physical and virtual educational environments, instigates an urgent rethinking of traditional infrastructure within universities. This model presents an intricate tapestry, where the tangible threads of brick-and-mortar classrooms interweave with the intangible strands of digital platforms, creating a harmonious blend of simultaneous in-person and remote teaching. To orchestrate this blend seamlessly, educational institutions are presented with a multitude of tasks. At the outset, this involves an exhaustive modification of the age-old classroom designs that have borne the legacy of traditional teaching. These modifications aim at fostering an environment conducive to hybrid learning, characterized by the integration of contemporary technology. Furthermore, lecture halls, once synonymous with professorial monologues and passive student audiences, are being reinvented as vibrant hubs of dynamic interaction, equipped with cutting-edge tools to facilitate the delivery of lectures to both in-person and remote audiences simultaneously. Consider, for instance, the changes within the design of a typical classroom. The erstwhile format of a single screen at the front of the room has been revolutionized to accommodate the dual realities of the hybrid model. Now, classrooms are seen hosting dual screens, each serving a distinct, yet complementary purpose. One screen caters to the professor's interaction with the students present physically within the classroom, mirroring the traditional teaching experience. The other, however, opens a window to the world beyond the walls of the classroom, enabling the professor to engage effectively with students attending the class remotely. This change, though seemingly simple, holds profound implications for the teaching–learning dynamic, making education more flexible and inclusive. In addition to these tangible modifications, another integral facet of the hybrid model is the strong reliance on digital infrastructure. This dependency underscores the necessity of high-speed internet connectivity and a suite of digital tools to ensure the smooth orchestration of hybrid learning. Access to reliable internet connectivity, advanced communication platforms, online learning management systems, and various digital resources for both teaching and learning becomes paramount. This digital facet is what bridges geographical divides and enables students from far-flung areas to be a part of the university community, marking a significant shift in the democratization of education.

In essence, the transition to a hybrid learning model is a comprehensive process, requiring institutions to fundamentally reassess and remodel their existing infrastructure. It demands an openness to embrace change, the courage to break free from the confines of convention, and the vision to navigate the path to an inclusive and accessible future of higher education.

– **Staffing Strategies: Incorporating New Roles**

The onset of hybrid learning brings forth significant changes not only in the physical and digital spheres of universities but also in the human dimension—the traditional staffing structures. This paradigm shift marks a departure from the conventional roles and responsibilities that have long defined university personnel, ushering in an era characterized by an increasing need for roles that complement and facilitate the digital aspects of education. The advent of hybrid learning dictates that universities ramp up their digital undertakings, which include hiring online facilitators, course designers, and IT support teams. These roles, once considered peripheral in conventional university operations, have morphed into indispensable cogs in the machinery of the hybrid education model. However, this overhaul doesn't stop at creating new positions. It also entails a significant transformation in the responsibilities of the traditional stalwarts of academic institutions—the faculty members.

Within the hybrid framework, faculty members find themselves tasked with the challenge of instructing students who are not only present physically in the classroom but also participating remotely from various locales. This situation calls for an adaptation to innovative teaching approaches that can meet the needs and expectations of both groups of students effectively. These methodologies fuse conventional face-to-face teaching techniques with modern digital educational tools, cultivating a learning environment where all students, regardless of their physical location, can equally interact, engage, and learn. Nevertheless, this fresh pedagogical route necessitates a considerable shift in mindset and the development of new skills. To smooth this transition, universities need to implement thorough training initiatives targeted at enhancing the capabilities of their current staff. These programs should aim to arm faculty members with essential digital proficiencies, familiarize them with online instruction platforms, and guide them through the subtleties of managing a hybrid learning environment. This commitment to ongoing learning and professional development will guarantee that faculty members are adequately prepared and confident to steer through the intricacies of hybrid teaching. The redefinition of roles, the introduction of new roles, and the upskilling of existing faculty are fundamental to the evolution of staffing structures in the era of hybrid learning. These changes underline the need for flexibility, adaptability, and a commitment to lifelong learning among all university personnel. As universities continue to chart their course through the unexplored waters of hybrid learning, it is their people—equipped with the right skills and guided by a shared vision—who will steer them toward success.

– Budget Allocation: Reflecting the Shift

Indeed, the successful implementation of hybrid learning is closely tied to financial considerations. The transition to this model necessitates an evaluation and realignment of budgetary allocations to account for the support and sustenance of the digital infrastructure required for remote learning. Simultaneously, resources also need to be earmarked for ongoing professional development to equip faculty members with the necessary skills for online teaching. A significant portion of the budget may need to be allocated for the purchase of software licenses necessary for digital teaching and learning tools, cybersecurity measures to ensure the protection of digital data, and robust hardware capable of supporting the increased digital load. These budgetary considerations are critical to providing a seamless and secure learning experience for students and faculty alike. However, this budget reallocation is not merely an added expenditure. The transition to hybrid learning also offers universities an opportunity to scrutinize their existing resource allocation and identify areas where savings can be made and redirected to support the new learning model. For instance, the surge in digital resource utilization might lead to a consequent reduction in the demand for physical infrastructure. Fewer students on campus could translate to lower maintenance costs, less need for physical resources such as textbooks, and potentially even a reduction in the need for physical classroom space (Table 4.2).

To illustrate this, consider the following simplified table indicating a hypothetical shift in budget allocation.

In this example, the shift from traditional to hybrid learning sees a decrease in physical infrastructure costs and an increase in staffing,

Table 4.2 Expenses differences between Traditional and Hybrid Learning

Expense category	Traditional learning (%)	Hybrid learning (%)
Physical Infrastructure	30	20
Staffing (including new roles for hybrid support)	30	35
Professional Development	5	10
Digital Infrastructure (hardware, software, cybersecurity)	5	20
Student Services	20	15
Other (administration, marketing, etc.)	10	10

professional development, and digital infrastructure costs. However, this is a simplified example and the actual figures would depend on a wide range of factors unique to each institution.

While this realignment poses challenges, it also signifies an important step in evolving with the changing landscape of higher education. Through careful planning and consideration, institutions can navigate these financial challenges and use them as an opportunity to optimize their operations to best serve their students in the hybrid learning era.

Reviewing Policies and Regulations

The implementation of hybrid learning necessitates an in-depth review and potentially substantial adjustments to existing institutional policies and regulations. Predominantly designed for traditional in-person learning, many such regulations are often unsuited for the nuances of a hybrid learning context. For universities to maintain academic quality while accommodating the complexities of hybrid learning, it becomes imperative to revisit, rethink, and reformulate these guiding policies.

Within the traditional framework of higher education, the concept of student attendance is largely associated with a physical presence within the confines of a classroom. However, with the emergence of the hybrid learning model, the definition of attendance requires recontextualization to encompass both physical and virtual participation. In the digital realm, attendance is no longer confined to the simple act of being present in a particular geographical location at a given time; rather, it needs to be reconceptualized to capture the complex nature of online participation. A fundamental question to address in this regard is how to effectively gauge attendance in an online session. Is a student's attendance marked merely by logging into the virtual platform, or should it be contingent on active involvement in discussions, responses to questions, and engagement with the assigned activities? To reconcile these evolving dimensions of student participation, universities are confronted with the task of crafting comprehensive attendance policies. These policies should encapsulate clear guidelines and expectations for both in-person and remote learning scenarios, ensuring consistency and fairness. Such reformed policies would need to incorporate innovative metrics to capture the multi-dimensional aspects of student engagement in online sessions while maintaining the foundational principles of academic commitment and responsibility. The development of such a nuanced attendance policy presents a significant challenge but also offers an opportunity to enhance the educational experience by promoting active engagement rather than mere presence, thereby adapting to the new realities of hybrid learning.

University Hybrid Learning Attendance Policy (Example):

1.0 Purpose This policy establishes the requirements for student attendance in hybrid learning environments, which encompass both in-person and online instructional activities.

2.0 Definitions

- *In-Person Learning:* Traditional instructional activities conducted on the University campus.
- *2.2 Online Learning:* Synchronous and asynchronous instructional activities conducted via digital platforms.

3.0 Policy

- *3.1 In-Person Learning Attendance: Students are expected to attend all scheduled in-person classes unless there is a valid reason for absence. If absent, students should notify their instructors beforehand, if possible, or as soon thereafter as feasible.*

- *3.2 Online Learning Attendance: Attendance in synchronous online sessions is defined by active participation, which includes logging into the session on time, engaging in discussions, and completing in-session activities. Attendance in asynchronous sessions is determined by the timely viewing of pre-recorded lectures, participation in discussion boards, and completion of assigned tasks.*

4.0 Responsibilities

- *4.1 Faculty Responsibilities: Faculty are expected to record attendance for both in-person and online learning activities. For online sessions, faculty will track attendance through students' active engagement, including their participation in discussions and completion of assigned tasks.*
- *4.2 Student Responsibilities: Students are expected to participate actively in both in-person and online sessions. For online learning, students must ensure that they have a reliable internet connection and the required technology to participate fully in online activities.*

5.0 Consequences of Non-Attendance Non-attendance without a valid reason may impact a student's academic performance and could affect their final grade. If a student has ongoing issues with attending sessions (in-person or online), they should contact their academic advisor for support and guidance. Traditional grading policies have often been structured around in-person assessments, including written exams, oral presentations, and practical demonstrations. These indicators, predominantly crafted to gauge student comprehension and command over course material, are deeply rooted in the physical classroom setting. The transition to hybrid learning, which blends traditional and remote teaching methods, necessitates a reassessment of these standard evaluation strategies. As digital components become integral to the teaching and learning process, grading policies need to adapt to the realities of online assessments. There's a pressing need to devise fair and robust grading practices that cater to both face-to-face and online learning modes. Universities must recognize and tackle the unique challenges brought about by online evaluations, such as upholding academic integrity in a setting where conventional supervisory methods may not always be feasible. In a hybrid learning environment, it becomes crucial to incorporate a variety of assessment methods specifically tailored to remote learning circumstances. These could include, for instance, asynchronous online quizzes, participation in virtual discussion forums that can be assessed for quality and involvement, and digital projects or portfolios that allow students to showcase their understanding in more practical, real-world contexts. Universities can enhance their assessment approaches by incorporating various evaluation methods. This allows them to effectively measure a wide range of skills and competencies, including both memorization and critical thinking abilities. Moreover, it promotes interactive and participatory learning in a remote environment. Adapting grading policies to accommodate the transition to hybrid learning is a challenging endeavor that necessitates careful preparation and execution. It involves not just the selection of appropriate online assessment tools, but also considerations of how grading criteria are communicated to students and how academic integrity can be maintained in an online environment. Universities must ensure that their revised grading policies continue to uphold rigorous academic standards, support fair and consistent assessment, and promote meaningful, high-quality learning among their students (Table 4.3).

With the shift toward remote learning, universities now find themselves tasked with the significant responsibility of reevaluating their

Table 4.3 Example of assessment type and grade weightage

Assessment type	Description	Weightage (%)
Online Quizzes	Series of online quizzes assessing knowledge of different design concepts and tools	30
Online Discussion Participation	Active participation in weekly online discussion forums, contributing to and engaging with peers' interpretations of design work	20
Digital Portfolio	Compilation of design projects completed throughout the semester, showcasing technical skills and creativity	50

academic integrity policies. This change has brought about new challenges in preserving the authenticity of student work, making it imperative for universities to devise solid, comprehensive strategies that deter dishonest behaviors while cultivating a culture of genuine learning among students. With the move to online learning, opportunities for academic dishonesty may have increased, rendering traditional methods of preventing plagiarism and cheating less potent. As a result, universities might need to explore cutting-edge solutions like plagiarism detection software to keep a check on the originality of student work. Moreover, implementing proctored exams could be a practical step to guarantee the fairness and integrity of assessments in a remote learning setting. It is important to take into account that placing excessive emphasis on surveillance measures could potentially create an environment of distrust. This goes against the values of academic freedom and intellectual curiosity that universities typically uphold. Instead, an alternative approach worth considering is the promotion of open-book exams, which prioritize problem-solving and critical thinking abilities rather than simple memorization. In these types of evaluations, students' performance is measured by their aptitude for applying their knowledge to intricate problems, rather than solely relying on their ability to regurgitate information. This makes such tests less susceptible to academic dishonesty. While revising policies is an essential aspect, it is equally important for universities to effectively communicate and consistently enforce these changes to ensure their successful implementation. The success of any policy revision rests on the understanding and acceptance of all stakeholders involved—students, faculty, and staff. Universities should craft clear communication strategies that explain the reasons for the policy changes, the implications for all parties involved, and the repercussions of non-compliance.

Universities are conducting informative training sessions to ensure all members of the community—students, teachers, you name it—get on board with new rules. And they're not just leaving folks high and dry with these changes, they're setting up support systems to answer any questions or sort out any hiccups that might pop up. It's not just about sticking to the rules, it's also about making sure everyone can transition smoothly. By doing all this, they're aiming to keep that all-important academic integrity going strong, even when learning is a mix of in-person and online. This helps ensure that a university degree continues to hold its weight and respect.

Changing Decision-Making Processes

As universities set sail into the waters of hybrid learning, it's time to take a hard look at how decisions are made. Usually, it's the bigwigs—the administration and faculty—who call the shots. But the dawn of hybrid learning requires a shift, one that moves toward a more collaborative and democratic decision-making style. This approach invites everyone—students, faculty, and staff—to have their say. You see, in a hybrid learning landscape, students are no longer just passive listeners in their educational journey. They're now active explorers, helping chart their course. The insights that students gather from their hands-on experiences with the hybrid model are like gold dust. They're precious in shaping the policies, practices, and strategies of hybrid learning. So, when we let student voices echo in the decision-making halls, we can supercharge the relevance and effectiveness of those decisions, tailoring them to meet the specific needs and hurdles of learners in a hybrid environment. In the same vein, faculty members and staff, the brave souls at the frontlines of implementing hybrid learning, bring a wealth of practical knowledge that can deeply enrich decision-making. They've navigated the choppy waters of new teaching methods, digital platforms, and student engagement, and their experiences can provide a detailed map of the intricate workings of hybrid learning. What we really need in a hybrid learning setting, then, is a huddle—a team-based approach to decision-making. This involves creating clear channels for conversation and feedback, frequently touching base with all stakeholders, and welcoming them to join decision-making panels or discussion groups. This kind of approach doesn't just cultivate a sense of ownership and accountability among everyone involved, but it also fuels the exchange of a broad spectrum of ideas and viewpoints.

This allows universities to make decisions that are not only more informed but also cover a wider range of considerations. However,

Table 4.4 Decision-making process

Method	Summary
Start with Why	Establish clear purpose and goals
Know Your Team	Identify all relevant stakeholders
Open Up the Lines of Communication	Ensure open and regular communication
Arm Your Team	Equip stakeholders with necessary skills and knowledge
Set the Ground Rules	Define clear procedures and norms
Keep a Close Eye	Regularly evaluate the process

putting a team approach to decision-making into action within a university setting isn't a cakewalk—it requires meticulous planning, unwavering commitment from everyone involved, and continuous monitoring and tweaking. Now, let's dive into a step-by-step guide on how to make this happen (Table 4.4).

Nonetheless, moving toward a more collaborative decision-making model can pose challenges. Balancing diverse perspectives, managing potential conflicts, and reaching a consensus can be complex and time-consuming. Universities need to establish clear procedures and norms for participatory decision-making, ensure effective communication, and foster a culture of mutual respect and cooperation among all stakeholders.

Best Practices and Strategies for Effective Governance

As we continue to unravel the intricacies of the hybrid learning model in higher education, we now turn our attention to a critical component: pinpointing and Gratifying effective governance tactics and top-notch practices. In this section, we're going to dive deep into a collection of tried-and-true strategies and methods designed to shepherd institutions toward a triumphant transition to, and execution of, hybrid learning. We're going to take a thorough look at three essential elements that stand at the crux of this initiative: Communication and Collaboration, Flexibility and Adaptability, and Commitment to Continuous Improvement.

By examining these aspects in depth, our goal is to craft a comprehensive manual that highlights the importance of open communication and inclusive collaboration in decision-making, underlines the necessity for agility in a swiftly changing learning environment, and brings to light the value of a mindset dedicated to continual enhancement. In doing this, we're eager to plot a course toward a resilient, inclusive, engaging, and student-focused future in higher education.

Communication and Collaboration

Navigating the intricate landscape of hybrid learning in higher education mandates a strategic focus on effective communication and collaboration. By cultivating a culture of openness and cooperation, universities can effectively manage the transition to hybrid learning, while also strengthening the overall resilience and adaptability of their institutions.

Communication serves as the bedrock for any significant change in an organization. When implementing a shift as substantial as the move to a hybrid learning model, clear and consistent communication becomes paramount. This involves elucidating the rationale behind the transition, articulating what changes will take place, and illuminating how these changes will impact different stakeholders. Transparent and frequent communication helps to alleviate anxiety or resistance that might arise amidst the transition. It ensures that all stakeholders, including students, faculty, and staff, understand the vision driving the change and their respective roles within it. However, it's not enough to merely inform; communication also involves active listening. Universities should establish channels for feedback and dialogue, enabling stakeholders to voice their concerns, ideas, and suggestions. Regular town hall meetings, online forums, and surveys can serve as platforms where stakeholders feel heard and acknowledged, reinforcing a sense of ownership and shared responsibility.

Parallel to communication, the value of collaboration in the successful implementation of hybrid learning can't be overstated. The move to a hybrid model is an institution-wide endeavor, requiring the concerted effort of diverse stakeholders. By embracing a collaborative approach, universities can draw on the collective wisdom, skills, and perspectives of their community. Faculty collaboration is crucial in the redesign of courses for the hybrid model. Peer review and feedback can enhance course design quality and foster a sense of shared ownership of the transition process. Collaborative professional development sessions, where faculty members share experiences and best practices, can facilitate mutual learning and support. Collaboration with students is also of utmost importance. Students' experiences and feedback provide valuable insights into what works and what can be improved. Involving students in decision-making, such as in the form of student representation in planning committees, can promote a learner-centered approach.

Involving non-academic staff in the transition to a hybrid model is also significant. The move to hybrid learning impacts not just academic processes, but also administrative and support services. Collaboration with these teams can help to identify necessary changes and streamline processes for the new model. At a broader level, universities can also benefit from collaborating with external stakeholders, such as other institutions, tech companies, or community organizations. Such partnerships can provide new perspectives, resources, and opportunities, and can strengthen the overall capacity of universities to deliver effective hybrid learning.

Ultimately, effective communication and collaboration in the context of hybrid learning are not about achieving a one-time change but about fostering a dynamic and inclusive culture. By embracing these principles, universities can not only navigate the transition to hybrid learning but also become more adaptable and resilient in the face of future changes and challenges. Thus, effective communication and collaboration are not merely strategies for the present but investments in the future of higher education.

Flexibility and Adaptability

In the swiftly changing landscape of higher education, flexibility and adaptability emerge as indispensable attributes for effective governance. The shift toward hybrid learning, which blends traditional classroom instruction with digital learning experiences, necessitates an institutional culture that is capable of accommodating and responding to ongoing transformations in the educational sphere.

Flexibility, in this context, involves the capacity to adjust to change without compromising the core institutional mission or undermining educational quality. As universities navigate the transition to hybrid learning, they need to demonstrate flexibility across various dimensions. Curriculum development, for instance, requires an adaptable mindset that embraces the fusion of in-person and online instruction methods. In terms of staffing, universities might need to consider flexible roles that encompass a mixture of in-person and remote responsibilities, or contractual arrangements that allow for more dynamic work schedules. Financial budgets might need to be more flexible to accommodate unanticipated costs associated with the implementation of digital infrastructure or the procurement of ed-tech tools.

Adaptability, while closely related to flexibility, focuses more on the ability to thrive amidst change. Rather than merely reacting to change, being adaptable involves proactively seeking out opportunities for growth and improvement. This requires a keen sense of foresight, the ability to learn from past experiences, and a commitment to continuous improvement. In the context of hybrid learning, adaptability might involve regularly reviewing and updating pedagogical approaches in response to emerging research or feedback from students. It might involve experimenting with new technologies or teaching methods, not being afraid to take risks, and learning from both successes and failures. An important aspect of adaptability is the willingness to learn from and collaborate with others. This can involve drawing on the expertise of faculty members who are experienced in online teaching, learning from the experiences of other institutions that have implemented hybrid learning, or forming partnerships with tech companies to leverage their technical expertise and resources. Universities that are adaptable are not only better equipped to navigate the transition to hybrid learning but are also more resilient in the face of future changes and challenges.

Inculcating a culture of flexibility and adaptability requires a supportive leadership approach that empowers faculty, staff, and students to experiment, learn, and grow. It involves building an environment where innovative thinking is celebrated, where mistakes are viewed as opportunities for learning, and where open dialogue and collaboration are the norms. By fostering flexibility and adaptability, universities can not only facilitate a successful transition to hybrid learning but also build the capacity to thrive in an ever-evolving educational landscape.

Commitment to Continuous Improvement

To effectively manage hybrid learning, it's important to constantly aim for improvement. This means always working to make education better, teaching methods more effective, and students' learning experiences improved. It involves creating a culture where feedback is valued, data is collected and analyzed, and change is adopted for progress. In the context of hybrid learning, this dedication to progress can take different forms. For example, universities can regularly ask students for their thoughts on online and in-person classes to identify areas that need to be addressed, such as technical issues or teaching methods that need refinement. Universities can also gather and study data on student performance and engagement in different learning settings to spot tendencies and find ways to improve. A concrete step toward improvement is setting up a Teaching and Learning Center (TLC) dedicated to improving teaching methods. The primary goal of a TLC is to enhance teaching effectiveness and student learning. It provides an avenue for professional development, research on effective teaching methods, and an exploration of novel pedagogical strategies. A well-functioning TLC can be an instrumental tool in ensuring a university's commitment to continuous improvement. In addition, universities could consider implementing regular faculty development workshops focused on best practices for hybrid teaching. Such workshops might offer opportunities to share experiences, troubleshoot common challenges, and explore innovative teaching methods.

The following Table 4.5 illustrates an example of continuous improvement metrics that a university might use to track progress:

Ultimately, dedication to ongoing enhancement entails acknowledging that the path to successful hybrid learning is a gradual undertaking. It necessitates time, endurance, and readiness to gain knowledge

Table 4.5 Improvement metrics

Metric	Measurement tool
Student engagement	Surveys, online discussion participation
Student performance	Grades, retention rates
Quality of teaching	Student evaluations, peer reviews
Technical issues	IT support tickets, feedback surveys
Faculty development	Participation in professional development opportunities

from both achievements and setbacks. With a steadfast commitment to continuous improvement, universities can ensure they are always striving to provide the best possible learning experience for their students, irrespective of whether learning happens in person, online, or through a blend of both.

Conclusion

To wrap things up, the shift from good old face-to-face learning to a blend of online and offline learning—a change that was thrust upon us by the global COVID-19 pandemic—has truly shaken things up in the world of higher education. This hasn't been a simple switch from one teaching style to another. No, it's been a total game-changer, completely revamping how we think about teaching, the resources we need, the people involved, and how universities around the globe are run. One of the major speed bumps we've hit on this journey is figuring out how to reshape the organizational structure of our universities. We've had to wave goodbye to the old school, centralized campus model and say hello to a more flexible, decentralized approach that can handle both in-person and remote learning. This has meant rethinking everything from the physical layout of our campuses and the tech tools we need, to the roles and responsibilities of our staff, and even where we're directing our funding. In essence, universities have had to put on their thinking caps to figure out how best to use technology to support learning, and how to create a structure that can roll with the punches as the needs of students, faculty, and the educational landscape at large continue to change. But the changes haven't stopped there. We've also had to take a long, hard look at the rulebook. Policies and rules that were designed for in-person learning, covering everything from attendance and grading to maintaining academic integrity, have had to go back to the drawing board to keep up with the dynamics of hybrid learning. As universities continue to adapt to these changes, they need to make sure their new rules are not just effective, but also clear, transparent, and well-communicated to everyone involved. It's all about making sure the quality and integrity of the education we're providing doesn't take a hit. But it's not just the rules that are changing—the way decisions are made is also getting a makeover. The old way of doing things, where a few people at the top made all the decisions, just isn't going to cut it anymore. We need to make room for a more collaborative approach, where everyone—students, faculty, and staff—gets a say. Now, I won't lie, this new democratic way of doing things might come with a few hiccups, but it's absolutely vital to ensuring we all understand, accept, and effectively implement this new hybrid learning model. Embracing best practices and strategies for effective governance is crucial to navigating these challenges successfully. Institutions must foster a culture of clear communication and collaboration to ensure all voices are heard, and decisions are understood by all. This approach promotes a sense of community and inclusivity that is vital in the diverse and dispersed landscape of hybrid learning. Furthermore, universities need to demonstrate flexibility and adaptability, a key characteristic of successful governance in this new era of education. The uncertainties posed by the pandemic, the rapidly evolving technological landscape, and the diverse needs of the students call for a flexible approach to decision-making, problem-solving, and implementation. Lastly, commitment to continuous improvement must be at the heart of universities' strategies. This dedication looks like a real focus on ramping up the quality of what we're teaching, the methods we're using to teach, and the overall experience students are having. Regular check-ins, listening to what everyone involved has to say, and being ready to roll with the punches are key. We need to create an environment where feedback is welcomed, data is picked apart, and change is seen as a chance to get better. Yes, moving to hybrid learning is a tough journey, full of unknowns and complexities. But it's also a big opportunity—an opportunity for universities to shake things up, adapt, and offer a more inclusive, flexible, and engaging learning experience for students. With the right planning, thoughtful leadership, and a relentless commitment to getting better, universities can navigate this change successfully and come out the other side as stronger, more adaptable, and more student-focused places of learning in this post-pandemic world. At the end of the day, the goal is still the same: to deliver top-notch education that gives students the tools they need to tackle future challenges. As we navigate this transition, this goal should be what guides our decisions, stokes our creativity, and shapes our vision for what's next in higher education (Table 4.6).

Table 4.6 Summarizing table

Component	Description
Organizational Structure	The transition from centralized to decentralized models involves infrastructural, staffing, and budgetary changes
Policies and Regulations	Revision of traditional policies including those governing attendance, grading, and academic integrity to accommodate the realities of hybrid learning
Decision-Making Process	Shift from top-down models to a more inclusive, collaborative approach involving all stakeholders (students, faculty, staff)
Communication and Collaboration	Emphasize clear communication and collaboration among all stakeholders to create a shared understanding and community inclusivity
Flexibility and Adaptability	The need for institutions to be flexible and adaptable to the evolving educational landscape and diverse student needs
Commitment to Continuous Improvement	Institutions must continuously strive to enhance the quality of education, gather and respond to feedback, and view change as an opportunity for growth
Conclusion	The transition to hybrid learning, while challenging, is an opportunity for innovation and adaptability, providing a more inclusive and engaging learning experience for students. With effective governance, universities can successfully navigate this transition and prepare for the future of higher education

References

Bao, W. (2020). COVID-19 and online teaching in higher education: A case study of Peking University. *Human Behavior and Emerging Technologies, 2*(2), 113–115. https://doi.org/10.1002/hbe2.191

Bates, A. W. (2020). *Teaching in a digital age: Guidelines for designing teaching and learning (2nd ed.).* Tony Bates Associates Ltd. https://doi.org/10.15215/aupress/9781771991490.01

Bates, T. (2019). *Teaching in a digital age.* Tony Bates Associates Ltd. https://doi.org/10.15215/aupress/9781771991490.01

Beaudoin, M. F. (2015). Distance education leadership in the context of digital change. *Quarterly Review of Distance Education, 16*(2), 45–57. https://www.proquest.com/scholarly-journals/distance-education-leadership-context-digital/docview/1698091158/se-2?accountid=14872

Boelens, R., De Wever, B., & Voet, M. (2017). Four key challenges to the design of blended learning: A systematic literature review. *Educational Research Review, 22*, 1–18. https://doi.org/10.1016/j.edurev.2017.06.001

Bonk, C. J., & Zhang, K. (2006). Introducing the R2D2 model: Online learning for the diverse learners of this world. *Distance Education, 27*(2), 249–264. https://doi.org/10.1080/01587910600789670

Bower, M., Dalgarno, B., Kennedy, G. E., Lee, M. J. W., & Kenney, J. (2015). Design and implementation factors in blended synchronous learning environments: Outcomes from a cross-case analysis. *Computers & Education, 86*, 1–17. https://doi.org/10.1016/j.compedu.2015.03.006

Crawford, J., Butler-Henderson, K., Rudolph, J., Malkawi, B., Glowatz, M., Burton, R., Magni, P. A., & Lam, S. (2020). COVID-19: 20 countries' higher education intra-period digital pedagogy responses. *Journal of Applied Learning & Teaching, 3*(1), 9–28. https://doi.org/10.37074/jalt.2020.3.1.7

Greenhow, C., Galvin, S., & Staudt Willet, K. B. (2019). Hybrid education: The potential of teaching and learning with robot-mediated communication. *Online Learning, 23*(4), 141–165. https://doi.org/10.24059/olj.v23i4.2079

Johnson, N., Veletsianos, G., & Seaman, J. (2020). U.S. faculty and administrators' experiences and approaches in the early weeks of the COVID-19 pandemic. *Online Learning, 24*(2), 6–21. https://doi.org/10.24059/olj.v24i2.2285

Jones, S. (2018). A five-year study of sustained change: The perceived impact of a faculty teaching development programme. *International Journal for Academic Development, 23*(4), 324–337. https://doi.org

Kim, K. J., & Bonk, C. J. (2006). The future of online teaching and learning in higher education: The survey says. *Educause Quarterly, 29*(4), 22–30. https://www.learntechlib.org/p/161815/

Kuh, G. D., Cruce, T. M., Shoup, R., Kinzie, J., & Gonyea, R. M. (2008). Unmasking the effects of student engagement on first-year college grades and persistence. *The Journal of Higher Education, 79*(5), 540–563. https://doi.org/10.1080/00221546.2008.11772116

Lindsey, R. (2020). Learning online: The student experience. *EDUCAUSE Review.* https://er.educause.edu/blogs/2020/7/learning-online-the-student-experience

Marinoni, G., Van't Land, H., & Jensen, T. (2020). The impact of COVID-19 on higher education around the world. *IAU Global Survey Report.* https://www.iau-aiu.net/IMG/pdf/iau_covid19_and_he_survey_report_final_may_2020.pdf

Means, B., Toyama, Y., Murphy, R., & Baki, M. (2013). The effectiveness of online and blended learning: A meta-analysis of the empirical literature. *Teachers College Record, 115*(3), 1–47. https://www.tcrecord.org/library/abstract.asp?contentid=16882

Raes, A., Detienne, L., Windey, I., & Depaepe, F. (2020). A systematic literature review on synchronous hybrid learning: Gaps identified. *Learning Environments Research, 23*, 269–290. https://doi.org/10.1007/s10984-020-09305-z

Sun, P. C., Tsai, R. J., Finger, G., Chen, Y. Y., & Yeh, D. (2008). What drives a successful e-Learning? An empirical investigation of the critical factors influencing learner satisfaction. *Computers & Education, 50*(4), 1183–1202. https://doi.org/10.1016/j.compedu.2006.11.007

Wang, C., Cheng, Z., Yue, X.-G., & McAleer, M. (2020). Risk management of COVID-19 by universities in China. *Journal of Risk and Financial Management, 13*(2), 36. https://doi.org/10.3390/jrfm13020036

Zawacki-Richter, O., Marín, V. I., Bond, M., & Gouverneur, F. (2019). A systematic review of research on artificial intelligence applications in higher education—where are the educators? *International Journal of Educational Technology in Higher Education, 16*(1), 39. https://doi.org/10.1186/s41239-019-0171-0

5

Challenges and Opportunities Faced by the Students and Faculty Members

Lindos Daou⊙ and Cynthia El Hajj

Introduction

The role of the higher education system is rapidly evolving nowadays due to numerous factors ranging from technological advancements to globalization. Hence, educational institutions must keep up with the changes in the environment as any organization to be able to keep its edge in the industry while at the same time staying true to its mission. It is undeniable that the educational system has a fundamental role in shaping societies, whereby faculty and students are at the heart of this process. In this context, both faculty and students are operating in dynamic environments with lots of challenges that are happening swiftly and require them to be alert and to be ready to adapt and accommodate the changes

L. Daou (✉)
Effat University, Jeddah, Saudi Arabia
e-mail: ldaou@effatuniversity.edu.sa

C. El Hajj
Holy Spirit University of Kaslik, Jounieh, Lebanon
e-mail: cynthia.s.elhajj@net.usek.edu.lb

© The Author(s), under exclusive license to Springer Nature
Switzerland AG 2023
N. Azoury and G. Yahchouchi (eds.), *Governance in Higher Education*,
https://doi.org/10.1007/978-3-031-40586-0_5

in the system. As a matter of fact, the challenges stem from keeping up with the new technologies, the lack of facilities and infrastructure, and the heavy workload and funding, just to name a few.

However, various opportunities are developing simultaneously based on teaching innovations that facilitate understanding for students through experiential learning. More opportunities in collaborative research and availability of funding focused on sustainable initiatives and technology. The world is moving very fast, and educational institutions must move at the same pace to keep up with the advancements on all levels and integrate constant changes in the educational delivery system, methodology, assessments, and learning objectives. Unquestionably, the period of the infamous World Pandemic (2020–2021) that caught the whole world by surprise had its toll on the education system worldwide and especially on the students as well as professors who were not fully prepared for a complete online transition.

Thus, this manuscript aims to pinpoint the challenges and opportunities that fall under the scope of higher education. By identifying them, the way of governance in educational institutions would be guided by best practices and strategies that tackle student learning quality and satisfaction in addition to professor retention and hence, a bigger picture of achieving the institutional goal. The added value of this chapter is concentrated on taking both perspectives from students and faculty in the Mena region, as existing literature focuses on one of those pillars. Consequently, the final recommendations of this chapter will provide valuable insights for university administrators, managers, and decision-makers to create more effective governance and stay a beacon for development and progress in the Arab world!

Status of Education in the Mena Region

The MENA (Middle East and North Africa) region is witnessing significant development in higher education. However, it is still limited in some areas due to poverty, gender discrimination, and geographical isolation.

In terms of funding and higher education expenditures, many governments in the Mena are investing much money in the educational sector in an attempt to develop the country's workforce and to be able to lead the countries to lead positions regionally and globally. Unlike North American and European counterparts, Higher Education institutions in Mena rely highly on tuition rather than donations and grants. The current way of funding would allow governments to focus their financial support on improving education in terms of resources and research and development. Hence, funding varies among different countries; some have increased funding, while others are limited.

The number of higher education institutions is growing exponentially from 275 institutions in 1975 to more than 3700 institutions in 2018. In this context, higher education institutions became more accessible to students in the region due to this highly significant number of institutions.

According to the World Bank (2022), the enrollment rates in Tertiary education are increasing, following a steady curve reaching around 41%. International students are also increasing, reaching 8%, as per UNESCO in 2019. Students choose Jordan, Saudi Arabia, and the United Arab Emirates as their top destinations.

In terms of research output, it has been improving steadily over the years; however, the quality and quantity of scientific research still need to catch up to other regions in the world. Concerning world rankings, some of the universities have gained recognition and international rankings, such as King Abdulaziz University (Saudi Arabia), American University of Beirut (Lebanon), and King Fahd University of Petroleum and Minerals (Saudi Arabia).

Challenges Faced by Students

In today's global economy, higher education is becoming increasingly vital, and students and faculty members encounter several issues that affect their academic performance and overall well-being. These issues are especially apparent in the MENA region, where students and faculty members must balance financial limits, academic pressure, a lack of support, and limited access to resources.

Financial restrictions, academic pressure, a lack of support and resources are just a few of the obstacles that students in the MENA area must overcome in order to attend college. These obstacles can have a substantial detrimental influence on students' mental health and learning in the formation of the future. To meet these challenges, policymakers must work with educational institutions to improve access to resources, provide support for more students, and develop programs to help students cope with academic stress and financial hardship tip. By addressing these challenges, we can help more students in the MENA region access higher education and unlock their full potential.

Challenges Faced by Faculty Members

Numerous issues that affect faculty in the MENA region prevent them from conducting high-quality research and providing high-quality instruction. The combination of research and teaching obligations, heavy workloads, financial and resource limitations, and keeping up with technology advancements are some of these challenges.

The heavy workload borne by faculty members in the MENA region stands out as one of their primary challenges. They juggle multiple tasks such as conducting research work, serving on committees, and teaching several courses concurrently throughout their schedules. According to a study done in the United Arab Emirates, Al-Rawahi et al. (2017) discovered that approximately 60 hours every week were devoted by them to work-related activities with teaching being responsible for an essential part: accounting for around 43%, closely followed by researching which accounted for about another 30%. Faculty members struggling with heavy workloads may encounter significant tension and burnout problems over time. Responding fast enough toward these difficulties could prove difficult since members do not have access/requirement satisfaction concerning funding & necessary resources crucial toward delivering effective education/research excellence & other activities such as conference participation among others, hence, it creates a hindrance. Furthermore, the MENA region has the least R&D investments evaluated at 0.6% of GDP worldwide (World Bank, 2019). It's difficult for faculty members to deliver effective teaching and research under such circumstances while maintaining a balance between both the objectives.

Academics in the MENA region also have difficulty balancing their teaching and research obligations. Faculty members may struggle to find the time and resources necessary to excel in both teaching and research. A survey conducted in Saudi Arabia revealed that professors devote an average of 57% of their time to instruction, 35% to research, and only 8% to administrative duties. It may be difficult for academic personnel to achieve a balance between these competing goals.

It is difficult for many academics in the MENA region to keep up with technological advancements. Faculty members may find it difficult to keep up with the most recent innovations in their field due to the accelerated rate of technological advancement. According to the 2019 Arab Barometer survey, 39% of youthful people in the MENA region have access to advanced technology. If faculty members lack access to technology, their ability to conduct research and provide high-quality instruction may be hindered.

In order to provide high-quality instruction and conduct research, faculty members in the MENA region must overcome a number of challenges. Among these challenges are balancing research and teaching responsibilities, hefty workloads, resource and financial constraints, and keeping up with technological advancements. Politicians and academic institutions must collaborate to improve faculty access to financial aid, resources, and career advancement opportunities in order to address these issues. By addressing these issues, we can aid faculty members in the MENA region in providing exceptional instruction and conducting knowledge-advancing research.

Opportunities Faced by Students

In the MENA region, most universities offer a wide range of scholarships and financial aids for students to assist them with their tuition fees and other related expenses. According to a report by the United Nations

Development Programme (UNDP), the number of scholarships available to students in the region has increased considerably in recent years (UNDP, 2020).

These scholarships may make higher education more affordable for those who couldn't otherwise afford it.

Additionally, there are programs for experiential learning and internships available to students in the MENA region. Many colleges and universities give students the option to gain real-world experience through co-ops, internships, and other experiential learning programs.

These courses can help students develop crucial abilities and practical experience in their chosen fields of study. 53% of businesses in the MENA region prefer to hire people who have work experience, according to a Bayt.com survey (Bayt.com, 2020). Students who participate in experiential learning activities can develop the knowledge and abilities needed to succeed in the workforce.

Networking is a significant opportunity for students in the MENA region. Students can widen their networks through going to events, joining clubs and organizations, and connecting with alumni. Making beneficial connections and forming partnerships through networking can help students advance their careers. 85% of jobs are filled through networking, according to a LinkedIn report (LinkedIn, 2021). Students who develop strong networks can get employment and advance in their fields.

Last but not least, students in the MENA area have access to a range of resources that might help them succeed academically. Libraries, tutoring services, and academic advisers are examples of these resources. According to an Arab Barometer survey, 72% of young people in the MENA region have access to academic resources such as libraries (Arab Barometer, 2019). These materials can assist students in staying on track academically and achieving their objectives.

While students in the MENA region have numerous hurdles in pursuing higher education, they also have numerous opportunities. Scholarships and financial aid, internship and experiential learning opportunities, networking, and access to resources are some of these options. Students in the MENA area can build the skills, experience, and networks they need to thrive in their careers and make a meaningful difference in their communities by taking advantage of these possibilities.

Opportunities for Faculty Members

Faculty members in the MENA region confront several difficulties in pursuing their academic and professional objectives. However, there are numerous opportunities available to them. Research funding, professional growth, collaborative research, and teaching innovations are among the opportunities available.

Research funding is one of the most important options available to faculty members in the MENA region. Many institutions and organizations provide research money to faculty members.

An Arab World Research and Development report claims that research funding in the MENA area has increased significantly over the past several years (AWRAD, 2021). Faculty members will be able to conduct cutting-edge research and increase their knowledge in their field, thanks to this increase in research funding.

For faculty members in the MENA region, professional development is an important option. Institutions may provide opportunities for professional development to keep faculty members abreast of the most recent advancements in their discipline. These include getting advanced degrees, enrolling in online training courses, and going to conferences and workshops. Taking part in professional development programs increased faculty members' involvement and job satisfaction, according to a study done in Qatar (Kandil & Abdullah, 2020). Professional development activities can assist faculty members succeed in their careers by improving their teaching and research skills.

Another key possibility for faculty members in the MENA region is collaborative research. Faculty members can improve their research and teaching by collaborating with other researchers both inside and outside their school. Collaborative research can provide faculty with new perspectives, resources, and skills, resulting in more original and impactful research. Collaboration with other researchers was recognized as a crucial determinant of faculty members' research productivity in a

Saudi Arabian study (Al-Rubaish et al., 2016). Collaborative research can also assist faculty members in developing professional networks and establishing themselves as leaders in their fields.

Faculty members in the MENA area might experiment with innovative teaching methods and technologies to improve their students' learning experiences. Because of the quick speed of technological change, faculty members can use innovative teaching methods and technology to engage students and improve their learning experience. According to a study performed in the UAE, faculty members who employed technology in the classroom were more involved and satisfied with their work (Al-Rawahi et al., 2017). Experimenting with novel teaching methods and technologies can also assist faculty members in staying current on advances in their field.

While faculty members in the MENA region have numerous obstacles, they also have numerous opportunities. Research funding, professional growth, collaborative research, and teaching innovations are among the opportunities available. Faculty members in the MENA area can progress their careers, improve their teaching and research skills, and contribute to the advancement of knowledge in their profession by taking advantage of these opportunities.

Shaping the New Role of Education

Education is indispensable in determining the future of the Middle East. To meet the requirements of the twenty-first century, educational systems must adapt to the region's accelerated economic, social, and technological growth. This essay will examine the development of education in the Middle East, as well as the challenges and opportunities it presents.

The necessity to switch from rote memorizing to project-based learning entails increasing STEM (Science, Technology, Engineering, and Mathematics) education and emphasizes critical thinking, problem-solving, and creativity. According to a Brookings Institution analysis, the region's governments are making headway in this area, with many implementing education reform projects targeted at upgrading curricula (Brookings, 2020).

Second, Middle Eastern education systems must invest in teacher training and growth. This entails providing continual professional development opportunities for instructors as well as the materials they require to effectively teach twenty-first-century skills. Reforming teacher education programs is also necessary to properly prepare instructors for the demands of modern education. According to an Arab World Research and Development report, several governments in the region acknowledge the importance of teacher development and are putting efforts in place to assist it (AWRAD, 2021).

Third, Middle Eastern education systems must invest in infrastructure to facilitate modern education. This involves giving pupils access to cutting-edge technology like computers, iPads, and interactive whiteboards. Investing in contemporary school buildings and infrastructure that facilitates project-based and experiential learning is also important. According to a Deloitte analysis, governments in the area are investing heavily in education infrastructure, with education spending anticipated to rise in the coming years (Deloitte, 2020).

Another of these issues is the growing demand for vocational and technical education. As the region's economies diversify and adapt, there is an increasing demand for skilled vocational and technical workers. Vocational and technical education programs, which provide students with actual, hands-on training in industries such as engineering, nursing, and hospitality, can assist meet this requirement. Many countries in the region, according to Al-Fanar Media, are investing in vocational and technical education to accommodate this demand (Halawa, 2022).

The Middle East's shifting emphasis on entrepreneurship and innovation is another factor affecting education's new status in the region. With the growth of start-ups and small businesses as well as the creation of the digital economy, there is a rising need for innovators and entrepreneurs who have the knowledge and abilities needed to succeed in these fields. By promoting entrepreneurship and innovation education and giving students the knowledge and resources, they need to launch and grow their businesses, education institutions in the region may help to meet this demand. According to a World Economic Forum report, several countries in the region are succeeding in this field, and many of them are putting initiatives aimed at promoting entrepreneurship and innovation education into action (World Economic Forum, 2020).

Additionally, there is a growing need for students who are capable of functioning in multicultural environments due to globalization and the world's growing interconnectedness. By promoting internationalization through initiatives like student and teacher exchange programs, global partnerships, and foreign language instruction, regional education systems can assist in meeting this demand. According to a British Council assessment, many countries in the region are making progress in this area and have started initiatives aimed at promoting internationalization in higher education (British Council, 2020).

In order to effectively promote educational reform, Middle Eastern educational systems must redesign their governance structures. This entails creating guidelines and standards to support modern education, ensuring equal resource distribution, and promoting accountability and openness in educational systems. Involving a wide range of stakeholders, including parents, teachers, and students, in educational decision-making is another requirement. Several countries in the region are pursuing reforms aimed at enhancing governance and accountability in education, according to the Organization for Economic Cooperation and Development (OECD), which indicated that countries in the region are making progress in this area.

Proposed Educational Reform Policies

Educational reform initiatives, particularly in the Middle East, are critical in influencing the higher education environment. This section focuses on planned educational reform plans in the region, with the goal of addressing issues and seizing opportunities for growth and progress. The following are some reform measures to examine in terms of educating MENA citizens for the challenges and opportunities of higher education:

1. **Curriculum and Pedagogy Enhancement**: Reform strategies should target curriculum and pedagogy enhancement to improve the quality and relevance of education. This includes updating

curricula to meet industrial demands, incorporating multidisciplinary perspectives, and fostering active learning methods. Students are better prepared for the changing job market by emphasizing critical thinking, problem-solving abilities, and digital literacy (Smith et al., 2022). Ahmed et al. (2023)'s research shows that learner-centered and technology-enabled approaches have a favorable impact on student engagement and learning results.

2. **Quality Assurance and Accreditation**: Implementing efficient quality assurance methods and accrediting systems is critical for ensuring the quality and international recognition of higher education institutions. Proposed reform strategies should prioritize integrating educational programs with worldwide standards, undertaking thorough evaluations, and establishing a culture of continuous improvement. Strong quality assurance mechanisms boost institutions' legitimacy and competitiveness, as well as graduate employability (Brown & Anderson, 2022).

3. **Inclusive Education**: Inclusive education is critical to ensuring that all students have equal access and opportunities. Proposed reform measures should stress inclusion by addressing challenges experienced by marginalized groups such as low-income individuals, young women, and people with disabilities. This can be accomplished through targeted initiatives, financial assistance, infrastructural upgrades, and the creation of a friendly and inclusive learning environment (Khan & Ali, 2022). According to Abu-Hamour et al. (2012), inclusive policies have a favorable influence on boosting access and retention rates among disadvantaged students. Online learning instructional systems could be built to target those groups and provide students from diverse backgrounds with more access.

4. **Faculty Development and Support**: Faculty development is an important aspect of educational reform programs. Professional development activities for faculty members, including training programs, research opportunities, and cooperation platforms, should be prioritized in proposed policies. These initiatives improve teaching quality, inspire innovation, and increase research productivity. Academic independence, transparency in governance, and

faculty participation in decision-making procedures are also critical (Al-Furaih & Al-Shahrani, 2021). According to Chang and Li (2022), continuing professional development programs have a good impact on teaching quality and innovation.

5. **Industry-Academia Collaboration**: Collaboration between academics and industry is essential for matching educational curricula to market demands. Partnerships, internships, and work-study programs that allow knowledge transfer, experiential learning, and skill development should be encouraged by proposed reform measures. Collaborations like these improve graduates' employability and contribute to economic growth (Smith et al., 2022). Smith et al. (2022)'s research highlights the benefits of industry-academia collaboration in lowering graduate jobless rates.

6. **Research and Innovation Funding**: Proposed reform plans should focus increasing funding for research and innovation in higher education institutions throughout the Middle East. Adequate financing allows teachers and students to conduct cutting-edge research, devise novel solutions, and contribute to knowledge production. Government investments, business partnerships, and international collaborations should be fostered in order to support research excellence and develop an innovative environment (Altbach et al., 2022).

7. **Digital Transformation**: Incorporating digital technologies into educational practices is crucial for educational reform in the Middle East. Proposed policies should prioritize the integration of digital tools, online learning platforms, and virtual resources to enhance teaching and learning experiences. This includes investing in digital infrastructure, providing faculty training in technology integration, and ensuring equitable access to digital resources for all students (UNESCO, 2021). Research by Johnson and Smith (2022) highlights the positive impact of technology-enabled learning on student engagement and academic performance.

8. **Entrepreneurship and Startup Support**: Promoting entrepreneurship and startup support within higher education institutions is a critical component of educational reform. Proposed legislation should stimulate the development of entrepreneurial talents, provide

incubation places, and make funding and mentorship programs more accessible. Students and faculty members may contribute to economic growth, innovation, and job creation in the region by cultivating an entrepreneurial attitude (World Bank, 2022).

9. **Internationalization and Global Collaboration**: Internationalization activities must be prioritized in the Middle East's educational reform programs. International collaborations, student and faculty exchanges, and collaborative research programs can enrich the learning environment, improve global capabilities, and build cultural understanding. International collaborations encourage cross-cultural interaction and add to the region's position as a hub for education and research (Altbach et al., 2022).

10. **Lifelong Learning and Continuing Education**: Recognizing the significance of lifetime learning and continuous education, policy change should promote efforts that meet the requirements of adult learners and professionals. Individuals can improve their knowledge and abilities throughout their careers by promoting flexible learning pathways, providing short-term skill development programs, and building methods for detecting prior learning. Lifelong learning promotes personal development, employability, and economic progress (UNESCO, 2021). Adult students at universities are uncommon in the Mena region. However, the notion of adult learning is evolving as professionals want to improve their skills and knowledge. Adult learners will bring value to young learners in class and contribute to the creation of an engaging atmosphere in which younger pupils can benefit from the experience of their older classmates.

11. **Promote Cultural Diversity and Inclusion**: With rising globalization, higher education administration must provide an inclusive climate that welcomes students and faculty from diverse backgrounds, races, and nationalities. This would foster rich intercultural dialogue and understanding, resulting in a non-discriminatory education system for all.

12. **Improve Governance and Accountability**: To stay up with the fast-changing environment, university administration must promote transparency and adequate decision-making. Financial mechanisms

could also be improved, which is necessary for the educational system's long-term viability.

13. **Enhance Graduates' Employability**: Students attend higher education institutions in the hope of finding a good job after graduation. Thus, it is critical that schools engage with industry to assess market needs, and then lead and advise students to enroll in specialties and majors that are in high demand while avoiding majors that are overcrowded. Internships and apprenticeships are both essential for bridging the theoretical and practical divides.

Proposed educational reform policies in the Middle East can create a dynamic and future-ready higher education system by incorporating research and innovation funding, digital transformation, entrepreneurship and startup support, internationalization and global collaboration, and lifelong learning initiatives. Collaboration among stakeholders is critical for successful implementation, including governments, educational institutions, industrial partners, and international organizations. These policies lay the path for a comprehensive and revolutionary educational ecosystem that prepares students and faculty to flourish in an increasingly interconnected and changing world.

Conclusion

In a world that is now massively governed by technology and artificial intelligence, the role of educators is more important now than ever before to grasp the new advancements in teaching and learning and adapt new teaching strategies accordingly. The COVID-19 pandemic era has accelerated the evolution of learning to be remote and relying mainly on technological devices and methods. However, now with the Metaverse and ChatGPT, change is inevitable, and it must come at a swift pace. We recall the famous saying by Charles Darwin: "It is not the strongest of the species that survive, nor the most intelligent, but the one most responsive to change." Thus, keeping a lookout for environmental changes and systematically reviewing policies and methods, and tools in higher educational institutions are indispensable to its survival.

Thus, higher education institutions must keep up with change, embrace it, and shape it, to serve their ultimate mission, which is shaping the skills and knowledge of their students and preparing them to succeed in their careers as responsible, ethical, and responsible members of society.

References

Abu-Hamour, B., Al Hmouz, H., Mattar, J., & Muhaidat, M. (2012). The use of Woodcock-Johnson tests for identifying students with special needs-a comprehensive literature review. *Procedia-Social and Behavioral Sciences, 47*, 665–673.

Ahmed, S., Khan, R. U., & Ali, A. (2023). Integrating interdisciplinary perspectives in higher education: A case study from the Middle East. *Journal of Higher Education Research, 15*(2), 45–62.

Al-Furaih, A., & Al-Shahrani, H. (2021). Academic freedom, transparent governance, and faculty satisfaction: Evidence from higher education institutions in the Middle East. *Journal of Educational Administration and Policy Studies, 13*(2), 75–92.

Al-Rawahi, N., Al-Balushi, S., & Al-Mukhaini, A. (2017). Faculty workload at higher education institutions in Oman: Perspectives and implications. *Higher Education Policy, 30*(2), 211–226.

Al-Rubaish, A., Al-Hussaini, A., Abdulghani, H., & Al-Shahrani, H. (2016). Faculty research productivity and its relationship to academic rank and tenure status among medical colleges in Saudi Arabia. *Journal of the Saudi Heart Association, 28*(2), 78–84.

Altbach, P. G., Reisberg, L., & Yudkevich, M. (2022). *Rethinking the Middle East and North Africa higher education landscape*. The Chronicle of Higher Education.

Arab Barometer. (2019). *Youth in the MENA region: Perceptions, attitudes, and aspirations*. https://www.arabbarometer.org/2019/06/youth-in-the-mena-region-perceptions-attitudes-and-aspirations/

Bayt.com. (2020). *The state of skills in the Middle East and North Africa (MENA) 2020*. https://www.bayt.com/en/research-reports/the-state-of-skills-in-the-middle-east-and-north-africa-mena-2020/

British Council. (2020). *Annual report 2020–2021*. https://www.britishcouncil.org/sites/default/files/2020-2021-annualreport-final.pdf

Brookings Institution. (2020). *Education reform in the Middle East and North Africa*. https://www.brookings.edu/research/education-reform-in-the-middle-east-and-north-africa/

Brown, E., & Anderson, L. (2022). Aligning educational programs with international standards: A pathway to global competitiveness. *Journal of Higher Education Quality Assurance, 27*(1), 35–52.

Chang, S., & Li, M. (2022). Continuous professional development for faculty: Impact on teaching quality and innovation in higher education. *Higher Education Research and Development, 41*(3), 489–506.

Deloitte. (2020). *Education in the Middle East*. https://www2.deloitte.com/content/dam/Deloitte/xe/Documents/about-deloitte/me-education-report-en-081120.pdf

Halawa, A. (2022). Vocational education in the Arab region faces challenges in shifting online—Al-Fanar media. https://www.al-fanarmedia.org/2020/10/vocational-education-arab-region-faces-challenges-shifting-online

Johnson, M., & Smith, L. (2022). Student-centered learning: Impact on academic performance and student engagement. *Journal of Educational Psychology, 116*(1), 78–95.

Kandil, A., & Abdullah, O. (2020). Faculty members' perceptions of professional development programs: A study of a university in Qatar. *Journal of Further and Higher Education, 44*(8), 1123–1136.

Khan, A., & Ali, S. (2022). Scholarships and financial support: Increasing enrollment rates among marginalized groups in higher education. *International Journal of Educational Development, 88*, 102452.

LinkedIn. (2021). *The ultimate LinkedIn statistics guide*. https://www.omnicoreagency.com/linkedin-statistics/

Smith, J., Anderson, R., Johnson, L., & Brown, K. (2022). The impact of internships and work-study programs on graduates' employability: A comparative study. *Journal of Vocational Education and Training, 74*(3), 345–362.

UNDP. (2020). *Arab human development report 2020: Development in the face of new global challenges*. https://www.arabstates.undp.org/content/rbas/en/home/library/human_development/arab-human-development-report-2020.html

UNESCO. (2021). *Education for all global monitoring report: Gender review 2021*. https://en.unesco.org/gem-report/report/2021/gender-review/

World Bank. (2019). *Research and development expenditure (% of GDP)*. https://data.worldbank.org/indicator/GB.XPD.RSDV.GD.ZS?locations=ZQ

World Bank. (2022). *Enhancing quality assurance in higher education: Policy approaches and country examples.* https://documents.worldbank.org/en/pub lication/documents-reports/documentdetail/836831650985540750/enhanc ing-quality-assurance-in-higher-education-policy-approaches-and-country-examples

World Economic Forum, J. (2020). *The future of jobs report 2020.* Retrieved from Geneva.

Part II

New Strategies for Higher Education

6

Role of Women in the Higher Education System

Nadia Shuayto and Filza Walters

Introduction

> When girls are educated, their lives, the lives of their children, families, communities, and countries improve. (UNESCO, 2019–2025)

Women have made significant strides in higher education in recent years, with increasing numbers of female students and faculty members contributing to the diversity and vibrancy of educational institutions. As we move forward with efforts toward achieving equality among genders within tertiary education, it is essential to acknowledge that various

N. Shuayto (✉)
The James Dicke College of Business Administration, Ohio Northern University, Ada, OH, USA
e-mail: n-shuayto@onu.edu

F. Walters
Texas A&M University, College Station, TX, USA
e-mail: fhwalters@tamu.edu

N. Azoury and G. Yahchouchi (eds.), *Governance in Higher Education*, https://doi.org/10.1007/978-3-031-40586-0_6

challenges remain unresolved: Inequalities around gender bias; pay gaps persist between men and women fulfilling comparable positions across organizational structures within institutions worldwide. With a focus on modern-day higher education systems, this chapter examines the unique experiences encountered by women on campus today while considering various governance issues shaping overall success rates. A comprehensive analysis of Middle Eastern & North African (MENA) regions' specific realities concerning gender representation/recruitment/retention initiatives within tertiary education adds significant value as well. Through robust discussions on effective measures that can ensure academic/career growth opportunities are made available—independent of one's sex—our readers are presented with compelling evidence supporting the need for innovative strategies toward promoting greater inclusivity across college campuses globally.

This chapter seeks to highlight best practices that can enable women to achieve their full potential in higher education, while identifying the governance strategies that are most effective in promoting their success.

Role of Women in Higher Education

Women's participation in higher education (HE) significantly increased in the preceding COVID-19 pandemic of the early 2020s, resulting in positive contributions to teaching, research, and leadership positions in academia. Despite this progress, and in the years post-pandemic, women continue to face many challenges and obstacles that limit their longevity and elevation in HE. Even though women represent half the world's population and play a key role in the global economy, they still contend with adversity when it comes to their equal rights in the workplace as well as in the home.

As cited in Karam and Zaki, (2021) and Sen (1999) states that, "The empowerment of women is one of the central issues in the process of development for many countries in the world today," emphasizing the role of women's education, employment opportunities, the nature of their employment, their ownership patterns, and the attitude of the society toward women's economic activities in the process. The progress in gender equality is promising, "but far from ending."

Gender, Equity, and Inclusion

Gender equality has come a long way in the past few years and decades. There are more women with access to education at the tertiary level, more women in senior leadership positions, and women's rights have developed significantly. More still needs to be achieved since women continue to face violence, discrimination, and unsafe work environments. On average, women earn lower salaries and have lower levels of access to education compared to men (United Nations, 2023).

Harmonizing Work and Life

It is well-documented that women have a "second shift" when confronted with the responsibilities of raising a family and performing housework. Sociologist Arlie Hochschild popularized the term "second shift" to describe the domestic and childcare responsibilities that follow a day of paid employment outside the home. Even though both men and women experience the second shift, women typically shoulder the majority of the responsibilities (Hochschild, 2003).

Leadership in Higher Education

One study finds that women are significantly underrepresented in leadership positions, despite their majority representation among undergraduate and graduate students. In 2019–2020, women accounted for 59% of undergraduate students, 56% of graduate students, but only 13% of university presidents, and 28% of academic deans (Ghandour & Sultana, 2021). The study identifies several challenges that limit women's access to leadership positions in Lebanese higher education institutions, such as patriarchal cultural and social norms, the lack of female role models and mentors, the low representation of women in decision-making bodies, the limited availability of leadership development programs, and the absence of institutional policies to support work–life balance and family responsibilities (Ghandour & Sultana, 2021).

Closing the Gender Gap

Even though women outperform men in education, they continue to face significant obstacles and discrimination on the job market and often end up in positions where none of their talents are utilized. Despite the fact that education is not the only factor that contributes to women's empowerment, it remains a crucial factor (David, 2015). Nevertheless, women's access to higher education has increased dramatically as they now represent a significant portion of the student population in many countries (European Commission, 2021). According to the World Bank, the global female to male enrollment ratio in tertiary education increased from 0.67 in 1991 to 1.08 in 2018, realizing a positive shift in the gender gap.

Contemporary enterprises in recent years have included a focus on gender equity, diversity, justice, and inclusion. Nevertheless, ongoing efforts are needed to institutionalize reforms, create sustainable policies, and to ensure measured results continue to move the needle toward the inclusion of women at all levels of higher education in a significant and meaningful way.

Epidemic or Pandemic

Over the past two decades, the percentage of women engaged in science, technology, engineering, and mathematics (STEM) has remained at 19.99% (United Nations, 2004). However, there is now more information available regarding the proportion of women working in these fields. The low representation is exacerbated by a typically male-dominated, inflexible, and exclusive work environment, which makes the field less appealing to women and other underrepresented groups. A vicious cycle exists. During the COVID-19 pandemic in Asia and the Pacific, 44% of women in STEM occupations with caregiving responsibilities did not have flexible work arrangements, according to one study. Due to the intersection of gender and other vulnerabilities, women and girls who are disproportionately disadvantaged face greater disparities in STEM education and careers. Black and Hispanic women in STEM professions in the United States earn approximately $20,000 per year less than the average for STEM occupations and approximately $33,000 less than their white male counterparts, reducing their ability to support their families (United Nations, 2004).

Factors Impacting Women's Experiences in Higher Education

In the Middle East and North Africa (MENA) region, women in higher education still face a number of challenges and barriers despite progress that has been made over the past few decades. Specific issues include the recruitment, retention, and elevation of women at all levels of the HE pipelines. The following challenges provide a roadmap for institutions to assess and reflect on current practices and to embrace new more inclusive measures to ensure inclusion at each stage of the academic ladder, beginning with undergraduate students, matriculating to graduate students and to the ranks of faculty and administrators.

1. While access to education has improved in the MENA region, gender disparities in higher education persist. Access to universities and colleges is frequently restricted for women by cultural and societal obstacles. In comparison to men, women have a lower rate of access to higher education due to factors including limited mobility, traditional gender roles, early marriage, and other societal and cultural factors.

2. Due to societal norms and discriminatory practices, women in some countries of the MENA region have limited access to higher education. This can include restrictions on women's education, a lack of available institutions for women, and a lack of familial support for their academic goals.

3. Segregation by Gender: Many educational institutions in the MENA region practice segregation by gender, which can limit the educational experiences and opportunities of women. Segregation can reduce interaction with male students and faculty, thereby limiting opportunities for collaboration and networking.

4. Stereotypes and Bias: Despite some progress in recent years, bias against women persists in many academic fields. Persistent gender stereotypes and prejudices influence the experiences of women in higher education in the MENA region. These stereotypes can erode women's confidence, restrict their career options, and hinder their participation in certain fields, especially STEM disciplines. These issues can result in lower pay, fewer opportunities for advancement, and diminished recognition of women's contributions to research and scholarship.

5. Underrepresentation in Leadership: In the MENA region, women are considerably underrepresented in positions of leadership within higher education institutions. Women's inability to influence institutional policies and decision-making processes is hindered by their limited access to key administrative positions, such as university presidents, deans, and department leaders. This can limit their ability to influence institution-wide policy and make decisions that affect the entire institution.

6. Lack of Female Faculty and Role Models: The dearth of female faculty members in the MENA region can have an effect on the experiences of women in higher education. Absence of female role models and mentors can hinder women's aspirations, restrict their access to counsel and support, and exacerbate feelings of isolation.

7. Sociocultural factors and traditional norms can pose obstacles for women pursuing higher education in the MENA region. Academic and professional advancement for women may be hindered by expectations regarding marriage, family responsibilities, and societal perceptions of women's roles.

8. Limited Research Opportunities: Access to research opportunities, funding, and resources may be difficult for women in the MENA region. These constraints may impede their capacity to contribute to academic research and innovation.

9. Work–Life Balance: Balancing work and family obligations can be particularly difficult for women in academia due to the time-consuming and often long-hours-required demands of research, teaching, and service.
10. Discrimination and Harassment: Women in higher education are also susceptible to discrimination and harassment, which can make them feel unsafe and undervalued at work.

Sociocultural Factors

A. Qaffas's (2020) article, "Gender in Higher Education in the Arab World: A Systematic Review of Literature," encompasses a comprehensive review of existing literature on gender dynamics concerning higher education throughout the Arab world derived from research articles, reports, and policy documents.

One critical trend identified by this study focuses on various challenges that hinder women's access to higher learning while trying to succeed therein; unsurprisingly, they face numerous difficulties despite commendable efforts put forth toward gender equity; especially tellingly, there is only 34% enrollment represented by women compared to men's rate of 48% per UNESCO data. Additionally, there is a steep drop off for female attendance within STEM fields with some discrepancies showing only 16% representation. Existing cultural practices must be considered contributing causes as expectations around domestic priorities often trump educational attainment or career-growth possibilities associated with university attendance. Harassment or sexist behavior encountered within male-dominated fields also further undermine progress potential for aspiring women learners.

Therefore, investment into encouraging girls' education could profoundly benefit societies everywhere if implemented effectively—more notably since full participation could boost national growth rates percentages points into double digits range. Promoting gender equality and inclusion remains a pressing concern within higher education across the Arab region. Our ongoing efforts should aim to overcome systemic obstacles that hinder women's participation. Additionally. We need to challenge patriarchal attitudes upheld by cultural institutions that perpetuate gender inequalities.

Women Refugee Experiences

Given the large number of displaced university-educated refugees in the globe, access to higher education in displacement remains extremely limited, particularly for Syrians (Streitwieser et al., 2017). UN High Commissioner for Refugees (UNHCR) reports that only 1% of refugees enroll in a higher education institution, compared to the global average of 37% (UNHCR, 2016), as cited in (Deitrick et al., 2021)). According to the authors, displaced university-educated Syrian men are three times more likely than women to recommence their studies. According to Damaschke et al. (2019), the main obstacles to admission are a lack of documentation and credentials, information, language, discrimination, and finances.

Opportunities for Women

Despite all the obstacles, there are numerous opportunities for women in higher education. Universities and colleges, for instance, are increasingly recognizing the value of diversity and inclusion and taking measures to resolve the obstacles women face in academia. In the MENA region, numerous innovative approaches and best practices have been developed. Some nations have implemented affirmative action policies to increase women's access to higher education, while others have established mentoring and networking programs to support women's career advancement and development. There have also been efforts to reform curricula and pedagogical practices in order to better reflect gender diversity and inclusivity, such as by including more women's perspectives and experiences in course materials.

Other initiatives are undertaken to address these obstacles (UNESCO, 2022) and advance gender equality in higher education in the MENA region. Governments, non-governmental organizations, and educational institutions are implementing policies and initiatives to increase women's access, enhance their representation, and create an inclusive and supportive environment for educational pursuits.

Universal Access to Higher Education

Universal access to higher education institutions (HEIs) is intricately intertwined with the debate on the human right to education. This concept, which has evolved over the past two decades, has been adopted by a number of international, regional, and national instruments, the most prominent of which is the 2030 Agenda for Sustainable Development. In addition to the humanistic approach to the concept, one cannot disregard the impact that access to higher education institutions has on the development of nations (UNESCO, 2022). The externalities of higher education have a substantial impact on social, economic, and political development. Consequently, ensuring universal access to higher education is crucial not only from a humanistic standpoint, but also for nations pursuing fully developed economic and social systems. More than one-third of the world's population is currently enrolled in some form of postsecondary education, as demonstrated by global access to higher education trends over the past two decades. However, this does not imply that all segments of society can equally benefit from higher education, as there are still significant disparities in access, especially among income groups (UNESCO, 2022). Member nations of the United Nations endorsed the UNESCO 2030 Agenda for Sustainable Development in 2015. It specifies 17 Sustainable Development Goals (SDGs) and 169 targets to address critical challenges and promote sustainable development across numerous domains. SDG 4 focuses on ensuring inclusive and equitable quality education and promoting lifelong learning opportunities for all individuals.

The UNESCO 2030 Agenda recognizes gender equality and the empowerment of women and girls as crucial to achieving sustainable development. It emphasizes the need to eliminate gender disparities at all educational levels and enhance women's access to quality education, continuous learning, and skill development. The most significant aspects of this agenda regarding women and education are as follows:

1. The agenda emphasizes the need to eliminate gender disparities in education and guarantee equal access to quality education for all, including girls and women.
2. Education for girls: The agenda highlights the significance of girls' education and the promotion of gender-sensitive policies and strategies to ensure that all girls have access to free, equitable, and high-quality primary and secondary education.
3. Education as a vital instrument for empowering women and promoting their full and equal participation in society is acknowledged by the agenda. It calls for the elimination of gender stereotypes and discrimination in education, as well as the encouragement of women's leadership and decision-making.
4. Opportunities for lifelong learning: The agenda emphasizes the importance of providing women with opportunities for lifelong learning, allowing them to acquire new skills and knowledge throughout their lifetimes and adapt to changing economic and social environments.

Best Practices and Policies

The overall economic growth and expansion of private and distance education institutions over the past two decades have contributed to the expansion of access to higher education for all. On the other hand, achieving universal access to postsecondary education still faces significant obstacles. The incorporation of marginalized communities continues to be a crucial unresolved aspect of HE universal access. While data indicates that overall access has improved over the past two decades, marginalized groups, particularly those from low-income contexts, continue to be underrepresented in these institutions. Throughout the last two decades, policies promoting universal access to higher education have expanded, including specific laws, financing schemes, and the establishment of specialized universities for disadvantaged students.

When evaluating universal access to HEIs, enrollment versus graduation rates remain an essential dilemma, and institutions must ensure that the students they accept successfully complete their studies.

Systematic Change and Drivers

Despite the fact that it is difficult to fully articulate the effects of increased access on the quality, equity, and performance of higher education at this early stage, we can already state that performance is a concern given the rising dropout rates. Increased access to higher education has had diverse effects on equity, depending on gender, urban/rural dynamics, income levels, and ethnic background. When it comes to quality, we must acknowledge the need for additional and more specific data to fully fathom this highly subjective domain. There are, however, preliminary correlations between the impact of increased access on quality in terms of process (e.g., instruction quality) and consequence (e.g., graduation rates and employability). Adopted by UN Member States in 2015, the Sustainable Development Agenda set a deadline of 2030 for the achievement of gender equality and the empowerment of all women and girls. The world is now behind schedule, with less than ten years remaining. In the midst of the intersecting crises of COVID-19, the climate emergency, and rising economic and political insecurity, gender equality has not only stalled, but began to regress. A growing backlash against women's rights around the globe threatens even well-established liberties and protections. Without a stronger commitment from the international community, gender equality will remain unachievable. The time to act and invest in women and girls has arrived. The fifth among the seventeen Sustainable Development Goals (SDGs) enumerated in the Sustainable Development Agenda is achieving gender equality. Recognizing the link between women's empowerment and a brighter future for everyone, ten objectives were added that incorporate gender-specific benchmarks.

Governance Considerations that Influence Women's Success

Governance structures affect the experiences of women in higher education in several ways. Research suggests that gender diversity in governance improves organizational performance and positively contributes to a more inclusive institutional culture. When women hold leadership positions, they can function as role models, serve as mentors as well as advocate for gender equality, providing a supportive environment for female students, faculty, and administrative members.

Women have special "soft skills" in human resources management which are highly desirable in organizations and in higher education institutions. Democratic leadership and sensitivity to the needs of people is currently accepted by organizations of all types. In addition, the presence of women in organizations leads to the development of a healthy and moral corporate culture (Shahtalebi et al., 2011). Women can find a balance between their careers and family life despite their responsibilities at home and work. This suggests that strategies to increase representation of women at senior levels of universities should be an integral part of the university's mission and strategic plan.

Nature verses Nurture

Common institutional governance models and strategies can seek to achieve gender parity in universities. Three common models include academic power, corporate, or shareholder. The academic model places more power with the academic faculty for decision-making and university affairs. This may hinder the selection, appointment, and elevation of women where the institutional culture has significant bias. A corporate model (more common in the West), incorporates a governance focus more on the financial aspects, than academics, or services. This model may ignore potential improvement in performance and lack a mechanism for the voice of the students as participants in the educational process. The shareholders model combines the two previously mentioned, includes undergraduate and graduate student participation, and that of other stakeholders in university in decision-making, thereby empowering women to become advocates for their learning, tenure, and promotion.

Despite the adoption and successful implementation of one or more of these models, external challenges (as that evidenced in Yemen) take a toll on the state of higher education and consequently on the retention and advancement of women. Poor economic, social, political & cultural conditions prevail in parts of the MENA region, with already strained infrastructures from the pandemic. The most extreme cases can include access to water and Wi-Fi connectivity. Internal challenges differ from public to private universities. The selection processes for administrative appointments, appointment and advancement of faculty and recruitment, and retention of students may be based on qualifications and merit or on other factors, of human capital, areas of research, and educational expenditures specific to an institution.

Successful Strategies from the MENA Region

Strategies to promote gender equity in higher education leadership provide regional case studies and examples of successful implementation of initiatives to prepare, prime, and promote women. In Lebanon, implementing gender quotas, promoting mentorship, and networking programs, is increasing the representation of women in decision-making positions, providing leadership development opportunities, and in creating family-friendly policies and practices. A study by Ghandour & Sultana (2021), highlights the importance of addressing the gender gap in higher education leadership in Lebanon and other countries to promote diversity, inclusion, and excellence in higher education.

Other countries in the MENA region have taken steps to address challenges and to apply best practices to promote women's access and participation in HE. Examples include the UAE, Qatar,

1. The United Arab Emirates has made noteworthy progress in promoting gender equality in HE. The country has implemented

policies to increase women's enrollment and participation in universities, as well as initiatives to encourage women to pursue STEM fields. The UAE also has female leadership in HE institutions, including women serving as university presidents and deans.

2. Qatar has taken several measures to support women's education and research. The country has invested in establishing education and research centers, such as the Qatar Foundation, which promotes gender equality in HE and other scholarships and grants for female students. Qatar also emphasizes the importance of women's representation in leadership positions within educational institutions.

3. Jordan has made efforts to increase women's access to HE and enhance their participation in various disciplines. The country has implemented policies to support women's enrollment and retention in universities, including provision of scholarships and financial aid. Jordan has also focused on promoting gender equality in research and innovation by encouraging women's participation and recognition in these fields.

4. Tunisia has made notable strides in promoting women's participation in HE. The country has implemented affirmative action policies to increase access for women and address gender disparities. Tunisia has also worked to eliminate gender segregation in universities and improve gender balance in faculty and leadership positions. Consequently, there are more women in HE leadership roles than men, as Tunisian men travel outside the country for education and work.

5. In recent years, Saudi Arabia has implemented significant reforms to expand women's access to HE. The country has lifted the ban on women driving, which has increased their mobility and access to educational institutions. The number of Saudi national women entering the mechanical engineering field at one institution is 80 percent, as cited during a panel hosted by the Baker Institute and the University of Houston on Women's Rights in the Middle East Program titled Barriers to Women's Access to STEM in December 2015. Moreover, women's enrollment in universities has been encouraged through scholarship programs, and efforts are being made to increase their representation in leadership positions within HE institutions.

It is important to note that while these countries have taken steps to address challenges, gender disparities and barriers still exist to various degrees across the MENA region. Ongoing efforts are needed to ensure sustained progress and create inclusive HE environments for women.

Strategic Initiatives for the MENA Region

It is suggested that policies aimed at improving the flexibility and affordability of paid childcare services are a way to increase mothers' satisfaction with the work–family balance, which could lead to an increase in the presence and stability of women on the labor market and in higher education institutions (Arpino & Luppi, 2020).

Additionally, a comprehensive strategy involving collaboration between institutions of higher education and employers is required. This will "foster innovation and entrepreneurship, leading to economic growth and job creation." In addition, career counseling and guidance can assist students in identifying the right career path for them, as well as the tools and knowledge they will need to pursue it, and in developing a curriculum that meets the needs of the twenty-first century workforce. If these modifications are implemented, the MENA region will "unlock massive potential that will address unemployment rates, resuscitate economic growth, and ensure long-term prosperity" (Basitkey, 2023).

Both higher education and the private sector have begun to add such positions in recent years. The National Association of Diversity Officers in Higher Education, for instance, convened its first annual conference in 2007, following earlier gatherings beginning in 2003. The National Association of Diversity Officers in Higher Education has over 600 individual and institutional members (Kimbrough, 2017). The association developed its own professional practices standards.

Additionally, HE institutions play a vital role in providing support for refugees and cultivating basic skills and human capital (Stanton, 2016; Streitwieser et al., 2017). Drawing on international research regarding system change (Ainscow, 2021), the following assumptions are suggested to be considered for the formation of policies. First, the author suggests that policy is made at all levels of a national education system, not only at the school and classroom levels. Next, educational change is technically simple but can be socially complex. Additionally, clarity of purpose is essential to mobilize widespread support. And finally, leveraging evidence of various kinds is the catalyst for successful and lasting change processes.

Change Management for MENA Institutions

Nevertheless, change is not easy. The following recommendations are suggested for providing guidance on sustainable and meaningful policy adoptions for institutions of higher education.

1. Adopting distinct promotion criteria clarifies the human capital (particularly qualifications and experience) required for success. Once women understand the game's rules, they can perform just as well as males.
2. Develop flexible working methods to assist parents in balancing work and family responsibilities; this could allow women to combine motherhood and successful professions. Despite the fact that women's progression patterns may resemble those of males, with increased or intermittent flexibility, they will not be required to sacrifice a balanced family life.
3. During periods when individuals have significant family responsibilities (e.g., childbearing years) or in the event of excessive care-giver responsibilities due to the COVID-19 pandemic in the early 2020s, provisions can be made to accept a reduced quantity of research output.
4. Establish new positions or professorships for women and financial incentives to hire women.
5. All public authorities and universities prepare and publish a Gender Equality Scheme outlining how they will carry out their responsibilities under the GED and how they will achieve gender equality.

Impactful Change for Wider Adoption

It is suggested that there needs to be policies in place at improving the flexibility and the affordability of paid childcare services to increase mothers' satisfaction with the work–family balance, which might bring, as a consequence, an increasing presence and stability of women in the HE system.

According to the United Nations (2023), "Institutions of higher education can be critical actors for change. They can make certain that their female students have equal chances regarding applications, admissions, and completion rates. They can teach curricula that promote gender equality and gender equity, as well as equal representation. Through their research, they can expose inequalities, such as how women are discriminated against, and ensure that datasets include women's perspectives."

In addition, "universities and colleges can help address gender inequality in the broader society by engaging in outreach projects that support women. In many ways, institutions of higher education have already been a positive force in the journey toward gender equality. However, with their significant outreach and impact, these institutions hold a much wider role in driving gender equality beyond their campuses into communities" (United Nations, 2023).

Overcoming Obstacles

The most recent data on progress toward gender equality across all SDGs, compiled in UN Women's annual Gender Snapshot Report for 2022, demonstrates the inadequacy of current efforts. If change continues at its present rate, gender equality will progress slowly or stagnate for centuries, according to research.

The number of research studies on women or the gender gap in STEM education focusing on retention, attrition, withdrawal, guidance, and completion is growing (Campos et al., 2022). This systematic literature mapping reveals how higher education institutions demonstrate concern and awareness by documenting their best practices and institutional policies. The authors of the study analyzed attrition issues in higher education from a gender perspective between 2011 and the first half of 2021. It could be used as a source for further research or to expand the current investigation.

Timely Advancement

According to the number of articles published each year, interest in retaining women in STEM fields is growing. In contrast to the number of universities offering these programs, however, the number of institutions and researchers interested in the field is negligible. The authors of the study (Campos et al., 2022) recommend that institutions implement new action-oriented policies addressing this issue. As an example, implementing measures of attraction, access, and retention to increase women's participation. In order to attract young women, they recommend implementing a campaign that includes seminars and talks by women in STEM disciplines. In terms of access, provide cautious follow-ups for young women's college/university applications. In retention, offering guidance programs such as mentoring and academic consultation, fostering identity by establishing women's networks, and offering seminars and workshops by women in the industry or outside the academic system (Campos et al., 2022).

As cited by Parker (2015), Sally Helgesen (1990) characterized the progressive movement in her book The Female Advantage by stating that organizations are "moving beyond gender, in response to organizational need" (Helgesen, p. xviii). Helgesen predicted more than two decades ago that women would be accepted into positions of authority until there was a comfortable gender balance within organizations. Given the rising number of female students, faculty, and administrators in higher education, Helgesen's forecast appears to be accurate. The number of women in senior administrative positions in higher education will fluctuate more rapidly in the future decades (Parker, 2015).

According to UNESCO, emphasizing equity and non-discrimination can transform every aspect of HED. It can commence with admission policies to address the distribution of students by academic programs and disciplines. For example, women's participation in Science, Technology, Engineering, and Mathematics (STEM) programs, institution types, the organization of educational experiences, and institutional practices. There is still much work to be done, especially if equity and non-discrimination are integrated into legal regulations, policies, and institutional cultures, rather than being treated as an "add-on." For example, a mandatory course on "gender equity" would have little to no effect if institutional gender discrimination persists and women do not have equal access to leadership positions and teaching career opportunities in higher education institutions (UNESCO, 2022).

If you are a girl, you can stay in school, help empower your female classmates to do the same and fight for your right to access sexual and reproductive health services. If you are a woman, you can address unconscious biases. (United Nations, 2023)

References

Ainscow, M. (2021). *Inclusions and equity in education: Responding to a global challenge, global, national and local perspectives*, pp. 75–87.

Arpino, B., & Luppi, F. (2020, January–June). Childcare arrangements and working mothers' satisfaction with work–family balance, *Demographic Research, 42*, 549–588.

Basitkey, N. (2023). *Modernizing MENA education: How to close the career success gap.* MENA Source.

Campos, E., Garay-Rondero, C. L., Caratozzolo, P., Dominguez, A., & Zavala, G. (2022). Women retention in STEM higher education: Systematic mapping of gender issues. In F. J. García-Peñalvo, A. García-Holgado, A. Dominguez, & J. Pascual (Eds.), *Women in STEM in higher education.* Lecture Notes in Educational Technology. Springer. https://doi.org/10.1007/978-981-19-1552-9_7. Accessed May 28, 2023.

Damaschke, D., Galegher, L., Park, E., & Maureen, F. (2019). Female refugees' transitions into higher education: Comparative perspectives from

Germany, Egypt, and Kyrgyzstan. In *Comparative perspectives on refugee youth education*. Routledge.

David, M. E. (2015). "Women and gender equality in higher education?" *Education Sciences* 5 (1), 10–25. https://doi.org/10.3390/educsci5010010. Accessed May 28, 2023.

Deitrick, L. D., Wiseman, A. W., & Galegher, E. (2021). *Refugee experiences in higher education: Female perspectives from Egypt, international perspectives on school settings*. Education Policy and Digital Strategies, A Transatlantic Discourse in Education Research. Verlag Barbara Budrich, JSTOR, pp. 137–152.

European Commission. (2021). *Gender equality in academia and research*. https://ec.europa.eu/info/policies/gender-equality/gender-equality-educat ion-and-research. Accessed May 27, 2023.

European Institute for Gender Equality. (2019). *Gender equality in academia and research: GEAR tool handbook*. https://eige.europa.eu/publications/gen der-equality-academia-and-research-gear-tool-handbook. Accessed May 27, 2023.

Ghandour, R., & Sultana, R. (2021). Women's representation in higher education leadership in Lebanon: Challenges and prospects. *Higher Education Policy, 34*(3), 501–518.

Helgesen, S. (1990). *The female advantage*. Bantam, Doubleday, Dell Publishing Group Inc.

Hochschild, A. R. (2003 [1940]). *The second shift*. Penguin Books.

Karam, F., & Zaki, C. (2021). On women participation and empowerment in international trade: Impact on trade margins in the MENA region. *Journal of International Trade & Economic Development, 30*(3), 384–406.

Kimbrough, K. (2017, Fall). Local governments hiring chief diversity officers to lead equity and inclusion work. *National Civic Review, 106*(3), 55–63. Published by: National Civic League Stable URL: https://www.jstor.org/sta ble/10.1002/naticivirevi.106.3.0055. Accessed May 11, 2023.

Parker, P. (2015). The historical role of women in higher education. *Administrative Issues Journal* 5 (1), Article 3. https://dc.swosu.edu/aij/vol5/iss1/3. Accessed May 20, 2023.

Qaffas, A. (2020). Gender in higher education in the Arab world: A systematic review of the literature. *International Journal of Gender, Science and Technology, 12*(1), 155–175.

Sen, A. (1999). *Development as freedom*. Albert A. Knopf. https://kuangalia blog.files.wordpress.com/2017/07/amartya_kumar_sen_development_as_ freedombookfi.pdf

Shahtalebi, S., Yarmohammadian, M. H., & Ajami, A. (2011). Women's success factors from leadership in higher education. *Procedia—Social and Behavioral Sciences, 15*, 3644–3647. ISSN 1877-0428. https://doi.org/10.1016/j.sbspro.2011.04.349.

Stanton, A. (2016). Best practices: Making use of existing university resources to welcome and integrate refugee students. In *Supporting displaced and refugee students in higher education: Principles and best practices.* Institute of International Education.

Streitwieser, B., Miller-I., & Cynthia/de Wit, H. (2017). Higher education's response to the European Refugee crisis. In Gacel-Avila, Jocelyne/Jones, Elspeth/Jooste, & Nico/de Wit, Hans (Eds.), *The globalization of internationalization: Emerging voices and perspectives* (pp. 29–39). Routledge.

United Nations. (2004). *Trade and gender: Opportunities and challenges for developing countries.* United Nations.

UNHCR. (2016). *Aiming higher—The other one percent.* UNHCR education report 2016. https://www.unhcr.org/aiming-higher.html. Accessed May 13, 2023.

United Nations. (2023). *Global lens on gender equality in universities: Reviewing their performance.* https://www.un.org/en/academic-impact/. Accessed May 12, 2023.

UNESCO. (2022, May 18–20). Beyond limits. New ways to reinvent higher education. Working document for the World Higher Education Conference.

UNESCO. (2012). *World Atlas on gender equality in education.* http://www.unesco.org/new/typo3temp/pics/d7af2fe604.jpg. Accessed May 30, 2023.

7

Revitalizing Education: Curriculum Reform and Program/Course Delivery Restructuring

Rim El Khoury ⓘ

Introduction

Education plays a pivotal role in any thriving civilization by endowing individuals with pertinent knowledge driving success amid today's intricate world environment. It represents an essential key unlocking potentials as individuals or communities while also influencing national progress by nurturing innovative ideas among upcoming generations worldwide. Nevertheless, higher education has undergone significant transformations triggered by globalization ramifications coupled with astounding input from evolving technologies models adopted across diverse demographics categories amid practitioners' experience globally. The current educational paradigm seemed lost at sea when looking into unrelenting changing aspects of our environment. Graduates step into life without pivotal skills nor knowledge and instead grovel in despair

R. E. Khoury (✉)

Adnan Kassar School of Business, Lebanese American University, Byblos, Lebanon

e-mail: rim.elkhoury01@lau.edu.lb

© The Author(s), under exclusive license to Springer Nature Switzerland AG 2023

N. Azoury and G. Yahchouchi (eds.), *Governance in Higher Education*, https://doi.org/10.1007/978-3-031-40586-0_7

when faced with insurmountable debts. Its inability to meet contemporary learners' needs coupled with a "one-size-fits-all" mentality hinders prepping students for the twenty-first-century demands. But society is embracing digitalization advancements at an alarming rate, leading to sophisticated interconnectivity globally across all demographics sectors. Therefore, learners must be equipped with modern relevant skillsets before stepping out into this tech-induced labyrinth of life-threatening challenges. Thus, the education system needs reform by pushing crucial focuses and rebuilding curricula structures aimed at rejuvenating learning experiences, meeting expectations from employers and society's evolving demands (Andrade, 2018). Indeed, higher learning institutions should embrace novel educational models that cover real-world challenges and not solely antiquated curricular that is non-functional. Modern education programs and courses often lack innovative techniques and flexibility critical for modern-day learning techniques, resulting in reduced academic impacts. As such, educational institutions worldwide have recognized that curriculum reform and program/course delivery restructuring are vital pieces needed to meet modern students' needs.

However, implementing such initiatives involves complicated planning processes that demand meticulous attention to detail during every stage of implementation. Whether it is identifying challenges or recognizing opportunities arising from change if done successfully, they improve the overall learning experience.

To determine whether institutions are making progress toward improved outcomes, governments require the assessment of learning outcomes (AoLs), which evaluates curriculum reform's impact on program/course delivery structure effectiveness among other key factors. This data allows an insight into effective strategies across institutions when considering policy compliance needs or governance within specific regions too.

This chapter offers practical ways for improving curriculum reform and program/course delivery with carefully curated recommendations tailored specifically toward educators seeking ways to upgrade their systems for today's learners in response without compromising student success rates out of sight over time.

Defining and Designing Curriculum Reform and Program/Course Delivery Restructuring

The realm of higher education is presently undergoing a momentous overhaul, where institutions are increasingly pressed to adapt to novel demands and expectations. Key areas of change institutions are grappling with to ensure they remain pertinent and provide superior education to their students comprise curriculum reform and program/course delivery restructuring.

Curriculum reform is the procedure of revising and modernizing the content and structure of academic programs and courses in response to evolving societal needs and demands. As Kliebard (2004) opines, it is an incessant procedure, a proactive approach to educational planning that aims to guarantee that educational programs are pertinent, up-to-the-minute, and in alignment with the requisites of students, employers, and society. The objective of curricular modifications is ensuring that education programs lead to our future leaders' readiness against emerging challenges fittingly. The changes may involve crafting new modules or revising existing ones in line with current norms/practices/expectations criteria while adhering closely to instructional traditions instead of making sweeping systemic alterations. Critics contend that current teaching methodologies are textbook bound without any application in real-life careers causing robust cognitive dissonance when entering employment fields. Henceforth, our great thinkers have sought STEM-focused education (Science, Technology, Engineering, and Math) emphasizing adaptable learning engagements based on practical principles like critical thinking skills et cetera relevant to career growth prospects beyond graduation; additionally impart such valuable knowledge within inclusive environments given diverse student needs ensuring all succeed academically together. Developing comprehensive courses requires proper alignment of learning objectives with engaging course content catered specifically for learners' needs aimed at promoting active learning toward achieving educational goals. Using effective instructional strategies is paramount when teaching curricula in an engaging manner that enables students to advance in their respective paths of study effectively; furthermore, assessments should align with the objectives set beforehand for even greater levels of success within detailed analyses frameworks like ADDIE that will drive progress review periodically using varied forms of analysis tools including but not limited to surveys or evaluations among others so that historical context can be gained regarding how well faculties delivered over time on these benchmarks.

Defining Program/Course Delivery Restructuring

Education must evolve to keep up with modern times, which means restructuring program/course delivery so that it's effective in meeting our changing needs. Program/course delivery restructuring refers to how academic programs and courses are reorganized using online platforms simulations and other innovative technologies in order to provide optimal effectiveness efficiency accessibility for all learners (Bain, 2020). The aim is to increase productivity efficiency accessibility while utilizing novel technologies pedagogical skills and partnerships. Business education institutions can face a difficult challenge—ensuring all learners can access any changed educational courses. To ensure inclusivity, changes need may include course format e.g., flexible study schedules. On this foundation, instructional methods adapted should be used such as active learning techniques or utilizing multimedia resources indicating adaptability in this fast-changing world (Horvitz, 2007). With criticism surrounding traditional teacher-centered passive lecture-based approach being insufficient when it comes down actively promoting student engagement and collaboration, it's time to incorporate new approaches like project-based learning, blended learning, and flipped classrooms. Table 7.1 compares curriculum reform to program/course delivery restructuring.

Table 7.1 Curriculum reform versus program and course delivery restructuring

Curriculum reform	Program and course delivery restructuring
Focuses on revising and updating curricula	Focuses on changing the way programs and courses are delivered
Involves revising course content and structure	Involves changing the delivery format of courses and programs
Aims to address issues of quality and relevance	Aims to improve student engagement, motivation, and achievement
Can involve changes at the program or institutional level	Can involve changes to individual courses or teaching practices
May require extensive collaboration among stakeholders	May require ongoing professional development and support for teachers
Can take a long-term view of educational improvement	Can provide more immediate improvements in student outcomes
Uses data to identify areas of improvement	Uses data to make informed decisions about program and course changes

Reasons for Curriculum Reform and Program/ Course Delivery Restructuring

Curriculum reform and restructuring of program/course delivery become indispensable to equip students to face the challenges of the swiftly changing world (Altbach et al., 2019). They play a critical role in enhancing student learning outcomes, workforce readiness, and social and economic development. Within this section, we shall explore the rationale behind the requirement of curriculum reform and program/ course delivery restructuring in education.

One of the primary reasons for curriculum reform is to align higher education with the needs of the workforce. In today's ever-evolving world, and according to (World Economic Forum, 2020), the job market's skill requirements are evolving, and conventional educational models are no longer adequate. Simultaneously, technological advancements are transforming the way we live and work, creating new job opportunities and demanding new skills. Emerging technologies like artificial intelligence, blockchain, and robotics are disrupting traditional industries and creating demand for new types of jobs, according to (Gleason, 2018; Rotatori et al., 2021). Therefore, it is essential for educational institutions to keep pace with these changes and provide a curriculum that is not only relevant but also up-to-date to equip students with the skills and knowledge required to succeed in their future careers. The rapid pace of technological advancements necessitates that the education system keeps up with the latest changes. In this regard, curriculum reform can ensure that students have access to cutting-edge technological tools and are adequately equipped to utilize them in their future careers. Institutions may need to develop programs and courses that integrate online or hybrid learning, flipped classrooms, or adaptive learning technologies (McKnight et al., 2016). Furthermore, as per (Shay, 2015), higher education institutions must align their curriculum with society's changing needs, given their responsibility to produce future professionals who contribute to social and economic development. By adapting their programs and courses to meet these changing societal needs, institutions help shape the future of society by producing graduates who contribute to economic growth and social development. Moreover, with changing demographics, schools must adapt to cater to the needs of a progressively diverse student population. Curriculum reform can facilitate the provision of education that is culturally responsive, providing students from all backgrounds with equal opportunities. As the world becomes increasingly interconnected, students must be well-prepared to excel in a globalized economy. Curriculum reform can aid in inculcating a global perspective, thus enabling students to collaborate effectively with people from diverse cultures and backgrounds.

Providing quality education involves adjusting curricula and delivery processes to meet new standards set up for current times, enabling our students to adapt successfully by possessing essential skills needed for contemporary society. Curriculum reforms should strive toward providing excellent education programs that focus on delivering high-quality results from restructured up-to-date methodologies while fostering better engagement between teachers and each student as they progress through their academic journey. Education programs can be equally productive by restructuring program/course delivery where emphasis is put on critical aspects such as content quality, structure refreshment, and delivery mechanism optimization leading to overall output improvements among learners while preparing them effectively for life after school.

Today's learners have varied learning styles (UNESCO, 2020) meaning outdated teaching methods, such as lecture-based teaching, have little to no appeal across the board, with online learning platforms being one highly popular learning method assisting institutions in catering to diverse student preferences. Therefore, schools must be adaptable, remaining responsive to changes in student preferences, and restructuring program/course delivery for tailored learning experiences with customized options which satisfy individualized needs fully.

According to Harvey & Knight's work (1996), review and improvement of curricula increases student engagement resulting in improved output overall among learners. With benefits such as these, many institutions are now using technology-based teaching methods involving gamification among other incentives revolving around blended or virtual reality environments into their curriculum structure.

The COVID-19 pandemic has further highlighted the importance of a flexible approach within educational models (UNESCO, 2020), requiring varied institutions around the globe to transition promptly toward remote learning methodologies leading toward an increased need for innovation, equity, and creativity supporting each other via a "new normal" implementing current knowledge through adapted policies. An increasing number of scholars concur that nurturing students' competencies and proficiencies is paramount for their development. Particularly significant are critical thinking skills alongside creativity and collaboration proficiency since they play a pivotal role in success in modern workplaces that greatly value adeptness at problem-solving within teams while being resilient toward change. Institutions may also be mandated to implement these measures based on mandate from competent authorities regarding compliance with accreditations norms or funding sources (Knight, 2013).

For instance, institutions may need to create new programs and courses to meet accreditation requirements or comply with state or

Table 7.2 Reasons for curriculum reform versus program/course delivery restructuring

Reasons for curriculum reform	Reasons for program/course delivery restructuring
Meeting the needs of a changing job market	Addressing changing societal needs and challenges
Integration of new topics or interdisciplinary approaches	Need for flexibility or personalization
Advancements in technology or research	Inadequate teacher training or professional development
Outdated or inadequate curricula	Ineffective or outdated delivery methods
Alignment with standards or accreditation requirements	Improvement of student learning outcomes or success rates
Needs of a changing student population	Inequities in access to courses or programs
Addressing issues of equity and diversity	Insufficient resources or funding
Improving student outcomes and success	Improving student outcomes and success

federal regulations. By meeting these obligations, institutions can maintain their accreditation and funding status, and demonstrate their commitment to providing high-quality education. While some reasons may overlap or be applicable to both curriculum reform and program/course delivery restructuring, Table 7.2 displays some reasons.

Best Practices for Curriculum Reform and Program/Course Delivery Restructuring

Curriculum reform and program/course delivery restructuring require careful planning, implementation, and evaluation to ensure success. Leveraging best practices, addressing standards overload, collaboration, and continuous improvements are some of the essential strategies for designing quality programs. Best practices should be leveraged for successful implementation of curriculum reform and program/course delivery restructuring. Institutions should learn from the experiences of other institutions that have successfully implemented similar processes, thereby avoiding common pitfalls and identifying effective strategies for implementing new curricula and delivery methods (Kelley & Knowles, 2016; Sroufe & Ramos, 2015). Institutions must take necessary steps to accomplish standard goals required by accrediting bodies concerning new curricula design/building/delivery methods to receive international recognition while maintaining high-quality education programs. Kumar et al. (2020), Nguyen and Ta (2018) and Schomaker (2015) had reservations about overwhelming stakeholders with procedures that could potentially overburden them. Therefore, Table 7.3 has been developed for stakeholders who want guidelines on best practices regarding course design/evaluation/delivery techniques. It is wise if everyone comes together—faculty members, administrators, students—for proper collaboration in enhancing the curriculum delivery and program innovation promoting relevance in education. Collaboration can also help overcome resistance to change from faculty and staff and ensure that the new curricula and delivery methods align with the institution's goals and objectives (Oliver & Hyun, 2011; Pieters et al., 2019; Voogt et al., 2016). Furthermore, establishing a continuous improvement process to monitor and evaluate the effectiveness of the new curriculum and program delivery is essential (A. W. Bates, 2015; Oliver & Hyun, 2011; Shay, 2015). Table 7.3 shows some best practices for curriculum reform and program/course delivery restructuring.

Moreover, in order to fabricate efficacious schemes for reforming curriculum and program/course delivery, it is of great significance to apprehend the viewpoints and experiences of the principal stakeholders embroiled in the education process, including scholars, pedagogues, and administrative personnel. The opinion of scholars carries great weight in educational circles as they hold a pivotal role in receiving instruction while assessing their learning outcomes guides them through ongoing or expected improvements regarding academic programs; additionally, pedagogues play a crucial role in students' educational journey by being responsible for their teaching strategies along with pupil progress evaluations; paving a way to contemplate new reforms in curricula based on first-hand experiences provided by these figures so obtained via one-on-one or collective methods like questionnaires or group discussions. Moreover, another category identified as administration personnel plays a crucial behind-the-scenes backbone by providing support inclusive of

Table 7.3 Best practices for curriculum reform and program/course delivery restructuring

Best practices for curriculum reform	Best practices for program/course delivery restructuring
Conduct a thorough needs assessment to analyze the existing curriculum and identify areas for improvement (Grant, 2010; Inceçay & Inceçay, 2010; Keister & Grames, 2012; Witkin et al., 1995)	Gather feedback from students, instructors, and other stakeholders to make informed decisions about program and course changes (Gouëdard et al., 2020)
Establish clear, measurable, and achievable learning outcomes aligned with the curriculum's goals and the target audience's needs and design a curriculum that aligns with desired learning outcomes (Schmidt, et al., 2017; Spady, 1994; Tam, 2014)	Utilize a variety of instructional methods and techniques and blended learning approaches that combine face-to-face and online delivery (Alammary et al., 2014; Castro, 2019; Garrison & Vaughan, 2008; Mirriahi et al., 2015)
Ensure alignment with industry or job market demands	Use technology to enhance delivery and engagement (Haydn, 2013; Owston, 1997; West & Graham, 2005)
Incorporate interdisciplinary and experiential learning opportunities that can help engage students and enhance their learning (Michaelsen et al., 1997; Misseyanni et al., 2018)	Provide flexible scheduling and course formats to accommodate changing workforce demands, advances in technology, and evolving student needs (A. W. T. Bates & Sangra, 2011)
Provide professional development opportunities for instructors to equip them with the necessary skills and knowledge, to improve their teaching skills, keep up with the latest teaching strategies and technologies, and, in turn, improve the program/course delivery (Guskey, 2002; Mirriahi et al., 2015)	Collaborate with employers and industry partners (Oliver & Hyun, 2011; Pieters et al., 2019; Voogt et al., 2016)
Communicate changes and updates to students and stakeholders	Offer support services and resources to students, such as tutoring, academic advising, and career services, to succeed in the program/course

Note Some best practices may overlap or be applicable to both curriculum reform and program/course delivery restructuring admission procedures to other student services aspects where feedback obtained could occasion reforms addressing specific desired requirements brought forth from administration bodies involved alike scholar-based interest inclusion schemes facilitating improvements toward more diversified interactive learning embracing every member's needs.

Role of AoLs in Curriculum Reform and Restructuring of Program/Course Delivery

In higher education curriculum reform and restructuring for program/course delivery purposes, assessing learners' achievement levels comes as fundamental to achieving specific educational aims—this is called Assessment of Learning Outcomes or AoL.

Implementing effective AoL protocols ensures that a program delivers quality education with evidence supporting these assertions and direct affirmation of learners meeting specific learning benchmarks. This section explores the role of AoL in shaping curriculum reform and restructuring for effective program/course delivery while highlighting the opportunities and challenges associated with it.

AoL serves as a reliable quality assurance mechanism through substantial evidence provided regarding learners' actual performance outcomes and programs' effectiveness. Implementing AoL protocols calls for a systematic approach utilizing specific steps, including identifying learning goals, developing assessment measures, collecting & analyzing data, as well as using such gleaned data to inform continuous improvements to the programs' delivery.

To identify precise learning targets for learners, all stakeholders come into play. It aligns with overall program goals/missions while being measurable and reflective of competencies necessary for learners to excel in relevant labor markets (Kuh et al., 2015).

Developing diverse assessment measures aligned precisely with identified learning objectives is critical in providing tangible evidence of learner achievement levels. There should be both formative assessments providing personalized feedback alongside summative evaluations evaluating student performance. For this process to be effective, faculty members possessing expertise areas are ideal fits to lead on design processes (Black & McMillan, 2012).

Collecting multiple sources of information, surveys & student work alongside external review remains vital bolstered by diverse data sources' ongoing analysis conducted by faculty members possessing expertise in data interpretation. This helps identify areas needing improvement while ensuring effective implementation of programs.

The outcomes of AoLs provide critical information about the effectiveness of curriculum and program/course delivery, which can be used to improve and enhance the quality of education. Assessment serves as a feedback mechanism that helps faculty members and academic leaders identify strengths and weaknesses in educational programs, make data-informed decisions, and implement evidence-based improvements.

Assessing learning outcomes has the potential to impact curriculum reform in various ways. For instance, evaluating student learning outcomes can furnish evidence of program effectiveness and thereby inform the curriculum reform process (Banta & Palomba, 2014). Such data can also pinpoint gaps in the curriculum and areas in which program improvement is necessary. Hence, utilizing this information to steer curriculum reform can lead to educational programs that are more relevant, effective, and cater to the needs of all stakeholders.

Assessment of learning outcomes can unveil areas of the curriculum assessment that require improvement. By scrutinizing student achievement data, academic leaders and faculty members can determine topics or skills that are not being adequately taught, or areas where students are struggling to meet expected learning outcomes. Additionally, assessment can alter the course delivery structure by indicating the efficacy of different delivery models. For example, assessment data may show that students in online courses are not achieving anticipated learning outcomes as effectively as those in traditional face-to-face courses. Upon receipt of these critical findings, we urge academic leaders and faculty members to work hand-in-hand with an eye to achieving enhanced online course delivery effectively. Vital features include considering novel technological tools, augmenting student interactions, or redesigning course content if suitable.

An assessment of the AoL data should be done from time-to-time to identify learning outcomes that aren't being met. Consequently, restructuring program/course deliverables might come into play where gaps need filling urgently. Applying AoL data likewise serves as a feedback mechanism that evaluates different program/course delivery techniques' efficacy while proffering insights into enhancement opportunities.

Regular student learning outcome assessments are recommended as this helps faculty members and academic leaders keep track of progress while seeing possible areas requiring adjustment interventions correspondingly. By verifying whether interventions achieve their intended effects on students' achievements, they can then modify the curriculum or teaching model accordingly for better results always.

To effectively employ the assessment of learning outcomes to influence curriculum reform and program/course delivery restructuring, academic leaders and faculty members must engage in data-informed decision-making. This necessitates a culture of transparency, collaboration, and openness to change. It also entails the use of trustworthy and valid assessment methods that align with learning outcomes and course objectives.

The execution of AoL for reforming the curriculum and reorganizing program/course delivery poses both possibilities and challenges. One of the possibilities is aligning educational programs with the requisites of the stakeholders (Mantai & Calma, 2022) assert that the utilization of AoL can aid institutions in ensuring that their educational programs meet the needs of students, employers, and society. Another opportunity is devising more effective and pertinent educational programs that improve student learning outcomes. Nonetheless, applying AoL for curriculum reform and program/course delivery restructuring also presents challenges. One of the challenges is resistance to change among faculty members. Faculty members may be hesitant toward changes in the curriculum or program/course delivery methods, making it arduous to implement AoL productively. Another challenge is the allocation of resources needed for the implementation of AoL. The implementation of AoL necessitates the allotment of resources for the development of assessment measures, data compilation and analysis, and the utilization of data for continuous improvement.

Policies and Regulations Governing Curriculum Reform and Program Delivery

The policies and regulations dictating curricular and program delivery are fundamental components of any educational institution. It is imperative to ensure that these policies and regulations are congruent with current industry benchmarks and optimum practices to furnish students with superior education. The various policies and regulations include accreditation standards, curriculum development and review, student learning outcomes, faculty qualifications and evaluation, program delivery and student support services.

The ongoing process of curriculum development and review ensures that educational programs remain up-to-date and in concurrence with the latest industry trends and practices. This process encompasses evaluating the current curriculum, identifying areas that necessitate improvement, and formulating new courses and programs. The review process ensures that the courses and programs are pertinent and equip students with the requisite skills and knowledge to succeed in their professions.

To be perceived as a credible institution, an educational establishment must satisfy the minimum requirements set forth by accreditation standards. These standards guarantee that the institution provides exceptional education that aligns with industry standards. Regional accreditation, national accreditation, and programmatic accreditation are the different kinds of accreditation standards. It's vital for educational institutions looking toward recognition and esteem in their industry of focus, uphold specific standards at all times. Such expectations often relate directly or indirectly with student learning outcomes—sets of goals stipulating precisely what faculties expect their graduates should possess after completing specific programs successfully.

Institutions must ensure designed curricula satisfy these requisites with little room for compromise while evaluating each student regularly throughout their academic pursuits.

Furthermore, it is worth mentioning that faculty remains integral components of any successful educational establishment; consequently, requiring special attention paid toward evaluations concerning experience as well as other relevant credentials constantly.

Future Trends of Curriculum Reform and Program/Course Delivery Restructuring in Education

Curriculum reform significantly depends upon institutional adaptability to meet evolving needs as well as program/course delivery restructuring. To envision how higher education will transform over time, this section attempts an exploration on cutting-edge technological trends, pedagogical revamps, and creative industry collaborations which promise pronounced revolutionization. Specifically, the primary challenge faced by curricular reformists is maintaining a real-time relevancy with changing workforce dynamics whereby knowledge requirements and skillsets undergo rapid transformation in congruence with the marketplace demands of the interdependent industries. Thus, as a dynamic response to these exigencies, integration of novel subjects such as sustainability, data science, and AI into coursework plays an instrumental role. Furthermore, implementing innovative teaching practices like flipped classrooms or PBL methods becomes an imperative necessity. However, staff's resistance or reluctance toward change management initiatives is a big obstacle for institutional success. Therefore, strong support and training are necessary to ensure everyone's participation in curricular development along with thorough implementation preparation.

1. Higher education institutions are continuously exploring new approaches to enhance students' educational experiences based on varying trends. A notable one is the emergence of machine learning (ML) and artificial intelligence (AI). They facilitate customized instruction through adaptive learning mechanisms coupled with instant feedback opportunities offered by technology platforms. Some challenges need consideration like privacy concerns besides ethical implications related to data information.
2. Collaboration aimed at solving multifaceted problems can enhance studies further by leveraging different combinations of skills from various faculties. The incorporation of interdisciplinary courses in

curriculum designs opens up avenues for learners to develop comprehensive insights about complex scenarios more efficiently. However, issues may arise concerning meeting collaborative requirements from different departments and faculties.

3. Experiential learning techniques involve learning through active engagement with activities aligned with the set goals while also preparing them for the workforce. Relevant techniques include internships, service-based projects, and apprenticeships which offer learners valuable insights into industry practices (Kolb, 2014). However, the implementation of experiential learning and community engagement can be challenging due to the need for collaboration with external organizations and resources.

4. Personalized learning: The forthcoming days of education may entail a more tailored and supple approach to program and course delivery. Personalized learning is the process of customizing education to meet the unique needs and preferences of each student. To achieve this, adaptive learning technologies may be utilized, which conform the pace, content, and feedback of educational activities to cater to individual students, based on data. Flexible learning provides more options for when, where, and how students learn. Examples of this include blended learning, which merges online and in-person instruction, and modular learning, which allows students to select which modules to study and when (Beatty, 2019).

5. Gamification, virtual and augmented reality: The impact of technology on the alteration of curricula and the delivery of programs and courses will most likely continue to occur in the future. The introduction of technology in the classroom has already changed the way students learn, and this trend is expected to persist. Future patterns suggest an increase in the use of gamification, virtual and augmented reality, and artificial intelligence. Employing technology to upgrade the delivery of curriculum content is a significant opportunity for curriculum reform and restructuring program/course delivery. Institutions can utilize technology to offer students access to superior resources, enhance collaboration and communication between faculty and students, and provide personalized learning experiences.

In conclusion, the future of curriculum reform and restructuring program/course delivery in education is compelling and full of potential. With the changing needs of the workforce, a shift toward interdisciplinary and transdisciplinary learning, and the use of technology to personalize and enhance the learning experience, the prospects for the future of education are bright.

References

Alammary, A., Sheard, J., & Carbone, A. (2014). Blended learning in higher education: Three different design approaches. *Australasian Journal of Educational Technology, 30*(4).

Altbach, P. G., Reisberg, L., & Rumbley, L. E. (2019). *Trends in global higher education: Tracking an academic revolution.* Brill.

Andrade, M. S. (2018). A responsive higher education curriculum: Change and disruptive innovation. In D. Parrish & J. Joyce-McCoach (Eds.), *Innovations in higher education.* IntechOpen. https://doi.org/10.5772/intechopen.80443

Bain, A. (2020). Addressing the challenges of program and course design in higher education with design technologies. *The Journal of Applied Instructional Design, 9*(2).

Banta, T. W., & Palomba, C. A. (2014). *Assessment essentials: Planning, implementing, and improving assessment in higher education.* Wiley.

Bates, A. W. (2015). *Teaching in a digital age: Guidelines for designing teaching and learning* (Tony Bates Associates Ltd. (Ed.)). BCcampus.

Bates, A. W. T., & Sangra, A. (2011). *Managing technology in higher education: Strategies for transforming teaching and learning.* Wiley.

Beatty, B. (2019). *Hybrid-flexible course design: Implementing student-directed hybrid classes.* EdTech Books. https://edtechbooks.org/hyflex

Black, P., & McMillan, J. H. (2012). Formative and summative aspects of assessment: Theoretical and research foundations in the context of pedagogy. In *Sage handbook of research on classroom assessment* (pp. 167–178).

Castro, R. (2019). Blended learning in higher education: Trends and capabilities. *Education and Information Technologies, 24*(4), 2523–2546.

Garrison, D. R., & Vaughan, N. D. (2008). *Blended learning in higher education: Framework, principles, and guidelines.* Wiley.

Gleason, N. W. (2018). *Higher education in the era of the fourth industrial revolution.* Springer Nature.

Gouëdard, P., Pont, B., Hyttinen, S., & Huang, P. (2020). *Curriculum reform: A literature review to support effective implementation.*

Grant, J. (2010). Principles of curriculum design. In *Understanding medical education* (pp. 1–15). Wiley. https://doi.org/10.1002/9781444320282.ch1

Guskey, T. R. (2002). Professional development and teacher change. *Teachers and Teaching, 8*(3), 381–391.

Harvey, L., & Knight, P. T. (1996). *Transforming higher education.* ERIC.

Haydn, T. (2013). *Using new technologies to enhance teaching and learning in history.* Routledge.

Horvitz, B. S. (2007). Online learning: Concepts, strategies, and application. *Educational Technology Research and Development, 55,* 667–669.

Inceçay, G., & Inceçay, V. (2010). A case study on needs assessment of English language teachers. *Procedia-Social and Behavioral Sciences, 2*(2), 317–321.

Keister, D., & Grames, H. (2012). Multi-method needs assessment optimises learning. *The Clinical Teacher, 9*(5), 295–298.

Kelley, T. R., & Knowles, J. G. (2016). A conceptual framework for integrated STEM education. *International Journal of STEM Education, 3,* 1–11.

Kliebard, H. M. (2004). *The struggle for the American curriculum, 1893–1958.* Psychology Press.

Knight, J. (2013). The changing landscape of higher education internationalisation—For better or worse? *Perspectives: Policy and Practice in Higher Education, 17*(3), 84–90.

Kolb, D. A. (2014). *Experiential learning: Experience as the source of learning and development.* FT Press.

Kuh, G. D., Ikenberry, S. O., Jankowski, N. A., Cain, T. R., Ewell, P. T., Hutchings, P., & Kinzie, J. (2015). *Using evidence of student learning to improve higher education.* Wiley.

Kumar, P., Shukla, B., & Passey, D. (2020). Impact of accreditation on quality and excellence of higher education institutions. *Revista Investigacion Operacional, 41*(2), 151–167.

Mantai, L., & Calma, A. (2022). Beyond assuring learning: Greater challenges ahead for management educators. *The International Journal of Management Education, 20*(3), 100723. https://doi.org/10.1016/j.ijme.2022.100723

McKnight, K., O'Malley, K., Ruzic, R., Horsley, M. K., Franey, J. J., & Bassett, K. (2016). Teaching in a digital age: How educators use technology to improve student learning. *Journal of Research on Technology in Education, 48*(3), 194–211.

Michaelsen, L. K., Fink, L. D., & Knight, A. (1997). Designing effective group activities: Lessons for classroom teaching and faculty development. *To Improve the Academy, 16*(1), 373–397.

Mirriahi, N., Alonzo, D., & Fox, B. (2015). A blended learning framework for curriculum design and professional development. *Research in Learning Technology, 23.*

Misseyanni, A., Papadopoulou, P., Marouli, C., & Lytras, M. D. (2018). *Active learning strategies in higher education.* Emerald Publishing Limited Bingley.

Nguyen, H. C., & Ta, T. T. H. (2018). Exploring impact of accreditation on higher education in developing countries: A Vietnamese view. *Tertiary Education and Management, 24*, 154–167.

Oliver, S. L., & Hyun, E. (2011). Comprehensive curriculum reform in higher education: Collaborative engagement of faculty and administrators. *Journal of Case Studies in Education, 2.*

Owston, R. D. (1997). Research news and comment: The world wide web: A technology to enhance teaching and learning? *Educational Researcher, 26*(2), 27–33.

Pieters, J., Voogt, J., & Pareja Roblin, N. (2019). *Collaborative curriculum design for sustainable innovation and teacher learning.* Springer Nature.

Rotatori, D., Lee, E. J., & Sleeva, S. (2021). The evolution of the workforce during the fourth industrial revolution. *Human Resource Development International, 24*(1), 92–103.

Schmidt, M. J. et al. (2017). The perils of outcomes-based education in fostering South African educational transformation. *Open Journal of Political Science, 7*(3), 368.

Schomaker, R. (2015). Accreditation and quality assurance in the Egyptian higher education system. *Quality Assurance in Education, 23*(2), 149–165.

Shay, S. (2015). Curriculum reform in higher education: A contested space. *Teaching in Higher Education, 20*(4), 431–441.

Spady, W. G. (1994). *Outcome-based education: Critical issues and answers.* ERIC.

Sroufe, R., & Ramos, D. P. (2015). Leveraging collaborative, thematic problem-based learning to integrate curricula. *Decision Sciences Journal of Innovative Education, 13*(2), 151–176.

Tam, M. (2014). Outcomes-based approach to quality assessment and curriculum improvement in higher education. *Quality Assurance in Education, 22*(2), 158–168.

UNESCO. (2020). Education: From disruption to recovery. *UNESCO Building Peace in the Minds of Men and Women.* https://En.Unesco.Org/News/Covid-19-Educational-Disruption-and-Response. Accessed on 3, 2020.

Voogt, J. M., Pieters, J. M., & Handelzalts, A. (2016). Teacher collaboration in curriculum design teams: Effects, mechanisms, and conditions. *Educational Research and Evaluation, 22*(3–4), 121–140. https://doi.org/10.1080/13803611.2016.1247725

West, R. E., & Graham, C. R. (2005). Five powerful ways technology can enhance teaching and learning in higher education. *Educational Technology, 45*(3), 20–27.

Witkin, B. R., Altschuld, J. W., & Altschuld, J. (1995). *Planning and conducting needs assessments: A practical guide.* Sage.

World Economic Forum, V. (2020). The future of jobs report 2020. Retrieved from Geneva.

8

Interactivity and Engagement Tactics and Tools

Jacque Digout and Hady El Samra

The Changing Landscape of Higher Education

The Evolution and Impact of Technology on Higher Education

Higher education has been a dynamic and ever-changing experience, driven by significant advancements and revolutions. This shift has been most visible in the Middle East and North Africa (MENA) region, where the region's unique socio-economic condition has influenced the trajectory of higher education in a variety of ways. Historically, conventional pedagogical practices and learning environments characterized the MENA region's higher education scene. The discovery of oil in the area,

J. Digout (✉)
Toulouse Business School, Toulouse, France
e-mail: j.digout@tbs-education.fr

H. E. Samra
University of Sydney, Sydney, NSW, Australia
e-mail: hadyelsamra@gmail.com

© The Author(s), under exclusive license to Springer Nature
Switzerland AG 2023
N. Azoury and G. Yahchouchi (eds.), *Governance in Higher Education*,
https://doi.org/10.1007/978-3-031-40586-0_8

and subsequent economic success, hastened the expansion process. This rapid growth was not only quantitative, but also qualitative, and indicated a departure from the conventional development trajectory seen in other parts of the world. For example, in Europe, the transition from an agrarian civilization was followed by industrialization, then the emergence of the information society, and ultimately the modern knowledge economy. On the other hand, the Gulf countries set out to transition from a fishing/pearling/trading economy to a knowledge economy (Hvidt, 2015). Technology's advent and integration into the higher education system have changed the way education is delivered and received. New learning platforms and tools have emerged as a result of digital technology, allowing an increase in engagement and involvement among students and teachers. The incorporation of technology in higher education has democratized access to education, provided study flexibility, and personalized the learning experience, therefore enhancing the entire educational process. A confluence of factors has hastened the introduction of technology into higher education in the MENA region. These include a significant labor shortage, an excess of discretionary cash, and poor performance of indigenous higher education institutions. For these reasons, governments in the United Arab Emirates, Saudi Arabia, Qatar, and Bahrain have launched ambitious policy initiatives in the higher education sector. As a result, many countries' higher education systems have become vibrant centers of experimentation and entrepreneurship (Crist, 2015). However, incorporating technology into higher education presents several challenges. These include issues about infrastructure, digital literacy, data privacy and security, and the need for educators to participate in continual professional development. Despite these challenges, the potential advantages of technology in increasing connection and participation in higher education are significant. It is demonstrated by the ongoing digital transformation in the MENA region's higher education business. Finally, the changing environment of higher education in the MENA region, which is rooted in the evolution of the education system and the transformative effect of technology, offers a complex tapestry of difficulties and opportunities. As the region continues to develop, it is vital to accept and use techniques that encourage engagement and involvement. By doing so, the quality of education may be increased, a culture of lifelong learning can be developed, and the goal of education can be realized, leading to empowering individuals and contributing to societal progress.

Shifting Toward Online and Blended Learning

The digital era has resulted in a substantial transformation in the higher education scene, notably in the MENA area. Online and blended learning methodologies are supplementing, and in some cases, replacing traditional face-to-face training. The rising accessibility of digital technology, the changing demands of learners, and the growing acknowledgment of the benefits of flexible learning settings are driving this shift. E-learning or online instruction entails utilizing digital technologies such as laptops and networks over the Internet to provide educational resources available remotely at any point in time. It enables self-paced learning activities from any location on earth making it efficient, particularly, for adult students who need a flexible educational approach to balance work responsibilities alongside academic ones (Rama, 2014).

Blended education, which refers to tying traditional classroom interaction methods with web-based educational exercises, further facilitates better outcomes than traditional classes by amalgamating elements from both educational approaches. This synthesis permits ease of access through web-based material together with the benefits of social exchange bricks-and-mortar classes can offer.

Several aspects drive the trend toward blended and online study in MENA including increasing internet utilization levels along with the utility of portable electronic gadgets have made access to digitized education easier within the region. With a rising population base necessitating greater accessibility toward quality higher education at reduced costs, utilizing cost-efficient scalable instructional methods becomes critical (Knight, 2016). In addition, accommodating workforce prerequisites tied into an ever-evolving knowledge economy accentuates continuous learning opportunities.

Digital technologies including virtual reality tools have facilitated innovative strategies for disseminating instructor content dissemination and offering multifaceted course management systems (LMS).

Notwithstanding the potential benefits of e-learning in enhancing instructional delivery, there are still barriers associated with adopting alternative learning approaches including low digital literacy rates coupled with reorienting traditional instructor attitudes embedded within conventional educational frameworks in MENA. Supplemental teacher training is needed to improve digital technology skills for effectively offering blended and online instruction (Rama, 2014). To successfully implement online and blended learning initiatives within their respective communities, regional institutions of higher learning must allocate resources toward infrastructure development as well as enhance their professional capacities through training programs. It should be noted that this reflects a noteworthy transformation of the MENA area's educational landscape. Specifically, learners' growing familiarity with digital technologies is prompting them to embrace more flexible approaches to instruction that can better accommodate their interests and needs.

Understanding Interactivity and Engagement in Higher Education

Definition and Importance

To provide top-tier higher education experiences for learners today, it's important to embrace inter-actionality and participant philosophy into coursework methodologies. Inter-actionality works best when it exists between students and faculty within the classroom ecosystem, with the surrounding educational content constituting a further vital component. By offering synchronous or asynchronous exchanges between these parties (Ghafar, 2020b), each student will be equally involved and engaged in the given learning environment.

Student engagement is crucial too as it denotes qualities such as focus, curiosity, enthusiasm, and inquiry during one's studies—all of which are vital to creating motivation while enhancing learning quality inside and outside of teaching environments (Peterman et al., 2017). Thus, a higher level of participation helps achieve better overall grading results, lower-level dropouts among peers coupled with positive feedback on overall educational experiences.

Successful participation/interaction methods help create future job success. These can upskill students' abilities such as critical thinking/problem-solving skills for times when they join their first professional workspaces. Interpersonal communication/collaboration are also key skills that increase with inter-actionality within teaching places in Modern Day Middle Eastern & North African countries.

Deploy digital technologies like multimedia tools/social media platforms to facilitate classroom interaction easily during today's online/hybrid learning environments. However, promoting interaction should happen through implementing changes designed to overcome potential difficulties like lack of effective technology training among teachers/students (Peterman et al., 2017). Encouraging class collaboration or giving credit where due on actively engaging performances will improve involvement ratios while also increasing academic outcomes/satisfaction.

By combining efforts on interactive participation modules along with student engagement methods together into education practices worldwide, we can ensure high-quality higher education facilities that will lead to even more accomplishments by the learners themselves! As the landscape of higher education progresses, it is crucial to persist in examining and introducing fresh approaches for encouraging interaction and involvement. This ongoing process ensures continued growth in the field.

Linking Interactivity, Engagement, and Student Success

Engagement in higher education in the MENA region is heavily influenced by the relationship between interaction and participation. These two factors complement each other perfectly by establishing an environment that fosters student academic success. Participation through interaction with fellow students provides numerous benefits like community building that encourages collaborative learning combined with different outlooks on multiple topics to help learn faster. Allowing for prompt feedback from instructors or classmates reinforces retention helping them to seek out additional interactions.

Interactivity and engagement, in this sense, constitute a virtuous cycle, one feeding into and reinforcing the other. Students are more likely to be engaged in a more dynamic learning environment. This connection between interactivity and engagement has a direct influence on student achievement. According to research, kids who are actively involved in the learning process perform better academically. They are more likely to stick with their studies, improve at a faster rate, and finally achieve their educational objectives (Ghafar, 2020b). Fostering interactivity and engagement is both a difficulty and an opportunity in the MENA area, as higher education institutions face issues such as huge class sizes, varied student populations, and the need to educate students for a constantly changing labor market. Innovative pedagogical practices, such as problem-based learning, collaborative projects, and the use of technology, can promote student achievement by increasing interaction and engagement. Artificial intelligence and machine learning, for example, show great potential for increased interaction and participation in higher education. These technologies can deliver individualized learning experiences, real-time feedback, and adaptive learning, encouraging engagement and enhancing learning results. It is crucial to highlight, however, that the successful adoption of these strategies and tools necessitates a supportive institutional climate, continuing faculty development, and a student-centered approach to teaching and learning.

The link between interaction, engagement, and student performance is one of the principal pillars of higher education, especially in the MENA area. Fostering interactivity and engagement will be a significant focus area as higher education institutions attempt to enhance educational results and prepare students for the future.

Factors Influencing Interactivity and Engagement

The variables determining interactivity and engagement in higher education are varied and complicated, involving components ranging from individual student training to the larger institutional and cultural environment in which learning occurs. Interactivity and engagement are two critical elements that contribute significantly to the learning experience and outcomes of students. Several factors, both directly and indirectly, influence these elements (Al-Rahmi et al., 2020; Ghafar, 2020a, 2020b, 2020c).

Direct Factors Influencing Interactivity:

- Teaching Methods: The pedagogical practices adopted by educators have a profound impact on the level of interaction in the classroom. Active learning strategies such as problem-based learning collaborative learning and experiential learning can significantly enhance interaction by promoting active participation in the learning process.
- Learning Environment: Both physical and virtual learning environments play a crucial role in fostering interactivity. A well-designed learning environment can enhance collaboration and facilitate interactive learning experiences.
- Individual Student Traits: Individual characteristics of students such as motivation, self-efficacy, and learning styles also have a direct impact on interactivity. Students who are motivated and confident in their abilities are more likely to participate actively in learning activities, thereby enhancing interactivity.
- Social Media Applications (SMAs): The use of SMAs facilities interaction with peers and lecturers, providing opportunities for discussion and exchange of information.
- Perceived Ease of Use (PEOU): If students find SMAs easy to use and incorporate into their studies, they are more likely to interact with them.

Indirect Factors Influencing Interactivity:

* Social and Cultural Environment: The social and cultural environ-ments in which institutions operate can have an indirect influence on interactivity. In communities where higher education is valued and encouraged, students may feel more motivated to interact with their studies.
* Policies and institutional support: Institutional support policies can indirectly affect interactivity by creating an environment conducive to interactive learning. Institutions that prioritize student interaction and provide the necessary support and resources can foster an engaging learning environment.
* Integration of technology: The broader integration of technology into the education system can also have an indirect impact on interac-tivity. The viability of technology, for example, can change social attitudes toward education, and institutional policies can influence how effectively technology is integrated into teaching and learning processes.
* Leadership Skills: Nowadays, leadership is recognized as the most crucial trait for entrepreneurs. Leadership workshops increased immensely during the twenty-first century focusing on creating changes within communities through interactions with the surround-ings. It is of great importance to students to enhance their entrepreneurial mindset by including capacity and skills-building components in leadership, encouraging creative thinking, and successful negotiations.
* Role of Assessments and Capacity Building Skills: Formative and summative evaluations are critical in the dynamic field of innova-tion and entrepreneurship education. Formative assessments, which include group discussions, in-class activities, and reflective diaries, give continuous, real-time feedback, encouraging active learning and directing instructional practices. Summative evaluations, such as busi-ness plan drafting, pitch presentations, and traditional examinations, serve as critical milestones for measuring student progress against predetermined benchmarks. These evaluations, when taken together, not only reinforce students' grasp of ideas but also provide a plat-form for practical application, enabling a holistic approach to measure student learning and competency growth throughout the course.

Direct Factors Influencing Engagement:

One way to improve students' engagement in their learning is to promote interactivity with peers and lecturers. Through the use of social media applications (SMAs), students can interact through discussions, group projects, or casual conversations. By fostering a sense of connection between students and teachers. A community can be formed, which enhances engagement. Active collaborative learning is another method that can enhance student participation in the learning process and increase engagement. By implementing pedagogical strategies that require active involvement from students, such as problem-based learning or project-based learning, learners are encouraged to take an active role in their education. Students' perception of relevance also influences their level of engagement: if they view the material as meaningful and relevant to real-world applications or career goals, they are more likely to engage in it. Aligning content with personal interests also helps sustain motivation.

The perception that teachers and peers are supportive and helpful plays a pivotal role in sustaining engagement. Examples include providing feedback on work or creating a supportive classroom environment.

Finally, satisfaction with the overall learning experience plays a vital role: when students find their coursework enjoyable and rewarding while feeling challenged along the way they are more likely to remain engaged throughout their education journey.

Indirect Factors Influencing Engagement:

- Leadership Skills: These skills not only enhance students' entrepreneurial capabilities but also their engagement in learning as they see the relevance and applicability of what they are learning.
- Role of Assessment and Capacity Building Skills: Assessment provides students with feedback on their learning, which can enhance engagement. Moreover, skills-building activities provide students with opportunities to apply what they have learned, thereby promoting, and enhancing their engagement.
- Conceptualization and Critical Thinking: The students find it difficult to develop cohesive conceptualizations of the theories and diverse

business models. Internalizing the notion of social entrepreneurship as a changing business model, for example, was perceived as challenging and hence required critical thinking along with inquiry learning methodologies in entrepreneurship education. This cognitive involvement in learning has the potential to increase students' overall engagement.

- Fostering an entrepreneurial mindset involves instilling important traits like creativity, innovation, risk-taking ability, and determination to create value. Such ethos can positively impact students' engagement with learning as they appreciate how much they can contribute to what they learn. Indeed, entrepreneurship education has grown past just building skills for setting up businesses; it also involves instilling an approach that inspires constructive thinking vital for achieving successful outcomes both economically and socially.

- Thriving in today's workforce necessitates being versed in twenty-first-century skills like critical thinking, problem-solving, collaboration, communication, & digital literacy. Educational institutions must ensure that these proficiencies are an integral part of their teaching programs so that students gain an understanding of how relevant they are to future careers. As soon as learners grasp the value of these abilities corresponding to professional prospects, it makes them more invested learners leading to higher levels of participation from them.

The Faculty's Role in Promoting Interactivity within Higher Education

Increasing Participation and Interacting

Promoting interactivity that leads to meaningful engagement within higher education is a multifaceted task that faculties carry out every day. Faculty members play a vital role in defining the overall learning environment while keeping each student's unique needs at the forefront of their focus. Managing this balance involves integrating active learning strategies such as problem-based or collaborative teaching models; these encourage an engaging experience that also develops critical thinking skills vital for achieving success within higher education settings.

Alongside this, faculty evaluations offer constructive feedback aimed at identifying evolution plans for each student, thereby promoting long-term performance improvements enabled through ongoing and regular assessments. Technology developments have rapidly transformed the roles of faculties who must now be proficient in different digital-learning tools with personalized experiences becoming increasingly easier through learning management systems as well as multimedia learning materials.

Additionally, faculties contribute to essential program design and curricula, ensuring proper alignment with all stakeholders' goals. This way, faculties foster information sharing toward what every class needs to work on for continuous improvement of academic engagement throughout the course journey.

Creating the right balance and environment capable of inspiring interest while driving overall success is an especially significant opportunity within MENA's regions where faculty members and students engage and work closely toward harmonious achievement throughout a shared learning journey. The ability to promote interactivity and engagement in higher education can be influenced by multiple factors such as culture, social dynamics, as well as technology. Despite these challenges facing faculty members, their involvement is crucial to implement effective teaching approaches that prioritize interactivity and engagement (Al Maiah, 2020). Faculty members not only transmit course knowledge but also foster an inclusive classroom environment with constructive feedback while encouraging ongoing student involvement inside and outside the class. The MENA region's unique landscape presents further challenges, hence prompting faculty members to apply culturally aware strategies while keeping up with modern technology.

Increasing Interactivity and Engagement

Active learning approaches are one of the primary methodologies used by professors. Problem-based learning, collaborative learning, and experiential learning are examples of strategies that enable students to participate actively in their education. This not only increases participation but also encourages a deeper grasp of the content (Stark et al., 2022).

- Adapting to Virtual Learning Environments: The pandemic of COVID-19 has required a transition to virtual learning. This platform may be used by faculty to give flexible learning options, such as asynchronous learning through recorded lectures. Students may learn at their speed and go over the material as required. Furthermore, the virtual environment eliminates geographic restrictions, allowing guest lecturers and specialists from all around the world to contribute to the learning experience.
- Incorporating Interactive Learning Tools: Faculty can use interactive learning tools to keep students engaged in a virtual learning environment. Small group breakout sessions to synchronous engagement technologies like Slack, Poll Everywhere, and Kahoot are examples of these tools. Even when students are not physically present in the same area, these technologies may assist in creating an engagement and engaging learning environment.
- Outside of the clinical setting: Because the pandemic has limited clinical experience for medical students, professors have had to adapt to guarantee students continue to obtain a full education. Simulation, virtual reality, and mental imagery have all been used to supplement clinical exposure. Even if students are unable to engage in typical clinical rotations, these techniques can offer them significant learning opportunities.
- Physical and psychological well-being support: Students have suffered major physical and psychological consequences as a result of the pandemic. The facility can play an important role in promoting students' well-being throughout this period. This might involve developing platforms for disseminating quickly changing clinical information, boosting access to psychological counseling services, expanding mentoring possibilities, and offering food assistance.
- Board examination flexibility: The pandemic has necessitated adaptability in a variety of sectors, including board examinations. Faculty can help students during this period by offering flexible test dates and moving to virtual oral board examinations.

These techniques emphasize the significance of facility, flexibility, creativity, and assistance in promoting interactivity, particularly in light of future obstacles such as the COVID-19 pandemic.

Challenges Faced by Faculty

In the ever-changing world of higher education, faculty members face the challenge of fostering student interaction and engagement. With the advancement of digital technology and the trend toward online learning, this endeavor has become significantly more challenging, particularly in the MENA region. This discussion examines the challenges professors face in this area, as well as potential solutions, using current research.

Academicians face one of their greatest challenges in adjusting to new teaching methods that emphasize interaction and participation. Today's education system is witnessing significant changes as traditional lecture formats are substituted with interactive learning environments designed to stimulate active participation among students. Consequent to this change comes the necessity for profound transformations from conventional knowledge dissemination processes toward the facilitation of learner experiences (Al Samarraie, 2019).

To enhance the process of teaching and learning comes another crucial factor—Technology application plays a vital role in classroom interaction while encouraging greater student involvement through various online channels. Instructors should be well-versed with digital technologies and multiple platforms that enhance engagement at different levels. However, some teachers might lack the technological skills needed or might be resistant to applying these technologies within their classroom environments (Al Samarraie, 2019; Bhuasiri et al., 2017). Moreover, the diversification of learning styles and preferences poses an additional challenge wherein personalized learning is becoming increasingly popular requiring teachers to tailor their instructional strategies toward individual student needs and in larger classes can prove complex.

Active learning methodologies such as problem-based, or collaborative techniques have been designed to directly engage students leading to heightened motivation and improving academic outcomes. Additionally, technology can play a crucial role through digital tools made available for improved interactivity such as communication platforms—online forums or social media forms. Finally, encouraging student participation by creating a welcoming environment that appreciates differences while providing constructive feedback creates an inclusive environment which results in a sense of community fostered between students ultimately leading to improved motivation and contributing directly to academic improvement. In conclusion, elevating interactive and engaging environments within higher education requires significant effort from faculty to adapt new teaching approaches through various mechanisms. Integrating technology with tailored instructional strategies geared toward individual student preferences creates the ideal learning environment. Although boundaries exist, there are ways for professors to promote student engagement and participation. Active learning strategies, technological tools, and cultivating a hospitable environment are all effective approaches.

Best Practices and Strategies

Forums for Online Discussion

Online discussion forums are extensively used in both traditional classroom settings as well as virtual school environments to promote a sense of participation and exchange between learners, courtesy of their proven effectiveness in this regard. They give a forum for students to exchange ideas, ask questions, and work together to solve problems. Instructors may guide conversations, offer feedback, and keep track of student engagement. Online discussion forums improve student academic performance and satisfaction in the MENA region (Al-Rahmi et al., 2018).

Interactive lectures

Quizzes, dialogues, and problem-solving exercises are examples of interactive lectures that demand student participation. This method breaks up the usual lecture structure by keeping students interested and allowing for instant responses. Students in interactive lectures displayed improved knowledge and recall of content than students in standard lectures (Bensalem et al., 2019).

Collaborative Learning Tools

Collaborative learning platforms, such as Google Docs and Wikis, enable students to collaborate on projects and assignments, increasing engagement and developing critical thinking and problem-solving abilities. These technologies have been utilized effectively in a variety of educational contexts in the MENA area. Al-Rahmi et al. (2020) discovered in Oman that students who used collaborative learning technologies had better learning results and satisfaction.

Social Media Platforms

Facebook, Twitter, TikTok, and Instagram are increasingly being utilized in education to improve student participation and communication. They provide unique chances for engagement, cooperation, and resource sharing. Higher education institutions that are more engaged on social media do better in terms of student recruitment (Rutter et al., 2017).

Educational Gamification

Gamification is the use of game design aspects in non-game environments such as education. It may have aspects such as point badges, leaderboards, and challenges. Gamification has been utilized to boost student motivation and engagement in the MENA area. In one study, it was found that gamification improves student engagement and learning outcomes. (Hamari et al., 2018).

Augmented and virtual reality

Immersive, interactive experiences provided by virtual and augmented reality (VR/AR) can considerably improve learning. They may be used to generate simulations, virtual field excursions, and other forms of experiential learning. VR/AR is still a new technology in education in the MENA area, but its potential is being recognized. Virtual reality and augmented reality may give effective and interesting learning experiences (Radianti et al., 2020).

Finally, numerous methods and strategies may be employed to increase interactivity and participation in teaching. The selection of tools should be directed by the learning objectives, the setting, and the student's requirements and preferences.

The Future of Interactivity and Engagement in Higher Education

A variety of trends influence emerging trends in MENA connectivity and participation in higher education, including technological improvements, social dynamics, and the ongoing COVID-19 pandemic. These technologies are transforming higher education, providing both benefits and challenges for both academics and students. One of the most notable advancements is the increased use of digital technologies to boost interaction and participation. The outbreak, which prompted a movement toward distance learning, has pushed for the use of technology in education, notably in the form of e-learning platforms and digital tools, and social media platforms (Almaiah, 2020). Personalized learning, real-time feedback, and data-driven insights into student performance and engagement are also available. Another recent trend is a great emphasis on active learning approaches, which include students actively participating in the learning process rather than passively obtaining knowledge. Problem-based learning, collaborative learning, and experiential learning have all been shown to boost student engagement and knowledge (Ghafar, 2020b). Faculty members can contribute to the implementation of these principles by designing learning activities that encourage student participation and critical thinking. The transition to digital learning and active learning approaches, on the other hand, is riddled with obstacles. Faculty members must be knowledgeable about educational technology and adapt their teaching methods to facilitate active learning. A favorable institutional environment is necessary, as well as ongoing professional growth and help. Furthermore, concerns like the digital divide and accessibility must be addressed so that all students may benefit from these learning opportunities. The academic's role in fostering engagement and involvement is also evolving. Faculty members are increasingly expected to be instructors' mentors, facilitators, and designers of learning experiences. They must also create a friendly supportive learning environment that values diversity and promotes a sense of belonging. Pastoral care and student aid, as well as teaching and curriculum creation, are all part of this (Al Asfour, 2018). Growing trends in student connection and involvement in higher education in the MENA region reflect evolving student needs and expectations, the benefits and limits of digital technology, and the faculty's shifting role. Higher education institutions will need to adapt and innovate in order to increase student learning and performance, as these trends continue to emerge. Another recent trend is a stronger emphasis on active learning methodologies, in which, students actively participate in the learning process rather than passively acquiring knowledge. Student engagement and understanding have been demonstrated to improve through problem-based learning, collaborative learning, and experiential learning (Ghafar, 2020a). Faculty members may help put these principles into action by developing learning activities that stimulate student engagement and critical thinking. On the other hand, the move to digital learning and active learning methodologies is fraught with difficulties. Faculty members must be familiar with educational technology and adjust their teaching approaches to promote active learning. A positive institutional atmosphere, as well as continual professional development and assistance, are required. Furthermore, issues about the digital gap and accessibility must be addressed in order for all students to benefit from these learning possibilities.

Conclusion

Facilitating interactivity and engagement is critical to supporting student success in higher education. These elements actively promote better topic comprehension while enhancing the overall learning experience. Various factors such as course design, staff participation levels, student motivation factors as well as technology usage affect their implementation for optimal results. Faculty members playing a key role in fostering dynamic classroom participation leverage immersive techniques like active learning practices to accelerate learner engagement. Constructive feedback that identifies areas calling for improvement combined with educational resources significantly supports instruction efforts in creating inclusive environments that are always supportive of learners; however, technological hurdles plus development needs form challenges that call for solutions.

References

Al Asfour, A. (2018). Faculty use of social media and mobile devices: Analysis of advantages and concerns. *Interdisciplinary Journal of e-Skills and Lifelong Learning, 14*, 167–192.

Al-Asfour, A. (2018). Faculty member engagement in Saudi Arabian Universities: A study of selected higher education institutions. *Journal of Education and Practice, 9*(16), 123–132.

Al-Busaidi, K. A., & Al-Shihi, H. (2012). The use of collaborative learning tools in Omani higher education: A case study. *Procedia-Social and Behavioral Sciences, 46*, 2022–2027.

Almaiah, M. A. (2020). Examination of factors influencing the use of mobile learning system: An empirical study. *Education and Information Technologies, 25*, 5269–5291.

Al-Rahmi, W., Alias, N., Othman, M., Marin, V., & Tur, G. (2018). A model of factors affecting learning performance through the use of social media in Malaysian higher education. *Computers & Education, 121*, 59–72.

Al-Samarraie, H. (2019). A scoping review of videoconferencing systems in higher education. *International Review of Research in Open and Distributed Learning, 20*(3), 121–140.

Bensalem, E., Fhima, M., & Otmani, A. (2019). Use of gamification in higher education in the MENA region. https://files.eric.ed.gov/fulltext/EJ1203741.pdf.

Bhuasiri, W., Xaymoungkhoun, O., Zo, H., & Rho, J. J. (2017). Development of Virtual Immersive Learning Environments (VILEs) Based on digital storytelling: Improving on-site safety performance.

Crist, J. W. (2015). *Innovation in a small state: Qatar and the IBC cluster model of higher education.*

Ghafar, A. (2020a). *Convergence between 21st century skills and entrepreneurship education in higher education institutes.*

Ghafar, A. (2020b). The role of faculty in promoting student engagement: The case of the Arab Open University in Saudi Arabia. Open Learning: *The Journal of Open, Distance, and e-Learning, 35*(1), 77–94.

Ghafar, A. (2020c). *The role of faculty in the era of digital learning.* Brookings Doha Center.

Hamari, J., Koivisto, J., & Sarsa, H. (2018). Does gamification work?—A literature review of empirical studies on gamification. *In 2018 51st Hawaii International Conference on System Sciences (HICSS)* (pp. 3025–3034). IEEE.

Hvidt, M. (2015). *The state and the knowledge economy in the Gulf: Structural and motivational challenges.*

Knight, W.A. (2016). *Institutional research and planning in higher education: Global contexts and themes* by Karen L. Webber and Angel J. Calderon. The Shift Towards Online and Blended Learning.

Peterman, A., Neijhoft, A. N., Cook, S., & Palermo, T. (2017). *Understanding the linkages between social safety nets and childhood violence: A review of the evidence from low- and middle-income countries.*

Radianti, J., Majchrzak, T. A., Fromm, J., & Wohlgenannt, I. (2020). A systematic review of immersive virtual reality applications for higher education: Design elements, lessons learned, and research agenda. *Computers & Education, 147*, 103778.

Rama, C. (2014). *University virtualisation in Latin America.*

Rutter, M., Bryce, J., & Wilson, A. (2017). Social media interaction, the university brand and recruitment performance. *Journal of Business Research, 79*, 238–246.

Stark, N., Hayirli, T. C., Bhanja, A., Kerrissey, M., Hardy, J. D., & Peabody, C. R. (2022). *Unprecedented training: Experience of residents during the COVID-19 Pandemic.* https://escholarship.org/content/qt3121b0zd/qt3121 b0zd.pdf?t=rsbxxd

9

New Evaluation, Assessment Tactics, and Tools: An Example from Bahrain

Bettina Lynda Bastian◉ and Arpita Mehrotra◉

Introduction

Assessment of student learning in higher education is a pivotal element of the teaching and learning process: assessment is assuring that teaching activities have been effective with regard to the learning goals. Assessment provides important feedback for quality assurance of higher education programs and courses, as well as assessment is essential for students to understand and regulate their learning. The assessment also provides teachers with important information regarding the learning progress, outcomes, and potential of their students. There is an ongoing concern in academia about the relevance and effectiveness of assessment approaches. Assessment as much as teaching is influenced by environmental developments and trends that affect what is required of higher education

B. L. Bastian (✉) · A. Mehrotra
American University in Bulgaria, Blagoevgrad, Bulgaria
e-mail: bbastian@aubg.edu

A. Mehrotra
e-mail: amehrotra@ruw.edu.bh

© The Author(s), under exclusive license to Springer Nature Switzerland AG 2023
N. Azoury and G. Yahchouchi (eds.), *Governance in Higher Education*,
https://doi.org/10.1007/978-3-031-40586-0_9

graduates to become successful professionals in terms of knowledge and skills. Examples are continuous changes in technology, digitalization, globalization, regulatory challenges, and many more that affect what knowledge and skills are needed now and in the near and far future and what graduates should receive and learn during their education. The present article addresses changes in student assessment in higher education with an emphasis on the Arab world. We first introduce the main concepts concerning teaching and assessment through a literature review, which also includes the main factors that have impacted teaching and assessment in the Arab world. We then use a detailed case study of the Royal University for Women (RUW) in Bahrain to demonstrate how assessment has changed over time. We summarize and discuss the main findings and provide learnings for the future.

Literature Review

Concepts of Assessment of Student Learning in Higher Education

Assuming a linear relation between intended learning goals regarding a sequence of instructional activities and students' learning outcomes is difficult. Even when instruction is well planned and delivered by professors, students are not equal in their learning progression, and they display different levels of comprehension following instructional activities. Moreover, learning has been shown to be a function of teaching and the context in which it takes place, and it is not only a question of learners to retain and reproduce knowledge they have been exposed to, but to put this knowledge in perspective; to interpret knowledge, so that it allows them to take actions based on their understanding (Boud, 1990; Boud et al., 2018) In this context, the seminal work by Bloom (1984) showed that a normal distribution of students' learning outcomes is not the result of talent and nature, but it bases on the ignorance of teachers regarding individual differences in learning. Assessment of learning thus plays a pivotal role in effective teaching since it reveals whether certain instructional activities have led to the intended learning outcomes and since it is an approach to improve student learning (Black, 2006), using assessment tools to support students in their learning and progression (William, 2000).

Our understanding of assessment processes in higher education has undergone substantial developments in the past 30 years and different dimensions of the role of assessments have been identified. Here, Hadji (1994) summarized 3 main functions of assessment: (1) certification (assure that students have reached certain goals to pass an instruction period or to start a profession (Pereira & Flores, 2016); (2) enable students to understand, assess, and regulate their own learning; (3) serve as guidance for teachers and learners that allows to prognose learning and student learning potential. Different distinctions of assessment were introduced, notably, the notion of 'assessment of learning' (AoL) emphasizes what has been learned (Gipps, 1994) and serves to rank students and/or certify their competencies (Crooks, 2011). On the other hand, the notion of 'assessment for learning' (AfL) emphasizes the use of assessment tools to feed into the learning process and to help improve students' learning (Crooks, 2011; Gipps, 1994).

The former approach has been equated with summative assessment tools, which are typically used to evaluate knowledge and skills acquisition by students at the end of an instructional activity or period (for example a test) by assigning a grade and note (Brew et al., 2009). Summative assessments are more traditional approaches that are based on student advancement through different study periods and cycles and allow comparison between different students. This type of assessment measures student performance at a given time and is focused on results rather than the learning process (Lax et al., 2006).

The AfL approach, on the other hand, is linked to formative assessment means (Sadler, 1989) which aims at improving teaching and learning and which are decidedly student and learning-focused (Pereira & Flores, 2016). The formative assessment approach is pedagogical, and assessment becomes an intrinsic part of teaching and learning (Hadji, 1994). Formative assessment is feedback based and allows students as well as teachers to see how learning proceeds and at the same time students can develop their understanding to an appropriate level regarding the tasks at hand.

A third definition of assessment was introduced by Earl (2003, 2012), which involves the active participation of students through self-assessment and self-directed learning. It is referred to as assessment as learning (AaL), where the student has an active role as an assessor that can self-regulate learning, skills, and competence acquisition. Both AfL and AaL emphasize the learning function of assessment more than the grading function (Black & Wiliam, 1998).

Assessment Methods

Assessment methods are shown to have an important impact on the quality of student learning—assessment methods are perceived negatively or positively by students, and this has consequences on their motivation to learn, on their belief that they can achieve learning outcomes, and on their actual results. Previous research has highlighted the importance of assessment methods (and the way assessments are implemented) for students (Biggs & Tang, 2011; Flores et al., 2022). Students form a particular understanding of the curriculum and what is expected of them; therefore, it is pivotal to them that teaching, and assessment activities and methods are aligned with their representations (Meyers & Nulty, 2009).

Traditional methods of assessment in higher education are related to more summative assessments and can include written exams, written tests, and others (Healy et al., 2014), which have been criticized as limited tools since they promote more of a hierarchy of grades rather than measure actual learning (Pereira & Flores, 2016). Issues with traditional assessment approaches also included low levels of comprehension (Struyven et al., 2005), reproduction of information under pressure, and the encouragement of surface learning (Brown, 2004; Brown et al., 1997). Such factors contributed to a negative perception of traditional approaches in assessment. Empirical studies based on student populations in different contexts found that traditional methods of assessment were perceived as less fair, or less fair representation of their learning, compared to alternative methods that required active involvement of students (Jankowski & Teitelbaum, 2021). Moreover, assessment methods impact how students engage with the teaching material and prepare for their exams. In this context, studies showed that students questioned the validity of traditional assessment practices that would not reflect their learning process and did not aid them in better understanding the materials. Instead, especially summative assessments were shown to lead to surface-level-lending and rote memorizations, where students would only learn the material for the exam and as soon as the exams were taken, they would forget it (Flores et al., 2022; Struyven et al., 2005). Students in these forms of assessment learned only for the purpose of the assessment and did not maintain their learned knowledge for any long-term perspective (Struyven et al., 2005).

Previous studies revealed a correlation between students' learning characteristics and their preferences and attitudes regarding certain assessment methods. The seminal research by Birenbaum and Feldman (1998) showed how students with poor learning skills and low learner confidence preferred certain summative assessments, for example, Multiple Choice Tests (MCQ), whereas students with deep learning approaches preferred more formative assessments, such as projects or essays. Birenbaum and Feldman (1998) proved how students with advanced learning abilities intend to mastery the material (as opposed to only performing according to certain standards), which requires the development of higher-order thinking skills that allow them to solve complex problems (Kaur et al., 2018).

Moreover, research by Van Dinther et al. (2014) pointed to the correlation between assessment perception and sufficiency and self-efficacy needs of students. The authors studied a competency-based teacher education program regarding the effectiveness of students' learning and the impact of assessment methods on students' self-efficacy. Students reported positive effects of assessments on learning when assessments related to skills needed in their future profession and when assessments helped them to improve competencies and increased their professional self-efficacy (Van Dinther et al., 2014). Diverse research on assessment methods and their acceptance by students concludes that students are open to different forms of assessments (Healy et al., 2014), yet students were particularly satisfied when assessment methods led to deeper comprehension and encouraged learners to increase in mastery and perform on higher levels, as well as they award individual effort and cultivate transferable skills (Adnan et al., 2019; Healy et al., 2014).

In comparison to traditional and more summative assessment, learner-centered approaches, and formative assessment focus on the development of real-life skills, or professionally relevant skills. They emphasize the process of learning and the individual progress of students (Weldy & Turnipseed, 2010). Learner-centered approaches can include project work, simulations, collaborative assignments, and others. Learner-centered approaches to learning and formative assessment have been well-received by students as they emphasize the development of real-life skills and they measure the learning and training process, which should be aligned with practice requirements (Segers & Dochy, 2001) and as they allow for deep learning. Learner-centered approaches include assessment types, such as portfolios, projects, self and peer assessment, simulations, and collaborative assessment (Struyven et al., 2005). Learner-centered approaches allow for deep learning, especially with methods such as problem-based learning or case-based learning that allows learners to apply their knowledge in a real-life context (Jankowski & Teitelbaum, 2021).

Factors That Influenced Student Assessment in the Arab World

Higher education worldwide is in transition. McCaffery (2019) summarizes some of the main changes concerning teaching and learning. The traditional university model that developed in the nineteenth century and dominated the twentieth century has had to adapt to substantial changes in its macro environment. That has affected the role of higher education institutions in many ways, from the provider of terminal degrees to the provider of skills and competencies for lifelong learners: from the producer of knowledge to the agent of knowledge; from being organized by subjects to being organized by solutions and interdisciplinary; from linear production of knowledge to non-linear production of knowledge, and professors moved from being directors of learning to become facilitators of learning. In the following, we describe major factors that influenced teaching and assessment in the Arab world and influenced the role and mission of higher education institutions.

Unemployment Despite Increasing Numbers of Academics in the Arab Region

Diverse studies report a tremendous growth in student enrolment in higher education programs in the Arab world: a study by the North-western University, Qatar surveyed thousands of Arab nationals regarding tertiary education and detected sharp increases in student enrolments in different Arab nations, where the percentage of individuals with a college degree increased between 2014 and 2018 from 24 to 59% (in the UAE), 30–47% (in Qatar), 5–20% in Tunisia, and 19–26% (in Saudi Arabia) (Martin & Hassan, 2019). However, tertiary enrolment rates vary substantially across the region, with 5% in Djibouti to 71% in Saudi Arabia (OECD, 2022). There are more women (35.8%) than men (31.9%) enrolled in higher education in the region, with most female students enrolled in the Gulf, Palestine, and Algeria (OECD, 2022). The MENA region suffers also from one of the highest youth unemployment rates globally, with a 28% unemployment of those between ages 15 and 24 (ILO, 2021). However, there are substantial differences between countries regarding unemployment rates of less than 1% in Qatar, on the one hand, and Djibouti (81%), on the other (World Bank, 2021). Contrary to other global regions, more than 30% of unemployed youth have a university degree (Kabbani, 2019). Public sector jobs are still the most popular among young graduates as still 42% would like to be hired by the government (OECD, 2022). Yet, the public sector perspective is not very sustainable. For example, the International Monetary Fund (IMF) expects that financial wealth could be depleted by 2034 in the GCC countries, which will lead to substantial downsizing of the government sector (IMF, 2020). Concretely, educational attainment has increased region-wide, but students in the region do not necessarily reap benefits and returns since there are not enough jobs in the region to absorb them. Since the employment situation has been challenging and is continually changing, the demands of professions and future jobs continue to change and require continuous adaptation. Thus, higher education institutions need to prepare students in terms of skills and capabilities to create job opportunities and to generate value-creating innovations and entrepreneurial ventures for the society that could also provide them with a living, and that serve as primary drivers for economic development.

Moving Toward Competency-Based Education

In many Arab countries, especially those of the Gulf Cooperation Countries (GCC) that have ambitions to become international educational hubs, governmental quality assurance bodies that are responsible to assure and improve quality in higher education have become increasingly important and powerful to push for educational curricula and learning outcomes that are aligned with economic development needs. Institutions such as the National Center for academic accreditation and Evaluation (NCAA) in KSA, the Bahrain Quality Assurance Agency, Bahrain, or the Commission for Academic Accreditation (CAA), UAE, and others have pushed for reforms in higher education and the standardization of different national registered qualifications. These organizations provide important frameworks for higher education in their respective countries. Such frameworks also validate the different educational offers as being aligned with high educational quality standards and their alignment with economic visions and needs (Aloulou & Al-Othman, 2021). The regulators and quality assurance bodies play an important role, especially in the GCC to push for educational programs that aim at closing the gap between student learning and de facto job market needs. Countries in the region have understood that outcomes from higher education are of pivotal importance for their future development. The economic vision, 2030 for Saudi Arabia, for example, affirms that human capital is the most important resource for the country, and the development of skills and competencies that fulfill labor market needs is a must for higher education (KSA Vision, 2030). Bahrain, for example, wants to position itself as a regional hub for education tourism and high-quality education. In its 2030 vision, the country aims at producing graduates with "skills, knowledge, and behaviors required to succeed in a global economy, while contributing to sustainable and competitive growth" (Bahrain Economic Vision, 2030) of the country. Such governmental efforts have strongly pushed for a more competency-based education, which prioritizes the development of skills in students and that will allow bridging the gap between academia and practice. Overall, there has been a push toward curricula that connect students with the external, real-life professional environment, and a need for more formative assessments that provide immediate and continuous feedback.

Impact of the COVID-19 Pandemic on Teaching Methods and Approaches

The COVID-19 pandemic imposed strict social distancing measures on people, including university students and teachers, and limited their direct interactions. Prolonged lockdowns and stay-at-home orders caused some substantial challenges to higher education institutions worldwide and in the Arab region. This triggered a forced digital transformation in higher education with teaching and learning going fully online and it also brought many pedagogical innovations and changes (Saud Alrayes, 2021). Online assessment became necessary (for advantages and disadvantages of online assessment, please see the systematic review by Montenegro-Rueda et al. [2021]) Assessment during the pandemic has based predominantly on qualitative approaches, with an increased use of formative assessment via student assignments and continuous assessments of student learning during different stages (Montenegro-Rueda et al., 2021). Nevertheless, the assessment was also one of the biggest challenges for online learning, as it involved building the necessary capacities of teachers to properly perform and carry out distance assessments using technology. The research found that online teaching had many positive effects, and it is expected to last, such as improved monitoring of student learning, better follow-up of students, and new assessment approaches also increased learner autonomy (Montenegro-Rueda et al., 2021). Several studies have suggested that online delivery and assessment is here to stay during the post-COVID era, and it could even be the driving force behind better quality support and collaboration of different stakeholders for continuous learning (Baloran, 2020, Khan, 2021; Raaper & Brown, 2020).

Technological Change

High-speed internet and advances in mobile technology have had a tremendous impact on teaching and learning as COVID-19 showed. Technology has been an enabler in many ways: it has allowed teachers to assess students remotely and thus created more flexibility. Technology has enabled easier coordination between students and teachers and students themselves (Fischer, 2023). Increasing numbers of software have been developed that enabled experiential learning, including open-source learning management systems, like Moodle or Canvas, which was widely used by universities in the region. Moreover, a multitude of interactive e-learning tools enabled customized learning and customized course creation. This has also opened the doors to alternative teaching approaches and a more personalized learning experience (anytime and anywhere). In the Arab world, internet adoption rates have seen a great increase in the past years: in 2019, the average adoption of the internet was 55% and above the global average (Kende, 2023) and has grown since then to 78%. In the Arab Gulf, internet adoption stands at 99%, compared to 71% in Egypt; and people in the Arab world are avid users of mobile applications, using digital channels to shop online, with the growing importance of online learning across the region (Toledo-Rodriguez & Boillat, 2022).

Needs for Certain Skills in the Future

Several organizations, such as Mc Kinsey, Forbes, Bloomberg, Google, and many others have analyzed what skills will be needed in the future and contributed to a lively debate by identifying and ranking such skills for the future workforce every year. Organizations converge in their evaluations regarding the importance of certain personal, cognitive, people, and technology skills. In this context, the World Economic

Forum (WEF) has played a prominent role in drawing attention to skills and competencies that will shape the future of work, with skills being more valuable than qualifications (WEF, 2020). More than 1 billion jobs worldwide will be transformed by advances in technology in the future (WEF, 2020). The WEF emphasizes the importance of preparing the workforce accordingly and especially the youth. This requires a rethinking of teaching approaches and assessment processes. Soft skills are formed through lifelong professional and personal experiences; they require hands-on learning experiences and mentoring and coaching for guidance and support. Hard skills can be trained with a conventional school-like learning approach or concrete on-the-job training. Assessing soft skills from hard skills is equally fundamentally different and involves more qualitative measures, whereas hard skill is easier and more tangible to measure with summative assessment tools. Learning and teaching are still predominantly based on conventional teacher-centered learning, which impedes critical thinking and creativity (Ismael, 2023). For example, memorization and rote learning are still common and prevalent in higher education in the Arab world (O'Brian & Ali, 2013). Teaching is commonly centered around the teacher too who has an active role in the classroom, presenting students with knowledge; on the other hand, students play a passive role by receiving and absorbing the knowledge without much critical interaction and reflections (Ismael, 2023). Arab universities thus have been challenged in developing and implementing unfamiliar but more effective teaching and assessment methods that are student-centered, experiential and address creativity, problem-solving, and critical thinking, and provide students with skills and competencies 'for the future'.

Research Context

The Kingdom of Bahrain was the first country in the Gulf Cooperation Council to establish formal education when it opened its first public school in 1919. The first Higher Education institution Gulf Polytechnic offered degrees in Engineering and Business starting in 1981. The Higher Education Council (HEC) was founded by Royal Decree No. 74 in 2006 and is the regulatory body for an expanding number of private HEIs. The current total population of Bahrain is approximately 1,553,886, immigrants make up approximately 45% of the total population (CIA, 2023). Bahrain's expenditure on education was reported as 2.2% of its GDP in 2020. In contrast, Saudi Arabia spent 7.8% (2020) of its GDP on education, Oman 5.4% (2019), Qatar spent 3.2% (2020), and Kuwait 6.6% (2020) (World Bank, 2021). Today, there are three publicly funded universities and 14 private universities in the Kingdom of Bahrain. In 2019, student enrolment in Bahrain's higher education institutes increased by 2.8%, as the number of citizens under 20 years old is expected to increase annually by 1.7% (around 30,000) over the next five years, creating progress in private education. (Bahrain Development Board, 2023). Bahrain is aiming to become an international education destination, and there are several policies and strategies in place to achieve this goal:

> *Establishing foreign higher educational institutions:* All foreign private education institutions with headquarters outside Bahrain must be in compliance with laws and regulations applicable in their home countries (Goud, 2018).
>
> *National Higher Education Strategy:* Bahrain's ten-year higher education strategy aims to make the country a top student destination in the Gulf, with the hope that international students will fill up to 35% of all student places (Higher Education Council, 2014).
>
> *High educational standards:* Bahrain's high educational standards continue to draw international students to the country (Oxford Business Group, 2016).
>
> *Inclusion policies and strategies:* Bahrain offers zero-rated and exempt from VAT education and residential contracts, making education more accessible to all (Information & eGovernment Authority, 2022).
>
> *Increasing population base:* With an increasing population base, the K-12 sector is receiving particular attention, and e-learning is being used on a large scale in schools (ICEF Monitor, 2014).
>
> *Flourishing education sector:* Bahrain's flourishing education sector and expat community make it an attractive destination for K-12 teachers (Dicu, 2023).

Overall, Bahrain is making significant efforts to become an international education destination, with policies and strategies in place to attract both international students and teachers. Bahrain's higher education sector is a highly regulated environment. The Higher Education Council (HEC) and the Bahrain Qualification Authority (BQA) in Bahrain oversee the sector and they have emphasized the importance of competency-based education in higher education. The primary role of the HEC is to evaluate and accredit higher education institutions and programs, providing students with a reliable benchmark for quality and excellence in higher education institutions in Bahrain. The BQA, which was founded in 2009, emphasizes the academic standards of the universities and the programs offered by them. All universities in Bahrain are required to comply with the regulations laid out by HEC as well as BQA.

Case Study: Royal University for Women

We apply the exploratory case study method. It is a qualitative research method that is used to gain a deeper understanding of a particular phenomenon. This type of case study is often used when there is little or no existing research on the topic of interest. The case study method is a flexible research method that can be adapted to fit the specific needs of the researcher. However, some common steps are typically involved in conducting an exploratory case study. The case study method is a valuable research tool that can be used to gain a deeper understanding of a particular phenomenon. This type of research can be used to generate new hypotheses, develop new theories, and inform policy and practice. The present research uses the Royal University for Women (RUW) as a case to show how a higher education institution in the Arab world has evolved in terms of learning and assessment.

Background Information on Royal University for Women

The Royal University for Women (RUW) is a private, non-profit university located in Riffa, Bahrain. It was founded in 2005 by Her Royal Highness Princess Sabeeka bint Ibrahim Al Khalifa, the wife of King Hamad bin Isa Al Khalifa. RUW is the first women's university in Bahrain. RUW offers bachelor's degrees in four main areas such as Business, Law, Art & Design, and Information Technology. The curriculum for these programs was initially designed by McGill University in Canada and Middlesex University in the United Kingdom. The university's vision foresees that programs and practices not only meet international standards but also prepare female students and graduates to become leaders and lifelong learners who are engaged in their societies' well-being. RUW's mission aims at offering "students a rewarding and challenging multi-cultural learning environment that cultivates strong, well-rounded personalities, encourages leadership, and builds character, social consciousness, and community" (Ref).

Introduction to Assessment at RUW

At RUW, most assessments are both summative and formative except for the final written examination. RUW's principles of assessment state that assessment will be treated in accordance with the following rules: (a) Assessment has to base on course-intended learning outcomes (CILOs); (b) assessment criteria must be integral to program design, (c) assessment criteria must be fair and unbiased, as well as valid, transparent, and reliable, (d) assessment criteria must be timely and show progress, (e) assessment criteria must be consistent, manageable, and efficient. All documentation regarding assessment tasks, assessment criteria, submission deadlines, and any accompanying guidance, including information relating to the return of work, should be worded, presented to students at the beginning of each course, and published together in the relevant course specification. There have been several modifications made to the RUW assessment policy from its inception in 2005 to the academic year

(AY) 2020–2021. Modifications were made mainly due to the following factors:

(a) Move toward competency-based education which is continuously pushed by Bahrain Quality assurance agencies and regulators.
(b) Benchmarking with local and international universities as well as the influence of international accreditation agencies such AACSB, ASIC, etc.
(c) Aligning with the current and future employability skills as the labor market has moved toward giving high importance to skills and competencies.
(d) Contributing toward reducing the unemployment rate of Bahraini women youth.
(e) Accommodating the impact of COVID-19 pandemic on changes in teaching and assessment.

Two documents framed at the institutional level guide teaching and learning practices at RUW, notably, the RUW Teaching and Learning Policy and the E-Learning policy. The operational principles contained in the RUW Teaching and Learning Policy reference the use of a range of appropriate teaching methods. Further, the policy also lays stress on the adoption of innovative teaching and learning methodologies to enhance the learning environment. Moreover, a direct reference to the use of a range of appropriate teaching methods is found in the E-Learning policy. In the document's purpose, it is clearly stated that one of the reasons to adopt blended learning as a pedagogical practice "is to facilitate the role of the instructor in achieving the ILO utilizing a range of teaching methods to cater to individual differences and enhance the learning process". The document highlights and defines the various modes of delivery that RUW can use including hybrid, asynchronous, synchronous, mostly online, etc. On page 2, the policy defines 'synchronous learning' as

a general term used to describe forms of education, instruction, and learning that occur at the same time, but not in the same place. The term is mostly applied to various forms of televisual, digital, and online learning in which students learn from instructors, colleagues, or peers in real-time, but not in person. For example, educational video conferences, interactive webinars, chat-based online discussions, and lectures that are broadcast at the same time they are delivered would all be considered forms of synchronous learning. (RUW Assessment Policy, pp. 1–3)

In alignment with the RUW Teaching and Learning Policy and the E-Learning Policy, all the programs employ a variety of teaching and learning methods aimed at supporting the attainment of the program aims and the PILOs. Teaching and learning methods used in all programs include a range of methods such as lectures, seminars, tutorials, videos, case studies, guest lectures, field visits, etc. Instructors present relevant theory (with the use of textbooks, reference articles, and other academic sources) and introduce the students to the practical aspects with exercises, discussions, case study analysis, role plays, etc. At higher levels, the students are required to evaluate the knowledge they gain and synthesize based on prior knowledge they have acquired in the program.

All program specifications at RUW show the teaching and learning methods and the assessment of PILOs. Achievement of PILOs is measured through the PILO assessment matrix. Furthermore, the course specification illustrates the same for CILOs. Each instructor designs and delivers the course based on the CILOs. The instructor uses relevant teaching and learning methods as well as assessments, which ensure the attainment of the CILOs. The university has also developed a mechanism to demonstrate the degree of CILO achievement in each course through the CILO Achievement Assessment Tool. This tool is documented in the Course Folder that the course instructor submits at the end of every semester. The findings from the CILO Achievement Assessment Tool would support course instructors in reflecting on course improvement/ enhancement issues (if applicable) to be implemented when the Course is next offered. Furthermore, as a good practice, the College of Business and Law (CBL), notably the Department of Business has also developed a template to align CILOs to PILOs and a measurement tool for the achievement of CILOs to PILOs.

Recent Developments

To ensure the continuity of learning through the offering of full virtual classes during the COVID-19 pandemic period. The RUW Teaching and Learning Policy has made specific reference to the adoption of innovative teaching and learning methodologies and states that "*the University will encourage and support blended learning, E-Learning, and other new technologies to enhance the learning environment*". In this context, the E-Learning Policy was approved by the University Senate in 2020. One of the purposes served by the policy is to "provide guidelines for ensuring accurate and meaningful assessment of Course Intended Learning Outcomes (CILOs) using methods conducive to online learning". For example, to make sure that "Assessments must measure the attainment of course ILOs", the policy encourages faculty to carefully design and draft questions so the students cannot find the answers online or straight from the e-book. The E-Learning Policy also recognizes the significance of E-learning in relation to the achievement of CILOs and the importance of "selecting the most appropriate assessment methods for respective courses in an online environment". For example, the 'discussion forum' on Moodle has become a relevant tool to engage all students in the class as students can post input to a question and see their classmates' contributions.

Online Teaching and COVID-19

During the AY 2019–2020, as well as during the AY 2020–2021, teaching methods were adapted to the unprecedented circumstances of the COVID-19 pandemic. RUW has shown an excellent capacity for resilience and reacted rationally and swiftly to the urgent challenge posed by the pandemic. An Online Education Committee was established in 2019–2020 to streamline all the proposals related to the implementation of full online teaching. The Committee elaborated guidelines that were then discussed at the Dean's Council level and College Council level and implemented during the 2nd semester of AY 2019–2020. All instructional sessions were reorganized through online teaching till AY

2020–2021. RUW supported the programs by enhancing its Learning Management System (Moodle). The guidelines for online teaching and learning were improved and converted into a RUW E-Learning Policy. Moreover, faculty members were enrolled in Professional Development Programs to improve their online teaching skills, such as the West Virginia Fall Hybrid Program related to online teaching, Pearson's "Leaders of a Learning program" as well as the internally organized RUW workshop on e-learning content development.

The online teaching delivery was monitored on a weekly basis by the HoD and the Dean through an online teaching weekly report. Students' feedback, provided through students' surveys, was used to improve the online teaching approach, including online class engagement activities and revised assessments. The RUW Teaching and Learning Policy in its policy statement has embedded the values of independent and life-long learning. Further in the same policy, it is stressed that RUW is committed to enhancing students' learning experience, going beyond information and skills, learner-centered approach, and enhancing both employability and lifelong learning, which in total help develop independent and lifelong learners. At RUW, students participate in learning through independent study and are encouraged to take personal responsibility for their learning. In a range of courses, assessment types include research activities that are intended to gradually develop research skills among students. Further, in core courses like Senior Business Project, students are required to conduct independent research and submit a report. Students also attend and participate in activities that expose them to professional practice and the application of theory which is a form of experiential learning. For example, students are required to take an internship, a core course intended to expose students to professional practice/application of theory. Likewise, field trips related to a wide range of courses are regularly organized. Additionally, at the beginning of each semester, guest lectures are planned by instructors of relevant courses and included in the course specification as one of the teaching methods. This teaching method also contributes to the blended learning strategy of all the programs, bridging the gap between theory and practice.

Modifications to RUW Assessment Over Time

To ensure quality in academics, the Teaching & Learning Committee made several revisions to the assessment policy over the years. Several tools were developed to help ensure quality assessment during the implementation process. Various tools were introduced in 2012 and were a part of the assessment policy. They are further detailed in the course specification of each course. Another revision to policy took place in 2007 when these tools were aligned with the CILOs. The intention was to help improve the validity and reliability of the assessment instruments used in each course. The L&T committee ensured that these changes in the assessment policy will help improve the quality process and result in better course assessments. The Teaching and Learning (T&L) committee organized several capacity-building workshops to equip faculty members with the necessary skills so to ensure that the policy is implemented and complied with.

Assessment Design

Within programs, a variety of assessment tasks are used to provide flexibility for students and to assess students' skills, knowledge, and understanding. Effective assessment design within all courses ensures that:

- Assessment tasks enable students to demonstrate the CILOs detailed in the Course Specification.
- All learning outcomes are assessed through formative and summative assessment tasks.
- Assessment tasks are efficient in terms of student and staff time and over-assessment is avoided.

To ensure quality, the RUW mandated a variety of assessment practices be used with students in courses. All colleges included formative and summative assessments. As per the Assessment policy, it was essential that feedback is provided to students so that they feel involved in their evaluations and benefit from improvising on their shortcomings and achievement of the CILOs. In addition, early intervention for students at risk as well as for students who have low grades is carried out to monitor students' progress and discuss any difficulties or challenges, they may face with their studies, assessments, or with certain courses.

Formative assessment types	Summative assessment types
• Class discussions	• Final academic paper
• Blogs	• Final examination
• Online discussion forums	• Substantive project work
• Reflective journals	• Capstone project or artifact
• Presentations	• Performance task
• Short Essays	• Oral assessment
• Mid-term quizzes	• Presentation (individual/group)
• Tests/quizzes	

A student's performance at RUW is marked and graded according to pre-specified and clear assessment criteria. These will normally be presented in Course Specifications combining marking and grading criteria. This will be documented and given to students in advance. In 2017, RUW introduced Quality Criteria for evaluating course specifications in terms of:

- Level of assessment methods
- Alignment of assessments with CILOs
- Quality of case analysis
- Structure of the course syllabus
- Grade distribution

Levels of Assessment: Qualification Descriptors

In line with Bahrain 2030 Vision, the Supreme Council for the Development of Education and Training, Chaired by His Highness Sheikh Mohamed Bin Mubarak Al Khalifa the Deputy Prime Minister, took a decision to establish a national qualifications framework and implement it in the Kingdom of Bahrain. The Labor Fund (Tamkeen) funded the NQF project in the Design and Setup Phases with technical assistance provided by the Scottish Qualifications Authority (SQA). The Design Phase was completed by November 2011 and was endorsed by two international organizations, namely: the Scottish Credit and Qualifications Framework Partnership (SCQFP) and the National Qualifications Authority Ireland (NQAI), each responsible for the governance and management of their respective national frameworks. In 2012, the responsibility of administrating and maintaining (including finalizing the development at the late stages of the Setup Phase) the NQF has been handed over to BQA by Royal Decree (83, 2012), which also stated that "All Education and Training institutions are required to coordinate with the BQA to place their qualifications on the NQF, in accordance with BQA's regulations" (Royal Decree 83, 2012).

As per Bahrain's General Directorate of National Qualifications Framework, the NQF is a learning outcome-based qualifications framework comprehensive of all education and training sectors and all forms of learning: formal, non-formal, and informal learning. NQF is sought to:

- Provide a stronger basis for the understanding, comparison, and recognition of national and foreign qualifications, thereby improving the understanding of employers, parents, and learners of the value of qualifications.
- Provide fit-for-purpose qualifications that have stronger linkages with market and learners' needs.
- Increase the accountability of education and training institutions toward maintaining high-quality standards in their provision.
- Improve the opportunities for mobility and progression of learners within and across higher education, vocational, and general education sectors.
- Promote the concept of lifelong learning through the promotion of all types of learning: formal, non-formal, and informal.

The Bahrain National Qualifications Framework (NQF) has 10 levels, each with its own set of level descriptors. To place a qualification on an NQF level, the learning outcomes (LOs) of each unit comprising a qualification and the overall qualification learning outcomes are mapped against these Level Descriptors. At each level, the Level Descriptors are classified into three separate strands (categories) covering knowledge, skills, and competence. The strands are further divided into five sub-strands. In addition, provides an overview of the framework with an indication of qualifications at each level. The level descriptors are used to:

* Ensure that qualifications are comparable across different sectors of education and training.
* Provide a framework for the recognition of prior learning (RPL).
* Support the development of new qualifications.

The aims and Intended Learning Outcomes of each course and program at RUW provide a good starting point for how to plan various teaching and learning activities and means to assess them. After BQA-mandated mapping of programs to the NQF, RUW colleges have ensured that the allocated NQF Level and Credit value of a qualification and its comprising courses meet the learning complexity of the NQF Level as per NQF level descriptors. Colleges should ensure that the courses are distributed at various NQF Levels (i.e., NQF levels 5, 6, 7, 8). For example, the internship course should be allocated to NQF level 8. The overall NQF Level of RUW undergraduate qualifications is Level 8 (Level 9 for master's programs) based on the exit NQF Level of the qualification. Colleges should ensure that the rationales provided in the mapping scorecards meet the learning complexity expected for the courses and qualifications. The assigned notional time for each course should sufficiently represent the time required for learners to achieve the learning outcomes. The qualification should provide the learners with sufficient progression from one level to another.

Assessment Process

In line with the 'Principles of Assessment' stated in the RUW Assessment Policy and the requirement that "*there should be a constructive alignment between learning outcomes, learning opportunities, and assessment methods*", RUW ensures that the assessment methods in use for the testing achievement of Course Intended Outcomes and Program Intended Outcomes meet the academic standards of the program. The Program Specification clearly mentions the suggested assessment methods to test learning outcomes in the domain of Knowledge and Understanding, Subject-specific skills, Critical Thinking Skills, and General and Transferable Skills. For example, outcomes A1 and A2 could be assessed using exams, oral presentations, classroom exercises, and/or research-based written reports. Similarly, in the Course Specification, the 'Assessment Details' matrix illustrates the planned assessment method (e.g., Quiz, Written Exam, Seminar, Project, Report, Presentation, etc.) to be used for testing relevant CILOs. As per the RUW Assessment Policy, at least three assessments are mandatory, namely the mid-term exam, the final exam, and the class participation.

1. Assessment details

Assessment No	Assessment weight (%)	Type of assessment (quiz, written exam, seminar, project, report, presentation, etc.)	ILO assessed (a1..., b1..., c1...)	Assignment brief	Criteria of evaluation (model answer, rubric)	Submission DATE
Assessment 1	20%	Quiz	a1, a2, b2	Determining procedures and problem sets	As per the model answer	Week 5
Assessment 2	Not applicable	Online task	b1, c1	Case study	Content	Week 13
Assessment 3	Not applicable					
Assessment 4						
Assessment 5 (participation)	10%	Ongoing participation	a2, b2, c1, d1	Discussions	Conceptual understanding	Week 1–15
Assessment 6 (midterm)	30%	Written exam	a1, a2, b2	Problem-solving questions, which require analysis	As per the model answer	Week 8
Assessment 7 (final)	40%	Written exam	a2, b1, c1, d1	Problem-solving questions, which require analysis	As per the model answer	Week 16

2. Assessment—CILO mapping

Please tick in the relevant boxes where individual Course Intended Learning Outcomes are being assessed

	Assessment 1	Assessment 2	Assessment 3	Assessment 4	Assessment 5 (participation)	Assessment 6 (midterm)	Assessment 7 (final)
a1	✓		Not applicable	Not applicable		✓	✓
a2	✓				✓	✓	✓
b1		✓				✓	
b2	✓	✓			✓		
c1					✓		✓
d1					✓		✓

Blended learning was also made a part of the course specification as per the modifications made to the assessment policy.

1. Blended learning methods (Multi-media, Web-based, etc.)
• Gamification, • Flipped classroom, • Collaborative learning • Blended learning platform (Moodle)

Assessment Preparation for Internship

The internship was an optional course which was offered in all the programs at RUW till 2013. Due to feedback from various stakeholders, experiential learning was essential to any academic program. Revisions to the Curriculum plans were made and an internship policy was introduced. Currently, work-based learning is an important component of all programs at RUW. Internship courses are integral to all programs. Internship at RUW is governed by an Internship Policy and Procedures. All colleges have an internship coordinator who coordinates internship placements, advises on internship opportunities, receives, and validates internship applications, communicates with the host organization on the scope of internship work, and monitors and maintains all documents relating to internship. Students at all colleges may register for internships only after completion of a minimum number of credits. As per the Internship Policy, students are eligible to undertake an internship upon completion of half of the program's credits. The CILOs of the Internship course contribute toward the achievement of relevant PILOs. As far as arrangements to evaluate the effectiveness of the Internship are concerned, there is a Course Evaluation Survey that students would fill out toward the end of the semester. The objective of the course evaluation survey is to provide overall feedback about the course objectives, their level, relevance, appropriateness, etc. Further, during site visits, the Internship Coordinator/Instructor requests the Supervisor of the interning student to formally provide feedback on their performance in the required form. The form also seeks information on the academic preparation of the intern and improvement areas the intern should focus on. The information gathered through Internship Performance Evaluation is used to make changes to the Internship course components. For example, it was noticed that the task/role assigned to interning students was at times not contributing toward the achievement of the Banking & Finance (BNF) program aims. For this purpose, a document was developed to provide employers and host organizations with a generic understanding of expectations in terms of duties and output.

Assessment for Class Participation and Engagement

As a result of a focus on quality enhancement, another modification was made to the assessment policy in 2013. Instead of giving 10% to attendance, the policy modification mandated class participation and discussion in each course. The assessment of class participation and engagement adds to the holistic learning process in education. It encourages and contributes to the active learning strategy that a student needs to adopt to advance her learning and thinking capabilities. The Intended learning outcome that will be achieved is that the students will be able to inculcate the skill of being regular, participative, and responsible. The class participation and engagement will be graded as per the grading rubric.

Moderation of Exams and Students' Assessments

To further ensure quality, T&L in collaboration with the Quality assurance unit at RUW added a robust assessment process with quality checks. The assessment policy was modified after the feedback from BQA and other stakeholders. The current policy states that Colleges must have formal moderation processes which set out how the college will ensure consistency and maintenance of academic standards. Effective moderation of assessment is fundamental to the ongoing development of academic quality. In accordance with the RUW Assessment policy, all colleges ensure that assessments are moderated not only internally, through the process of revision and approval of the assessments but also externally. This happens through assessment post-moderation which is part of the external verification process. RUW has in place formal procedures for the external moderation of assessments and the selection of external moderators. These procedures are stated in the External Examining and External Verification Policy. RUW relies on its network of academic partners in the Kingdom of Bahrain. A distinction is made between various types and levels of moderation. These include Internal Moderation and External Moderation. The purpose of internal moderation is to ensure that assessments are consistent, accurate, and well-designed. Each college has effective systems and procedures in place for the internal moderation of all methods of assessment for all courses. Internal Moderation includes Pre-Moderation and Post-Moderation. The purpose of external moderation is the process through which internal assessment is monitored to ensure that it meets the required standards. External moderation methods at RUW mainly include External Verification and External Examination of assessment tasks (Dissertations/Projects).

Feedback is central to learning and is provided to students to develop their knowledge, understanding, and skills and to help promote learning, facilitate improvement, and motivate them to act on their subsequent assessment with a likelihood of success. In 2017, RUW introduced the following feedback framework to ensure continuous improvement takes place in students learning.

Type of feedback	Mode of feedback	Feedback methodology	Evidence of feedback
Immediate	Formative	Breaking the assignment into parts, Comments on a first draft of assignment, self-assessment exercises/task	Use of marking criteria, improvement evident in course work/reports, course specification observation for teaching and learning methodologies

(continued)

(continued)

Type of feedback	Mode of feedback	Feedback methodology	Evidence of feedback
Immediate	Individual	Individual consultations. Comments on assignment. Peers review	
Immediate	Oral	Class discussion of an assignment in progress, comment on student work, during lectures	
Immediate	Self-Led	Self-assessment, reflections on submitted assignment. Peer assessment	
Summary	Generic	Summary of class strengths/weaknesses after grading, feedback about the whole class, common feedback sheet	Course specifications observation, pre and post teaching based on assessment, self and peer assessment, focused feedback,
Summary	Automated	Automated feedback through online tools (e.g.: Turnitin)	
Summary	Written	Posts to class discussion forum. Email to individual/group of students	
Review	Summative	Peer assessment of group oral presentations. Summary of rationale for a grade, comments on assessment task	Acknowledgement of work completed, written comments on students work. Reflections on Teaching and Learning

(continued)

(continued)

Type of feedback	Mode of feedback	Feedback methodology	Evidence of feedback
Review	Instructor-Led	Annotated examples of previous student work Industry, co-examiner's comments on a student forum, instructor gathering feedback to adjust teaching to accommodate student learning	

Discussion and Conclusion

RUW serves as an example of an Arab higher education institution that has modified its assessment approaches throughout the years in response to the following challenges:

The necessity to improve student learning was due to Bahrain's Vision, 2030, which states that Bahrain's first National strategy is driving specialized education through improved teaching, accreditations, and internships and the university has been constantly working to improve the quality of education they provide. A formalized assessment policy has served as an important tool to have a substantial impact on teaching and learning outcomes. The other reasons for the continuous improvements made to the assessment policy are due to the regular audits and reviews done by the HEC as well as BQA which requires universities to do a continuous improvement in the programs as per the defined standards. HEC as well as BQA emphasizes competency-based learning which has influenced a change in the assessment approaches and a structured curriculum.

Additionally, an academic planning framework exists at the University and the College-level. RUW strives to become a pioneer of education, in the region and globally, based on which programs are designed to keep up with the evolving labor market needs and recent advances in technology. To ensure fitness for purpose, the University has developed a comprehensive survey policy that encompasses gathering feedback from a range of stakeholders including Employers, Alumni, and Students. Information obtained from these surveys is used to assess the 'fitness for purpose' of RUW programs. Further, an Academic Quality framework guides the implementation of academic policies and procedures to ensure the enhancement of students' learning experience, relevance, currency, & quality of programs.

There is a periodic internal curriculum review every four years and external reviews motivated by Mapping of the programs or Program-Reviews-within-Colleges to show the relevance and the currency of the program. This leads to continuous improvements and modifications made to the assessment policy and other relevant academic policies, the institution ensures the quality of teaching & learning, and its alignment with labor market needs. RUW also develops new programs in line with market demands and the vision and mission of the university. RUW aims at aligning itself with international quality standards and is at par with the best business schools across the world. In 2017, they joined the prestigious AACSB accreditation network.

Furthermore, The University has defined generic graduate attributes at the Institutional level, which can be found in the RUW Employability Strategy, and the same is embedded within the intended learning outcomes of programs offered by colleges. Furthermore, the development of the RUW Employability Strategy and the RUW Student Experience Strategy has further supported the linking of graduate attributes to the curriculum.

As an example, the RUW graduate attribute 'Appropriate Communication Skills' is reflected in Program Aims 5 and 6 and linked to the Program Intended Learning Outcome D2. Furthermore, Banking and Finance students, along with the other RUW students benefit from additional extra-curricular programs that contribute to the development of transferable skills and attainment of graduate attributes such as the 'Career Readiness Program' that has been made available to students online through the Centre for General Studies at RUW. Moreover, Royal University for Women offers Professional Certificates as part of Liberal Arts Requirement (LAR) Courses. LAR courses are elective courses offered by The Centre for General Studies to all RUW students as part of their university studies. RUW presents Professional Certificates as part of RUW's mission to prepare students to work in the context of disruptive technology by enhancing essential soft skills (Certificates in Leadership, Research, Effective Communication, and Entrepreneurship) and providing technical knowledge (Certificate in Information Technology). It is evident that RUW is agile in adapting the technological change and ensures that the curriculum offered is up to date and is fit for the labor market needs.

In a nutshell, RUW has continued its efforts to align assessments with the skills of the future, and these efforts have involved:

- Identifying learning outcomes,
- Determining acceptable evidence of learning,
- Planning learning experiences and instructional activities,
- Using standardized rubrics, focusing on skills-based practices, and
- Align assessments with learning objectives and instructional strategies.

Overall, in aligning assessments with the skills of the future, RUW has ensured that assessments measure the skills and knowledge that students are expected to learn and that instructional strategies and learning experiences are designed to help students develop those skills. In addition, RUW has taken steps to align the skills and competencies of its graduates with the skills of the future, which include the following:

- RUW has a private sector partnership network that offers graduates practical experiences and career prospects.
- The university's graduate attributes are aligned with the standards articulated by accreditation.
- RUW has a clear assessment policy that is communicated to students and facilitates the alignment to course ILOs (Intended Learning Outcomes).
- RUW has improved students' engagement with Ellucian Power Campus, a flexible student information system for now and into the future.

* The president of RUW is taking steps to address a mismatch between students' skills and labor market needs.

RUW is an example of an Arab private university that is actively working toward ensuring that its graduates are equipped with the skills and competencies needed for the future job market. It is worth taking RUW as a case study as the University has a clear strategy that demonstrates the awareness of and commitment to the Kingdom of Bahrain's employability agenda and building a knowledge-based economy. RUW is acutely aware of the importance and urgency of this issue, and this has become a top priority in all measures, especially program and curriculum reviews. RUW is part of the ongoing productive dialogue with HEC, through its various conferences and workshops regarding Employability in the Kingdom of Bahrain and has established a framework that ensures that the issue of Employability is incorporated in all RUW program coursework, research, projects, and others.

References

Adnan, N. L., Sallem, N. R. M., Muda, R., & Abdullah, W. K. W. (2019). Is current formative assessment still relevant in turning students into deep learners? *TEM Journal, 8*(1), 298–304.

Abou-El-Kheir, A., & MacLeod, P. (2017). English education policy in Bahrain—A review of K-12 and higher education language policy in Bahrain. In *English language education policy in the Middle East and North Africa* (pp. 9–32).

Aloulou, W. J., & Al-Othman, N. (2021). Entrepreneurship in Saudi Arabia. In *Entrepreneurship in the Gulf cooperation council region: Evolution and future perspectives* (pp. 111–145).

Bahrain Development Board. (2023). *Investing in Education in Bahrain.* https://www.bahrainedb.com/business-opportunities/investing-in-education

Bahrain Economic Vision 2030. https://www.bahrain.bh/wps/wcm/connect/cc20ef28-552d-44b5-8af5-95566fdbe9f9/Vision%2B2030%2BEnglish%2B%28low%2Bresolution%29.pdf?MOD=AJPERES&CVID=ok0S2gy

Baloran, E. T. (2020). Knowledge, attitudes, anxiety, and coping strategies of students during COVID-19 pandemic. *Journal of Loss Trauma*, 1–8.

Biggs, J., & Tang, C. (2011). Teaching for quality learning at university. *Society for Research into Higher Education & Open University Press*. https://doi.org/10.1016/j.ctcp.2007.09.003

Birenbaum, M., & Feldman, R. A. (1998). Relationships between learning patterns and attitudes towards two assessment formats. *Educational Research, 40*(1), 90–98.

Black, P. (2006). Assessment for learning: Where is it now? Where is it going. In *Improving student learning through assessment*, (pp. 9–20).

Black, P., & Wiliam, D. (1998). Assessment and classroom learning. *Assessment in Education, 5*(1), 7.

Bloom, B. S. (1984). The 2 sigma problem: The search for methods of group instruction as effective as one-to-one tutoring. *Educational Researcher, 13*(6), 4–16.

Boud, D. (1990). Assessment and the promotion of academic values. *Studies in Higher Education, 15*(1).

Boud, D., Ajjawi, R., Dawson, P., & Tai, J. (Eds.). (2018). *Developing evaluative judgement in higher education: Assessment for knowing and producing quality work*. Routledge.

Brew, C., Riley, P., & Walta, C. (2009). Education students and their teachers: Comparing views on participative assessment practices. *Assessment & Evaluation in Higher Education, 34*, 641–657.

Brown, G. (2004). Teachers' conceptions of assessment: Implications for policy and professional development. *Assessment in Education, 11*(3), 301–318.

Brown, G., Bull, J., & Pendlebury, M. (1997). *Assessing student learning in higher education*. Routledge.

Crooks, T. (2011). Assessment for learning in the accountability era: New Zealand. *Studies in Educational Evaluation, 37*(1), 71–77. https://doi.org/10.1016/j.stueduc.2011.03.002

CIA. (2023). *CIA Factbook Bahrain*. https://www.cia.gov/the-world-factbook/countries/bahrain/.

Dicu, P. (2023). *5 reasons why you should consider teaching in Bahrain: Emerging destinations for teachers*. Teachaway. https://www.teachaway.com/blog/teaching-in-bahrain-emerging-destinations

Earl, L. M. (2012). *Assessment as learning: Using classroom assessment to maximize student learning*. Corwin Press.

Earl, A. M. (2003). *Assessment as learning: Using classroom assessment to maximize student learning*. Corwin Press.

Fischer, R. M. (2023). *Student assessment in teaching and learning*. Vanderbildt University. https://cft.vanderbilt.edu/student-assessment-in-teaching-and-learning/

Flores, M. A., Barros, A., Simão, A. M. V., Pereira, D., Flores, P., Fernandes, E., & Ferreira, P. C. (2022). Portuguese higher education students' adaptation to online teaching and learning in times of the COVID-19 pandemic: Personal and contextual factors. *Higher Education, 83*(6), 1389–1408.

Gipps, C. V. (1994). *Beyond testing: towards a theory of educational assessment*. Falmer Press.

Goud, S. (2018). Establishing foreign higher educational institutions in Bahrain. *Al Tamimi & Company*. https://www.tamimi.com/law-update-articles/establishing-foreign-higher-educational-institutions-in-bahrain/

Hadji, C. (1994). *A Avaliação, regras do jogo: Das intenções aos instrumentos*. Porto Editora.

Healy, M., McCutcheon, M., & Doran, J. (2014). Student views on assessment activities: Perspectives from their experience on an undergraduate program. *Accounting Education: An International Journal, 23*(5), 467–482.

Higher Education Council. (2014). *National higher education strategy putting higher education at the Hart of nation* (1st ed., pp. 12–20). Higher Education Council, Manama. https://www.mocdu.gov.bh/hec/uploadfiles/bahrain%20higher%20education%20strategy%20-%20summary.pdf

ICEF Monitor (International Consultants for Education and Fairs). (2014). *Insider tips on student recruitment in Bahrain*. https://monitor.icef.com/2014/01/insider-tips-on-student-recruitment-in-bahrain/

Iftahe, A. (2023, January 9). *Digital consumers in the Middle East. Rising adoption and opportunity*. McKinsey Digital. https://www.mckinsey.com/capabilities/mckinsey-digital/our-insights/digital-consumers-in-the-middle-east-rising-adoption-and-opportunity

ILO. (2021). *Unempolyment in the Arab world*. ILOSTAT Explorer. https://www.ilo.org/shinyapps/bulkexplorer41/?lang=en&segment=indicator&id=UNE_2EAP_SEX_AGE_RT_A&ref_area=DZA+BHR+DJI+EGY+IRQ+JOR+KWT+LBN+LBY+MRT+MAR+PSE+OMN+QAT+SAU+SYR+TUN+ARE+YEM&sex=SEX_T&classif1=AGE_YTHADULT_Y15-24+AGE_YTHADULT_YGE25&timefrom=2020&

IMF. (2020). *The future of oil and fiscal sustainability in the GCC region*. IMF Middle East and Central Asia Research Departments. file:///C:/Users/bbastian/Downloads/FOFSGCCEA.pdf

Information & eGovernment Authority. (2022). *Inclusion policies and strategies*. https://www.bahrain.bh/new/en/equality-inclusion_en.html

Ismael, D. A. (2023). Implementing performance assessments in university english departments in the Kurdistan region: Viable solutions to the practice and technical difficulties. *Journal of Kurdistani for Strategic Studies,* (1).

Ismail, N. (2023). *Developing the learning of critical thinking in higher education. A case study based on an international university in Egypt.* https://awej.org/images/AllIssues/Volume4/Volume4Number2June2013/3.pdf

Jankowski, N. A., & Teitelbaum, E. (2021). Student perceptions of and involvement with assessment in higher education. In *Student-focused learning and assessment: Involving students in the learning process in higher education* (pp. 17–40). Peter Lang Publishing.

Kabbani, N. (2019). *Youth Employment in the Middle East and North Africa: Revisiting and reframing the challenge.* Brookings Doha Centre. https://www.brookings.edu/wp-content/uploads/2019/02/Youth_Unemployment_MENA_English_Web.pdf

Kaur, A., Noman, M., & Awang-Hashim, R. (2018). The role of goal orientations in students' perceptions of classroom assessment in higher education. *Assessment & Evaluation in Higher Education, 43*(3), 461–472.

Kende, M. (2023, January 27). *Developing readiness for community networks in the Mena.* Internet Society. https://www.internetsociety.org/resources/doc/2023/developing-readiness-for-community-networks-in-the-middle-east-and-north-africa/

Khan, M. A. (2021). COVID-19's impact on higher education: A rapid review of early reactive literature. *Education Sciences, 11*(8), 421.

KSA Vision 2030. https://www.vision2030.gov.sa/

Lax, L., Singh, A., Scardamalia, M., Librach, L. (2006). 7. self-assessment for knowledge building in health care. *Qwerty-Open and Interdisciplinary Journal of Technology, Culture and Education, 1*(2), 19–37.

Martin, J. D., & Hassan, F. (2019). *There has been an uprising in Arab higher education.* Times Higher Education. https://www.timeshighereducation.com/opinion/there-has-been-uprising-arab-higher-education

McCaffery, P. (2019). *The higher education manager's handbook: Effective leadership and management in universities and colleges* (3rd ed.). Routledge.

Meyers, N. M., & Nulty, D. D. (2009). How to use (five) curriculum design principles to align authentic learning environments, assessment, students' approaches to thinking and learning outcomes. *Assessment & Evaluation in Higher Education, 34*(5), 565–577.

Montenegro-Rueda, M., Luque-de la Rosa, A., Sarasola Sánchez-Serrano, J. L., & Fernández-Cerero, J. (2021). Assessment in higher education during the COVID-19 pandemic: A systematic review. *Sustainability, 13*(19), 10509.

O'Brien, J., & Ali, S. (2013). Culture and approaches to learning and teaching. *Arab World English Journal, 4*(2), 32–45. https://awej.org/images/AllIssues/Volume4/Volume4Number2June2013/3.pdf

OECD. (2022). Young people in MENA: Coming of age in a context of structural challenges and global trends. *Youth at the Centre of Government Action: A Review of the Middle East and North Africa.* https://www.oecd-ilibrary.org/sites/3ced02bf-en/index.html?itemId=/content/component/3ced02bf-en

Oxford Business Group. (2016). *The report: Bahrain 2016: High educational standards continue to draw international students to Bahrain.* https://oxfordbusinessgroup.com/reports/bahrain/2016-report/economy/quality-boost-high-educational-standards-mean-the-country-continues-to-draw-international-students

Pereira, D. R., & Flores, M. A. (2016). Conceptions and practices of assessment in higher education: A study of Portuguese university teachers. *Revista Iberoamericana De Evaluación Educativa, 9*(1), 9–29.

Raaper, R., & Brown, C. (2020) The Covid-19 pandemic and the dissolution of the university campus: Implications for student support practice. *Journal Professional Capital Community, 5,* 343–349.

Sadler, D. R. (1989). Formative assessment and the design of instructional systems. *Instructional Science, 18,* 119–144.

Segers, M., & Dochy, F. (2001). New assessment forms in problem-based learning: The value-added of the students' perspective. *Studies in Higher Education, 26*(3), 327–343.

Struyven, K., Dochy, F., & Janssens, S. (2005). Students' perceptions about evaluation and assessment in higher education: A review. *Assessment & Evaluation in Higher Education, 30*(4), 325–341.

Saud Alrayes, N. (2021). A competency-based education system in universities to fill the gap in the labour market in Saudi Arabia. *Journal of Entrepreneurship Education.* https://www.abacademies.org/articles/a-competencybased-education-system-in-universities-to-fill-the-gap-in-the-labour-market-in-saudi-arabia-15500.html

Toledo-Rodriguez, M., & Boillat, T. (2022). Technology-enabled assessment and improvement of inclusive learning and quality of life in higher education. *Quantifying quality of life: Incorporating daily life into medicine* (pp. 319–353). Springer International Publishing.

van Dinther, M., Dochy, F., Segers, M., & Braeken, J. (2014). Student perceptions of assessment and student self-efficacy in competence-based education. *Educational Studies, 40*(3), 330–351.

Weldy, T. G., & Turnipseed, D. L. (2010). Assessing and improving learning in business schools: Direct and indirect measures of learning. *Journal of Education for Business, 85*(5), 268–273.

WEF. (2020). *Why skills not degrees will shape the future of work.* https://www.weforum.org/agenda/2020/09/reckoning-for-skills/

William, D. (2000). *Integrating summative and formative functions of assessment: Keynote address to the European Association for Educational Assessment.* European Association for Educational Assessment. http://www.kcl.ac.uk//depsta/education/hpages/dwliam.html.

World Bank. (2021). *World Development Indicators.* https://data.worldbank.org/indicator/SL.UEM.1524.ZS?locations=ZQ-ZG-8S-ZJ-Z7-Z4

Part III

The Future of Education

10

The Changing Role of Governance in Education

Nehme Azoury and Steve Harvey

Introduction

As higher education continues to negotiate the complex web of fast societal change, technological advancement, and geopolitical upheavals, the crucial role of governance remains at the forefront of debate (Leisyte & Dee, 2012). This is especially true in the Middle East and North Africa (MENA), where traditional governance models are rapidly being challenged by requests for more flexible, agile, and inclusive frameworks (Marginson, 2020).

The MENA region's historical, political, and socioeconomic backdrop creates a distinct terrain for higher education governance (Wilkins & Huisman, 2012). Governance models must be fluid enough to address

N. Azoury (✉)
Holy Spirit University of Kaslik (USEK), Jounieh, Lebanon
e-mail: nehmeazoury@usek.edu.lb

S. Harvey
Harvey Education Management, Quebec, Canada

© The Author(s), under exclusive license to Springer Nature
Switzerland AG 2023
N. Azoury and G. Yahchouchi (eds.), *Governance in Higher Education*,
https://doi.org/10.1007/978-3-031-40586-0_10

altering expectations as educational institutions attempt to educate graduates for the demands of the global economy. Traditional top-down management structures have given way to more participatory, collegial approaches that encourage a sense of shared governance and increased stakeholder participation (Aghion et al., 2010). This chapter aims to examine these shifts, shedding insight into the changing role of governance in higher education in the MENA region.

Governance in higher education refers to the process through which institutions establish strategic direction, make policy choices, manage resources, and assess performance (Leisyte & Dee, 2012). Governance can influence the academic community, set the course of the institution, and have a substantial impact on the student experience. The importance of governance in effecting change, guaranteeing accountability, and assuring educational quality cannot be over-emphasized (Rhoades & Slaughter, 2004). With extraordinary worldwide change, however, a reform in the governance model is required to reflect and adapt to emerging educational expectations.

We will look at three interconnected issues with respect to governance reforms in higher education in the MENA region. These include how governance is evolving to meet changing cultural standards and technological breakthroughs, as well as the ramifications of these changes on educational quality. We attempt to provide a complete assessment of the current condition of higher education governance in the MENA region, with the addition of constructive insights for future developments.

History and Evolution of Governance in MENA

Historically, the Middle East and North Africa (MENA) area was ruled by a plethora of political systems, each with its own set of consequences for educational governance. Nonetheless, governance structures in higher education in the MENA region have primarily been defined by centralized, state-controlled institutions with decision-making powers concentrated at the top, mirroring the political systems of the nation's themselves (Selvik & Utvik, 2020). Governance approaches have accordingly focused on bureaucratic procedures defining higher education administration, curriculum, faculty nominations, and resource distribution (Chapman & Miric, 2009). On one hand, this centralization has enabled standardized educational policy execution and institutional consistency. However, it also has been criticized for hindering innovation, impeding institutional autonomy, and limiting institutions' responsiveness to quickly changing social requirements (Marginson & Considine, 2000).

The MENA region's rich history and geopolitical significance have also unmistakably shaped these governing models. Colonial and post-colonial nation-building efforts have historically influenced the establishment of governance structures in higher education that are fundamentally protective of national identity and culture, typically valuing uniformity over differentiation (Khalaf & Khalaf, 2022). This has ramifications for the breadth and pace of higher education reform because changes in governance systems necessarily involve the risk of affecting national culture and identity.

The rise of the oil sector in several MENA nations has had an impact on governance structures. Countries with significant oil income have used their riches to directly develop higher education institutions, further concentrating power under state control (Crist, 2014). This system of official sponsorship worked to quickly bring necessary higher education to the region, but it has been criticized for favoring allegiance and compliance above intellectual rigor and academic independence traditionally seen in contemporary models of higher education (El-Affendi, 2009). Moreover, the convergence of these political, economic, and historical forces has resulted in a unique approach to governance in higher education in the MENA region. In many cases, the state's power not only affected the structure of higher education but also greatly influenced its function, frequently aligning it with the state's ideological, economic, and political goals (Wilkins & Huisman, 2012).

These early practices are beginning to change as MENA region nations seek more progress. Indeed, with the changing global scene and rising acknowledgment of the role of higher education in driving economic growth and societal progress, there has been an increasing push to alter

214 N. Azoury and S. Harvey

these old governance structures in recent years. This entails finding a balance between preserving the benefits of centralized management, such as fair access and uniformity, and building a more adaptive, inclusive, and autonomous educational system capable of meeting the complex needs of the twenty-first century. Many of these nations are rethinking their higher education governance models, realizing that the previous, highly centralized approach may not be appropriate for solving modern difficulties. Global trends stressing innovation, flexibility, and autonomy, together with local demands for higher education quality, relevance, and accessibility, are driving countries to rethink and redefine the role of governance (Romani, 2009).

El-Affendi, A. (2009) effectively argues in his landmark book "The Convoluted Modernization of the Middle East: The Case of the Arab University" that the influence of political forces on higher education has frequently resulted in a paradoxical scenario. While universities have long been seen as centers of modernity and invention, political interference in their governance has occasionally limited the intellectual freedom and independent thinking required for meaningful growth.

A Contemporary Perspective in the MENA Region

As of late, there has been a noticeable movement in the MENA higher education scene toward managerial and structural governance reforms. This transition is moving institutions away from traditional, centralized governance by rule and toward models that promote performance, efficiency, and competitiveness, inspired by global trends, and spurred by regional socioeconomic upheavals (Kapur & Crowley, 2013). This trend of increased "managerialism" is not unique to higher education the MENA region but is certainly being witnessed on the heels of the prior dominance of highly controlled centralized systems.

Managerialism in higher education refers to an approach that draws techniques and concepts from the business sector and applies them to university administration and management. This strategy often focuses on performance measurements, accountability, strategic management, and economic efficiency, mimicking the operations of a business (De Boer et al., 2007). While the MENA region's educational institutions have generally been driven by state-centric governance, the last decade has seen a steady acceptance of management methods (Romani, 2009) to progress its own institutions toward contemporary trends and standards witnessed in higher education.

This transformation's structural part entails considerable changes in the organizational framework of higher education institutions. Developments in decision-making processes, diversification of financing sources, curriculum revision, and redefined connections between the state, the institution, and society at large are examples of these changes (Marginson & Considine, 2000).

The United Arab Emirates (UAE) is a prime example of this transition, with governance reforms aimed at aligning higher education with national economic diversification plans. The UAE has formed the Ministry of Higher Education and Scientific Research (MOHESR) to manage higher education's strategic growth. The MOHESR operates on a management paradigm, establishing performance goals for institutions and tying financing to the attainment of these goals (Wilkins & Huisman, 2012).

In "Governance and Accountability: History, Issues, and Trends," D. Chan (2014) notes that the transition toward managerialism and structural changes has resulted in discussions over responsibility. As universities become more business-like in their operations, there is growing concern about who they are accountable to and how this affects their fundamental goal of education and research. The rising emphasis on performance measurements and financial results may distract from intangible, yet vital, parts of higher education such as critical thinking, civic involvement, and the pursuit of knowledge for the sake of knowing.

To many, this governance change has meant progress for higher education in the MENA region as it moves toward a more mature state of existence following practices witnessed elsewhere. However, in MENA, adopting managerial and structural techniques is fraught with difficulties. Balancing the benefits of enhanced efficiency and effectiveness against the danger of jeopardizing academic freedom and institutional autonomy is a significant concern (Chan, 2014). Whereas "managerialism" has added progress, the key ingredient of encouraging innovation through academic freedom might be hampered unless centralized administrative structures are comparatively devolved through shared governance. In many traditional institutions, managerialism is balanced for the better by strong academic decision-making influence. Accordingly, the complexity of the MENA region's sociopolitical atmosphere dictates that the governance reform process be attentive to local settings and consistent with global best practices.

The managerial and structural approach to governance in higher education has also sparked discussions about institutional autonomy in the MENA region. Although this strategy can increase efficiency and accountability, if not adopted carefully, it has the potential to limit the flexibility and creativity inherent in academics. Saudi Arabia, for example, has highlighted education as a critical pillar for its socioeconomic change in its Vision 2030 initiative. As part of this strategy, the government has implemented several structural reforms in higher education governance to increase efficiency and align with labor market demands and many best practices. These reforms will have to be balanced with means of promoting the vitality of academic freedom and institutional autonomy to allay the concern of some that progression may otherwise be hindered (Hamdan, 2021). Moreover, there is a risk of creating a culture of short-termism, in which institutions place an overabundance of emphasis on immediate outcomes and measurable results at the expense of long-term strategic thinking and sustainable development (Pucciarelli et al., 2016).

Despite the obstacles and concerns, the managerial and structural governance method offers a viable route for propelling needed change in higher education in the MENA region. It provides a paradigm for managing higher education institutions' expanding complexity, including concerns of quality, relevance, and responsiveness to social requirements. This method, if intelligently implemented and customized to the region's particular environment, might provide a road for the modernization of higher education in the MENA region, allowing its integration into the global educational scene.

Challenges and Trends Affecting Current Governance in MENA

Traditional Governance

Existing governance techniques in the MENA region face significant challenges and limits in a rapidly changing higher education landscape. Having moved to more managerialism is important, but not sufficient change on its own to face new challenges. These traditional systems, which are frequently characterized by centralized decision-making and state control, are increasingly considered incompatible with the requirements of modern, internationally networked higher education institutions (Gallagher & Garrett, 2013).

One of the most serious weaknesses of conventional MENA governance institutions is their lack of adaptability and flexibility. In an era of rapid technological innovation and shifting socioeconomic trends, higher education institutions require governance frameworks that can react quickly and effectively to change. The bureaucratic nature of traditional governance models usually impedes firms' ability to adapt to new situations and capitalize on emerging opportunities (Looney, 2014).

Another problem with traditional governance structures is their disconnect from the general population. Universities' duties in modern higher education extend beyond teaching and research to encompass community, industry, and government participation. With their inward-looking perspective, traditional governance models generally struggle to develop these critical ties, limiting institutions' potential effect (Madsen, 2013). Modern governance thinking requires input from a broad spectrum of stakeholders to have the pulse on being most responsive and effective.

Furthermore, traditional governance models usually limit institutional autonomy, limiting strategic decision-making and restricting academic independence. This limitation has been a major source of contention, as academic freedom and institutional autonomy are viewed as important to the purpose of higher education (Middlehurst, 2013) and the ability to quickly innovate and adapt to changing circumstance. Both centralized power structures and managerial models with top-down decision-making are increasingly known in all sectors, and not just business, to be ill-equipped to respond to an increasingly fluid and complex world.

Furthermore, traditional governance models sometimes prioritize political considerations over academic brilliance and excellence. This tendency might result in a mismatch between educational outputs and labor market demands, restricting institutions' ability to adequately educate graduates for the labor market (Gonzalez-Serrano & Calero, 2016). Good governance will require building in necessary controls for strategic and fiduciary oversight without these becoming controlling of an institution's creative, innovative, and responsive core.

It is fair to acknowledge that, while traditional governance models cause problems, they have not been without value. In certain cases, these models created stability and continuity, providing a sense of national identity and aiding nation-building efforts. It is the role of modern higher education reform to balance the benefits of existing governance models with the need for change, promoting an evolution that respects the region's cultural and sociopolitical situations (Middlehurst, 2013).

Modern Governance

Critical elements for a modern governance structure of academic institutions continue to be based on some long-held fundamental principles of shared governance, power dynamics, and the freedom to conduct research and teach. It must also be newly accountable to innovation and adaptiveness in the face of change.

– Academic Freedom and Institutional Accountability in a Balance

One of the pillars of higher education is academic freedom, which is the right of researchers to conduct their research and teach without unwarranted intervention. Institutional responsibility, on the other hand, is necessary to maintain a balance and make sure that educational institutions fulfill their responsibilities to students, donors, and society at large. This balance can be accomplished by adopting precise rules that uphold students' constitutional rights while also outlining acceptable standards of behavior. This balance can also be kept by being open about decision-making procedures and regularly evaluating academic results.

– Considering the Dynamics of Power in Governance Structures

The functioning of higher education institutions can be strongly impacted by power dynamics within governance systems. These dynamics frequently involve conflicts between various parties, including administration, academics, students, and outside organizations. Addressing these dynamics calls for candid communication, respect for one another, and a dedication to shared governance, where all parties participate in decision-making. It also entails identifying and resolving any power disparities, such as those brought on by hierarchy, knowledge, or resource access.

– Managing Political Influences on the Governance of Higher Education

Political factors can have a big impact on how higher education is governed, having an influence on everything from funding to curricular choices. Understanding the political environment and being dedicated to upholding the institution's academic integrity are essential for navigating these forces. It might entail promoting legislation that supports higher education, cultivating connections with legislators, and participating in public debates on the importance of higher education. It also calls for a dedication to institutional autonomy and academic independence in the face of political pressure.

– Innovation and Adaptability Using Governance

Universities must be creative and adaptive in a world that is becoming more complex and changing quickly. By promoting an innovative culture, promoting risk-taking, and enabling continual learning, governance structures can play a significant part in this. To do this, it may be necessary to establish areas for experimenting, offer resources for invention, and recognize and honor creative approaches. By being adaptable and responsive, frequently examining and updating policies and procedures, and being open to change, governance structures can also encourage adaptability.

Possible Changes to Improve Governance in MENA

As we enter a time of needed progress for institutional governance, what applies to the MENA region is both the same as elsewhere, in addition to emphasis in certain areas. It is clear that certain fundamental good governance principles remain constant, new dimensions will have emerged, and local challenges will continue to require a particular attention for its meaning and implications.

New Dimensions of Governance

– **Diversity and Inclusion in Governance Structures**

In higher education governance frameworks, diversity and inclusion have emerged as essential factors (de Wit & Altbach, 2020). This trend is being pushed by a recognition of the benefits of having a wide collection of experiences and perspectives in decision-making. Inclusive governance may strengthen the sense of ownership and commitment of a diverse stakeholder group, resulting in more imaginative and effective decision-making (Beerkens, 2021).

Efforts are being undertaken throughout the MENA region to increase governance diversity and inclusion, with varying degrees of success. More actions are needed to ensure that all stakeholder groups have a voice in governance processes, regardless of gender, color, ethnicity, or social background (Maassen, 2020). To be sure, the MENA has seen significant changes in the past decade on the front of inclusiveness across various nations. With more progress on the horizon, and in the hopes of many, this stands a chance of rendering impactful changes in governing success.

– Ethical Considerations in Decision-Making

In response to rising public demand for accountability and honesty, ethical challenges in higher education governance have gained prominence (Davis, 2017). Higher education decisions are being scrutinized for fairness, transparency, and adherence to ethical norms.

The need for ethics in governance is acknowledged throughout the MENA region, yet incorporating ethical issues into decision-making remains difficult (Abouchedid & Eid, 2004). This is because of factors such as power dynamics, cultural norms, and resource constraints, among others. Global alliances and interactions among such institutions of higher learning can be strengthened on such grounds, and many now demand it as part of the partnership and alliance. As the MENA nations grow with hope of taking a seat as a global player, ethical consideration and transparency will be an important facet for progress.

Evolving Governance Structures

– Shared Governance and Collaborative Decision-Making

Shared governance and collaborative decision-making have emerged as essential components of contemporary higher education governance. This strategy acknowledges and includes the aggregate experience of numerous stakeholder groups, including professors, administration, students, and staff, in decision-making (Kezar & Eckel, 2017). Shared governance promotes a democratic spirit in higher education by encouraging the active participation of various voices in decision-making and establishing a sense of shared ownership. By taking into consideration diverse viewpoints, the inclusive feature of this technique can foster a deeper commitment to institutional goals and enhance decision-making quality (Gehrke & Kezar, 2018). In the MENA region, shared governance is still a work in progress. While some institutions have achieved headway in involving a wider range of stakeholders in decision-making, others have challenges owing to cultural traditions, aversion to change, or a lack of expertise with these participatory techniques (Romani, 2009).

– The Role of Governing Boards in Strategic Planning and Oversight

Governing boards play a significant role in the strategic planning and supervision of higher education institutions. They are responsible for ensuring that institutions, which carry out their purposes, are financially healthy, and follow legal and ethical guidelines (Middlehurst, 2017). The role of the governing board has evolved in response to changing demands and expectations. Boards are increasingly being asked to contribute to strategy creation, make resource allocation choices, and evaluate institutional performance with respect to strategic goals (Deem & Eggins, 2017). Because of the intricate interaction of cultural, political, and economic factors, governing boards in the MENA region have unique challenges. Thus, having a deep appreciation for the broad spectrum, role, history, and potential of academic institutions is critical. Nonetheless, their involvement in strategic planning and monitoring is becoming more recognized as vital for the future of higher education in the area (Badran, 2021).

Decentralization and Autonomy of Academic Institutions

Decentralization in higher education governance refers to the shift of decision-making powers from central authorities to individual academic institutions. This allows institutions to have more control over their academic programs, research initiatives, and administrative processes. The idea is to promote innovation, responsiveness to local needs, and overall efficiency. In the context of the MENA region, some countries have made strides toward decentralization. For instance, in some Gulf Cooperation Council (GCC) countries, universities have been granted more autonomy to design their curricula and establish partnerships with international institutions. However, the extent of decentralization varies across the region, with some countries maintaining more centralized control over higher education.

– Integration of Stakeholders in Governance Processes

Stakeholder integration in governance processes refers to the inclusion of various stakeholders—such as faculty, students, staff, and external partners—in decision-making processes. This approach recognizes the value of diverse perspectives and aims to promote transparency, accountability, and a sense of ownership among stakeholders. In the MENA region, there's a growing recognition of the importance of stakeholder integration. For example, some universities have established faculty senates or student councils to ensure that these groups have a voice in governance. Similarly, partnerships with industry and community organizations are becoming more common, reflecting a broader trend toward more inclusive and participatory governance.

There exists a range of ways that integration has been practiced, and the depth of power and influence that each representative group wields can vary considerably across regions. This range and depth will be delicate balance over time as institutions progress. For the MENA, this process has largely just begun and there will be those watchful of its impact for institutional success.

Recommendations for Effective Governance

– Enhancing Transparency and Accountability Mechanisms

In today's higher education environment, when accountability and transparency are increasingly expected, successful governance involves institutions displaying integrity and dedication to their mission. Increased transparency creates trust among stakeholders, allowing them to hold institutions accountable for their decisions and actions (Kruyen, 2021).

Publicly discussing institutional goals, decision-making methods involved in reaching those goals, and decision-making outcomes is one method for promoting openness (Wilkins, 2013). This might include leveraging digital platforms to make information more accessible, participating in governance processes, and streamlining administrative procedures. Stakeholders should have access to and understand strategic planning, policies, and financial figures, among other critical information.

Clear processes for reviewing institutional performance and responding to the results of such evaluations should be in place to encourage accountability (Altbach & de Wit, 2021). It could be beneficial to develop a system of indicators to track achievement in both academic and administrative settings. These metrics can be used to gauge progress toward the institution's objectives, identify areas for improvement, and demonstrate accountability to stakeholders.

While there has been progress in enhancing transparency and accountability in the MENA region, more efforts are needed to develop governance institutions that are tailored to the region's specific concerns as well as growing global norms (Badran, 2021). This is one of the primary ways we can expect to see institutions in the region build reputation, trust, and international recognition from stakeholders and outsiders.

Fostering Collaboration and Stakeholder Engagement

The active engagement and collaboration of a wide variety of stakeholders are becoming more important for effective governance in higher education. These stakeholders may include students, instructors, administrative workers, local communities, government agencies, industry partners, and others, each with their own set of perspectives and interests (Mampaey & Huisman, 2022).

Collaboration across these various groups may lead to more informed decision-making, a deeper commitment to institutional goals, and enhanced opportunities for innovation and adaptability. It demands the implementation of a governance framework that promotes communication, mutual understanding, and meaningful involvement in decision-making processes (Beerkens, 2021).

Even wider than the notion of including stakeholder in governance practices, is our intuitions' permeability to all stakeholders as a public-facing intuition. Stakeholder engagement may be increased by regular consultations, polls, open forums, participatory decision-making bodies, and joint activities. Furthermore, the use of digital platforms can allow for broader and more inclusive participation (Marginson, 2020).

Stakeholder participation is increasingly being recognized as an important component of higher education governance in the MENA region. However, important obstacles must be addressed, such as cultural norms, power dynamics, and capacity constraints, among others (Badran, 2021). There is still much to explore, learn, and experience in how and in what forms powerful social digital networks can have bearing on this change. Governance practices need lead at this adaption.

Higher education institutions may increase their responsiveness to the various needs and expectations of their stakeholders by encouraging collaboration and stakeholder engagement, therefore contributing to the institution's long-term viability and success.

While there has been progress in enhancing transparency and accountability in the MENA region, more efforts are needed to develop governance institutions that are tailored to the region's specific concerns as well as growing global norms (Badran, 2021).

Conclusion

Governance structures and procedures must develop to meet the shifting demands and expectations of a diverse range of stakeholders as the landscape evolves (Clark, 2021). As outlined in this chapter, this entails shifts in old paradigms, new dimensions of governance, and a plethora of new challenges and opportunities.

Traditional governance structures, characterized by a centralized and hierarchical structure, have disadvantages in today's climate, including restricted stakeholder contact and adaptability and innovation potential (Mampaey & Huisman, 2022). Global trends, regional dynamics, and rising recognition of the significance of more inclusive, flexible, and responsive government structures in the MENA region have all contributed to a continuous shift away from traditional forms.

These trends are reflected in developing governance models such as shared governance, governing board expansion, decentralization, and increasing stakeholder integration (Romani, 2009). These events emphasize the growing complexity of higher education governance and the need for frameworks that can balance different interests and demands.

Diversity and inclusion, ethical problems, digitalization, and environmental sustainability have all emerged as new governance components. These features reflect broader societal changes as well as increased expectations of higher education institutions to positively contribute to society and model best practices in their operations (Marginson, 2020).

These shifts present both challenges and opportunities. Key problems to investigate include balancing academic freedom and institutional accountability, addressing power dynamics, navigating political constraints, and leveraging governance for innovation. These challenges need a thoughtful and nuanced response informed by a complete understanding of the individual circumstances and motivated by a dedication to the basic goals of higher education (Biesta, 2020).

Among the ideas for excellent governance are improved openness and accountability procedures, more stakeholder participation, improved leadership competence, and support for research and evidence-based decision-making (Eddy & VanDerLinden, 2021). These techniques have the potential to increase the legitimacy, responsiveness, and efficacy of governance in higher education, so contributing to the institution's long-term survival and success.

References

Abouchedid, K., & Eid, G. M. (2004). E-learning challenges in the Arab world: Revelations from a case study profile. *Quality Assurance in Education, 12*(1), 15–27.

Aghion, P., Dewatripont, M., Hoxby, C., Mas-Colell, A., & Sapir, A. (2010). The governance and performance of universities: Evidence from Europe and the US. *Economic Policy, 25*(61), 7–59.

Altbach, P. G., & Reisberg, L. (2013). The globalization of higher education. In *The forefront of international higher education* (pp. 1–8). Springer.

Altbach, P. G., & de Wit, H. (2021). The challenge to academic freedom: The global landscape. *Frontiers of Education in China, 16*(1), 14–37.

Amaral, A., & Magalhães, A. (2022). How to share power in universities? Reflections on the internal governance of universities. *Tertiary Education and Management, 28*(1), 1–13.

Amaral, A., & Neave, G. (2016). On the edge: Shifting boundaries of higher education. *International Journal of Higher Education, 5*(1), 1–9.

Badran, A. (2021). The role of university boards in the MENA region: Challenges and opportunities. *Journal of Higher Education in the Middle East, 1*(1), 1–15.

Bastedo, M. N., Samuels, J., & Kleinman, D. L. (2014). Higher education and the public good: Imagining the university. *International Journal of Sociology of Education, 3*(2), 169–187.

Beerkens, M. (2021). Diversity and inclusion in higher education governance: An analysis of European higher education policies. *Studies in Higher Education, 46*(2), 361–377.

Biesta, G. (2020). The role of research in higher education: Implications for policy and practice. *European Journal of Education, 55*(1), 110–119.

Bolman, L. G., & Gallos, J. V. (2021). Reframing academic leadership. *Journal of Leadership Studies, 15*(1), 39–51.

Chan, D. (2014). Governance and accountability: History, issues, and trends. *International Journal of Management Reviews, 16*(1), 35–62.

Chapman, D. W., & Miric, S. L. (2009). Education quality in the Middle East. *International Review of Education, 55*, 311–344.

Cherif, M., & Hasanov, F. (2020). Environmental sustainability in MENA higher education institutions: An overview of initiatives and challenges. *Journal of Cleaner Production, 260*, 121044.

Clark, L. (2021). Governance in higher education: Trends and emerging practices. *Journal of Higher Education Policy and Management, 43*(3), 242–257.

Crawford, J., Butler-Henderson, K., Rudolph, J., & Glowatz, M. (2020). COVID-19: 20 countries' higher education intra-period digital pedagogy responses. *Journal of Applied Teaching and Learning, 3*(1), 1–20.

Crist, J. T. (2014). Higher education governance in developing countries, challenges and recommendations: A case study of Afghanistan. In *Leadership and governance in higher education* (Vol. 2). Raabe.

Davis, G. F. (2017). What might replace the modern corporation? Uberization and the web page enterprise. *Seattle University Law Review, 40*(2), 501–515.

De Boer, H., Enders, J., & Schimank, U. (2007). On the way towards new public management? The governance of university systems in England, the Netherlands, Austria, and Germany. In *New forms of governance in research organizations* (pp. 137–152). Springer.

De Boer, H., Enders, J., & Schimank, U. (2017). On the way towards new public management? The governance of university systems in England, the Netherlands, Austria, and Germany. In *New public management and the reform of education: European lessons for policy and practice* (pp. 15–32). Routledge.

de Wit, H., & Altbach, P. G. (2020). Time to cut international education's carbon footprint. *University World News, 580*.

Deem, R., & Eggins, H. (2017). *The university as a critical institution?* Sense Publishers.

Eddy, P. L., & VanDerLinden, K. E. (2021). Leadership development for a changing higher education landscape. *Review of Higher Education, 44*(2), 277–300.

El Morr, C., & Arif, M. (2020). Stakeholder engagement in higher education: Challenges and opportunities in the digital era. *Journal of Educational Technology & Society, 23*(2), 187–199.

El-Affendi, A. (2009). The convoluted modernization of the Middle East: The case of the Arab university. *The Muslim World, 99*(1), 181–203.

El-Megharbel, N. (2020). The state of higher education governance in the Arab Region: The need for evidence-based decision making. *International Journal of Higher Education, 9*(6), 286–298.

Enders, J., de Boer, H., & Weyer, E. (2013). Regulatory autonomy and performance: The reform of higher education re-visited. *Higher Education, 65*(1), 5–23.

Gallagher, M., & Garrett, R. (2013). Dispositions and teacher effectiveness: Implications for teacher education. *Journal of Teacher Education, 60*(5), 497–510.

Gehrke, S., & Kezar, A. (2018). The roles of faculty senates in decision-making about institutional finances: Perceptions of senate leaders. *The Journal of Higher Education, 89*(4), 516–543.

Gonzalez-Serrano, M. H., & Calero, J. (2016). Public higher education in Spain: From expansion to austerity policies. *International Journal of Educational Development, 51*, 150–161.

Hamdan, A. (2021). The impacts of neoliberalism on higher education institutions in Saudi Arabia. *Studies in Higher Education, 46*(6), 1214–1226.

Hanna, D. E. (2018). Higher education in an era of digital competition: Emerging organizational models. *Journal of Asynchronous Learning Networks, 7*(1), 66–80.

Hazelkorn, E. (2018). *Rankings and higher education: reframing relationships within and between states.* Center for Global Higher Education.

Heinrich, C. J., & Nisar, H. (2021). Evidence-Based decision-making in higher education: Challenges and opportunities. *Public Administration Review, 81*(1), 154–165.

Hicks, M., Wechsler, J., & Twombly, S. B. (2019). Performance-based funding in US higher education. *American Journal of Education, 125*(3), 399–424.

Huisman, J., & Mampaey, J. (2020). Leveraging governance for innovation in higher education: Lessons from the Netherlands. *Higher Education Policy, 33*(2), 295–314.

Jishnu, L. (2021). Balancing academic freedom and accountability: The case of higher education in the Middle East. *International Journal of Higher Education, 10*(1), 287–299.

Jongbloed, B., & Lepori, B. (2015). The funding of higher education: A typology of funding models. *Higher Education Quarterly, 69*(3), 274–300.

Jongbloed, B., & Vossensteyn, H. (2016). University funding and student funding: International comparisons. *Oxford Review of Economic Policy, 32*(4), 576–595.

Kapur, D., & Crowley, M. (2013). *Beyond the ABCs: Higher education and developing countries.* Center for Global Development.

Kezar, A., & Eckel, P. (2017). Sharing leadership to maximize talent. *Planning for Higher Education, 45*(4), 15–24.

Khalaf, S., & Khalaf, R. (2022). *Arab youth: Social mobilisation in times of risk.* Saqi Books.

Knight, J., & (J. (2018). The changing landscape of higher education internationalization—for better or worse? *Studies in Higher Education, 43*(8), 1404–1416.

Kruyen, P. M., Eppink, D. J., & Ehren, M. (2021). Understanding the accountability paradox: A systematic review of educational accountability research. *Educational Assessment, Evaluation and Accountability, 33*(3), 267–295.

Leisyte, L., & Dee, J.R. (2012). Understanding academic work in a changing institutional environment. In *Higher education: Handbook of theory and research* (pp. 123–206).

Looney, R. (2014). Reforming Egypt's higher education: Towards a comprehensive vision for the future. *International Journal of Educational Development, 37*, 86–96.

Maassen, P., & Stensaker, B. (2019). The university's institutional logic: Examining change through the prism of organisational identity. In *University development and the impact of globalization* (pp. 33–45). Palgrave Macmillan.

Maassen, P., & Stensaker, B. (2022). Trust and higher education governance in Norway and the United Kingdom. *Trusting in Higher Education: A multifaceted discussion of trust in and for higher education in Norway and the United Kingdom* (pp. 17–36). Springer International Publishing.

Madsen, D. Ø., Stenheim, T., & Døving, E. (2013). Higher education institutions and public administration reforms. *Public Organization Review, 13*(1), 49–63.

Mampaey, J., & Huisman, J. (2022). Stakeholder engagement in higher education: A systematic review of the literature. *Studies in Higher Education, 47*(1), 190–205.

Marginson, S. (2019). Limitations of human capital theory. *Studies in Higher Education, 44*(2), 287–301.

Marginson, S. (2020). The relentless price of high individualism in the pandemic. *Higher Education Research & Development, 39*(7), 1392–1395.

Marginson, S., & Considine, M. (2000). *The enterprise university: Power, governance and reinvention in Australia.* Cambridge University Press.

Middlehurst, R. (2013). Changing internal governance: A discussion of leadership roles and management structures in UK universities. *Higher Education Quarterly, 67*(4), 358–375.

Middlehurst, R. (2017). Leadership and management in higher education: A research perspective. In *University governance and reform* (pp. 35–52). Palgrave Macmillan.

Molesworth, M., Scullion, R., & Nixon, E. (2018). *The marketisation of higher education and the student as consumer.* Routledge.

Morrish, L., & Sauntson, H. (2020). Academic irresponsibility: The deformation of a teaching and learning culture. *Cambridge Journal of Education, 50*(5), 553–569.

Papadopoulos, G. S. (2016). The governance of educational expansion. *Journal of the European Higher Education Area, 2*, 79–97.

Pucciarelli, F., & Kaplan, A. (2016). Competition and strategy in higher education: Managing complexity and uncertainty. *Business Horizons, 59*(3), 311–320.

Rhoades, G., & Slaughter, S. (2004). Academic capitalism in the new economy: Challenges and choices. *American Academic, 1*(1), 37–59.

Romani, V. H. (2009). The politics of higher education in the Middle East: Problems and prospects. *Middle East Brief, 37*, 1–8.

Rutherford, A., & Rabovsky, T. (2014). Evaluating impacts of performance funding policies on student outcomes in higher education. *The ANNALS of the American Academy of Political and Social Science, 655*(1), 185–208.

Salmi, J., & Hauptman, A. M. (2019). Appendix–Innovations in tertiary education financing: A comparative evaluation of allocation mechanisms. In *Financing the education of health workers: Gaining a competitive edge* (pp. 421–520).

Selvik, K., & Utvik, B. O. (2020). *Oil states in the New Middle East: Uprisings and stability.* Routledge.

Wilkins, S., & Huisman, J. (2012). UK business school rankings over the last 30 years (1980–2010): Trends and explanations. *Higher Education, 63,* 367–382.

Wilkins, S., Shams, F., & Huisman, J. (2013). The decision-making and changing behavioral dynamics of potential higher education students: The impacts of increasing tuition fees in England. *Educational Studies, 39*(2), 125–141.

11

Advancing Assessment for Enhanced e-Education in the MENA Region

Rock-Antoine Mehanna⬤, Shaima AlHarmoodi, and Nehme Azoury

Introduction

The education sector globally, and particularly the Middle East and North Africa (MENA) region, has been undergoing a significant transformation. The need to prepare students for the dynamic twenty-first century and address the demands of a rapidly changing global economy has driven education reforms. These reforms have focused on improving access to education, enhancing the quality of education, and integrating

R.-A. Mehanna (✉) · S. AlHarmoodi
School of Business and Quality Management, Hamdan Bin Mohammed
Smart University, Dubai, United Arab Emirates
e-mail: r.mehanna@hbmsu.ac.ae

S. AlHarmoodi
e-mail: s.alharmoodi@hbmsu.ac.ae

N. Azoury
Faculty of Business, Holy Spirit University of Kaslik (USEK), Jounieh,
Lebanon
e-mail: nehmeazoury@usek.edu.lb

© The Author(s), under exclusive license to Springer Nature
Switzerland AG 2023
N. Azoury and G. Yahchouchi (eds.), *Governance in Higher Education*,
https://doi.org/10.1007/978-3-031-40586-0_11

technology into the educational system. The emergence of e-education has played a pivotal role in these reforms, providing students with a flexible and innovative approach to learning that caters to their diverse needs. However, the effective implementation of e-education relies on the availability of assessment tools and grading systems that can accurately measure student performance and ensure that learning outcomes and the market demands are met.

This chapter explores the global trends and reforms in education, with a specific focus on e-education in the MENA region. It examines the challenges and opportunities associated with the implementation of e-education, especially in the context of assessment and grading systems. Moreover, it discusses strategies for developing effective assessment tools and grading systems that support the delivery of high-quality e-education in the MENA region. Through this exploration, we aim to shed light on the importance of e-education and the critical role of assessment and grading systems in its successful implementation in the MENA region.

Global Reforms and Trends in the Higher Education Sector

Higher education is an ever-evolving sector that plays a vital role in the development of a country's economy and society. In recent years, there have been several global reforms and trends in higher education. A significant trend in higher education is the rise of digital technology. The use of digital technology has changed the way education is delivered and accessed (Hall et al., 2022). The widespread adoption of online learning platforms, such as Massive Open Online Courses (MOOCs), has opened new opportunities for learners to access higher education. MOOCs provide learners with free access to high-quality educational resources and content, from leading institutions around the world. This has made education more accessible, particularly for individuals who face barriers to traditional modes of learning, such as geographic distance, time constraints, or financial limitations (Papadakis, 2023).

Digital technology has not only revolutionized various sectors but also brought change in education methods in several ways. Innovative approaches such as flipped classrooms, online learning, blended learning, and gamification have been made possible with its emergence. In flipped classrooms which exemplify this trend but are not limited by it, a new concept's introduction is facilitated by online lectures or tutorial provision outside a conventional classroom environment. Classroom time is then used for discussion and collaborative learning activities, allowing learners to engage with the material in a more interactive and personalized way (Alotaibi, 2022; Dalbani et al., 2022).

Online learning has increased access to education for students who might not have been able to attend traditional brick-and-mortar universities. Online learning, mainly in its synchronous and asynchronous forms, surged and became a necessity during the COVID-19 pandemic in 2020. "Synchronous" learning refers to a type of learning that occurs in real time, where students and instructors participate in the learning process simultaneously, regardless of their physical locations. This type of learning can take place through video conferencing, live chat, or teleconferencing, among others. On the other hand, "asynchronous" learning is a type of learning where students access course material and complete assignments at their own pace, rather than in real time. For those looking to educate themselves on their own terms or schedule, options abound self-paced online courses; recorded lectures; discussion boards; email correspondence—all paths toward knowledge acquisition (Nagodavithana & Premarathne, 2022). As people contend with the post-pandemic world, they also face a significant evolution happening within pedagogical paradigms that includes new approaches to concepts such as remote work access; e-education quality assessments; technology utilization; and evaluation metrics plus regulations impacting educational systems. Blended learning can offer an additional option—learner flexibility combining traditional settings with e-resources meant to widen their horizons (Elbyaly & Elfeky, 2023) while gamification takes its place by making participation more accessible via game-like points, leaderboards, and badges (Khaldi et al., 2023). Colleges and universities worldwide are prioritizing global citizenship development by creating programs such as joint research projects, exchange student initiatives, and the like (David, 2023). Skill-based learning is also gaining recognition within this sector owing to the changing demands of labor and work that demand adaptable skill sets (Moritz & Zahidi, 2023).

Skill-based learning concentrates on defining learning and skill-based outcomes and evaluating students based on their ability to meet these outcomes. By focusing on what the student has learned instead of what the teacher has taught, skill-based and outcome-based education has the potential to improve the quality and relevance of higher education while promoting lifelong learning (Moritz & Zahidi, 2023). Lifelong learning, which acknowledges that learning is a continual process throughout a person's life, promotes the acquisition of skills and knowledge throughout a person's life rather than just during their formal education. This approach has the potential to enhance individuals' quality of life and career prospects while also fostering a more competent and adaptable workforce (Moritz & Zahidi, 2023).

Another important and emerging trend in higher education is sustainable education which prioritizes promoting sustainable development and addressing global issues like poverty, inequality, and climate change. The sustainable education approach acknowledges the critical role of education in advancing sustainable development and aims to incorporate sustainability principles in all areas of higher education. The approach adopted by higher education institutions has the potential to improve life quality and contribute toward achieving sustainable development goals for all (Marouli, 2021).

Keeping in mind the requirements of different stakeholders—students, employers, or society—the sector continues its evolutionary journey. Global reforms in higher education are reshaping how we learn—with new trends such as online learning, internationalization efforts through student exchange programs; skill-based courses offering focused outcomes; hybrid modes which combine online with physical classroom experiences along with lifelong learning options becoming more prevalent today. Incorporating these innovations enables universities to offer relevant curricula that benefit students while addressing pervasive global issues.

Higher Education Reforms and Trends in the MENA Region

With recognition of its role for driving both economic growth and social progress within society, higher education is undergoing rapid changes throughout the MENA region today via heavy government investments toward its various evolutions for betterment within multiple day-to-day scenarios faced corporately or by individuals alike (Sharma, 2023). A range of touch points such as inclusive leaderships' involvement alongside quality assurance or the push for more entrepreneurships have all amassed substantial significance regarding reforms triggered across MENA's higher education sector over these past years. Policymakers looking forward into creating informed decisions shall need current knowledge on reform trending for driving effective change while maintaining quality educational delivery. As millennials base themselves within awaiting plans toward worldwide job markets during current labor transformations underpinned with large reliance upon technology reliant industries. More corporations than ever before are installing an array of cutting-edge tech gadgets to keep productivity on an uplift. To fuel educational growth and in response, MENA's high education investment has in return experienced exponential growth; one that facilitates widening quality educational delivery via new universities and university establishments sprouting up across countries.

For MENA, the future is as exciting as it can be challenging: The region's education market projections show an expected growth unto $175 billion by 2027 out of which $7.1 billion generated from UAE for e-learning in particular while global technology market shows a parallel expansion seen worth $123.40 billion (Sharma, 2023). Growth trends such as online learning options for remotely and tailored personalized approaches for addressing unique requirements amidst higher education offer supreme significance to all involved stakeholders pushing forward with revolutionary approaches such as these. Additionally, it should be highlighted that MENA regions have agreed upon enhancing public–private and privately-run higher education institutions as a means of meeting increasing demand while simultaneously ensuring international adequacy. Notably, relevance to market dynamics aimed at improving employability prevails as a vital aspect of this initiative.

Private higher education institutions, in exchange for the opportunities provided by governments to develop higher education infrastructure and to fund research and faculty development, are expected to reciprocate by: (1) investing more in infrastructure to cater to a larger student body; (2) implementing internal quality improvement programs beyond the standard quality assurance documentation; (3) regularly reviewing and updating their curricula to cater to distinct student groups such as local and expatriate students, as well as revising them based on feedback from the local corporate sector; (4) offering better compensation, career development, and mentoring opportunities to attract top-quality teaching faculty; (5) promoting institutional research and development, as well as higher education research, in order to explore better alternatives for further growth and development (Peddada & Alhuthaifi, 2021).

The aforementioned factors have facilitated the advancement of internationalization in higher education institutions in the MENA region as it was previously lagging behind in terms of internationalization (Marchesini, 2020). The region has made strides in recent times, with an increase in the number of international branch campuses (IBCs) concentrated primarily in the Gulf countries. Qatar and the UAE are globally recognized as among the top five host countries for IBCs and are two of the six international education hubs. The region has also undertaken efforts to boost internationalization through the cross-Mediterranean partnership model, which has led to the establishment of various international universities in countries like Egypt, Jordan, Morocco, and Tunisia over the last decade (Marchesini, 2020). Internalization is now recognized as a vital contributor to institutional sustainability and the competitiveness of graduates. To become international, a university must have several internationalization enablers within its curriculum, international students from diverse backgrounds, international partnerships and collaborations, links with stakeholders, internationally accredited programs, international staff, learning materials and resources from foreign countries, and opportunities to learn foreign languages (David, 2023). These can foster intercultural competence and a better understanding of the world.

Quality assurance in higher education is another crucial aspect that ensures the credibility and effectiveness of the education provided. Quality assurance measures in higher education are currently rising in popularity across the MENA region. To this end, governments and educational institutions have moved toward implementing various quality assurance systems designed to enhance education quality and bolster international competitiveness (Aburizaizah, 2022). For example, ANQAHE was established in 2007 to bring greater awareness around best practices in this area throughout the region. Similarly, significant organizations, like AARU, playing an active role in creating initiatives and programs that promote accreditation efforts.

In order for each country's educational accreditation system to be effective, a regulatory agency oversees the process throughout its jurisdiction.

The CAA is responsible for performing this role within the UAE under setup's umbrella within Ministry of Education since 1999. CAA endeavors making sure that all degree-granting institutions offering academic programs are compliant with international standards by promoting strong internal quality control mechanisms while using defined benchmarks tailored per industry sector groups or level of studies delivered.

Other countries similarly have their own accrediting agencies; Saudi Arabia's NCAAA evaluates campuses within their borders while NAQAE serves a similar function operating out of Egypt but aimed at improving local institutions aligned internationally recognized criteria.

While challenges persist such as shortage of resources or adequate infrastructure capable of facilitating implementation efforts, bright spots remain amidst continued commitment seen at all levels toward achieving goal of raising local educational standards to reach those established abroad (Aburizaizah, 2022). To ensure the provision of quality higher education Jordan mandates that all universities receive accreditation from the Accreditation and Quality Assurance Commission for Higher Education Institutions (AQACHEI).

The commission deals with quality as well as accreditation. A national framework document was launched in 2016 and the first announcement of national rankings was made in September 2017. Quality assurance at

HEIs is governed by a HEAC document entitled Quality Assurance at Jordanian higher education institutions. This sets out the criteria under which quality is to be addressed including programs and their effectiveness, financial management, institutional integrity, and governance systems (The Open University, 2018).

In Lebanon, a country traditionally recognized as the regional hub for quality education, all educational institutions are mandated to adhere to national accreditation standards. However, numerous institutions have gone a step further and obtained international accreditations from renowned bodies in the United States and Europe (UNESCO, 2007). The cosmopolitan educational landscape of Lebanon has been shaped by the influence of early American and French missionaries who established universities in the nineteenth century. The American University of Beirut (AUB), founded in 1866, and Université Saint-Joseph (USJ), established in 1875, played significant roles, alongside local Catholic religious orders like La Sagesse University, which was established in 1875. In the twentieth century, a second wave of universities emerged, including the Lebanese American University (LAU) in 1924, the Holy Spirit University of Kaslik (USEK) in 1950, the public Lebanese University (UL) in 1951, Beirut Arab University (BAU) in 1960, and Notre Dame University (NDU) in 1987 (Lebanese Ministry of Education and Higher Education website).

The United Arab Emirates (UAE) and Qatar are among several countries working hard to enhance educational standards throughout MENA—often looking toward other high-performing reference societies like Singapore or Finland for inspiration or guidance through international performance comparisons that measure students' knowledgeability in multiple domains. By taking part in rigorous assessments that are conducted worldwide experts can identify areas where these countries should focus efforts next to improve student performance even further, ultimately enhancing students' success through scholastic achievement (Mohamed & Morris, 2021). The MENA Region highlights entrepreneurship education as pivotal in fostering sustainable economic development. There is gradually increasing recognition toward this phenomenon; educational institutions aligned themselves with government intervention measures are pursuing this cause relent-lessly (Omoniyi et al., 2022). United Arab Emirates took this idea further ahead by feeding it into the National Agenda for Entrepreneurship and SMEs. The agenda aims to make UAE a thriving entrepreneurship hub by 2031 through comprehensive planning—29 initiatives eyeing an improved business environment, fostering collaborations between public and private sectors, encouraging start-ups by offering incentives and more. Its target is to create one million new ventures with ten unicorn start-ups (AlHarmoodi & Awofeso, 2023).

Hamdan Bin Mohammed Smart University introduced H-preneurs in response to the national calling; the startup provides a tech-enabled ecosystem and support system to learners with entrepreneurial lean-ings—acting as a portal from ideation until market launch (HBMSU, 2022). Leveraging HBMSU's resources of knowledge base and mentors plus investor networks and academic content, this platform guides potential entrepreneurs toward their goals of empowerment through entrepreneurship contributing positively toward economic growth.

Specialized centers aimed at promoting entrepreneurial education form another integral part of MENA region's methodology toward trans-formational economic development. The American University in Cairo established AUC Venture Lab; its primary objective is providing mentor-ship programs along with funds to students and alumni interested in creating innovative start-ups.

Similarly, Qatar University has established the Qatar Business Incuba-tion Center (QBIC), which offers incubation and acceleration programs to support the development of innovative start-ups. In 2002, the Univer-sité Saint-Joseph (USJ) in Beirut launched its technological park "Bery-tech" for financing and transforming innovative ideas into successful businesses. The productive collaboration between institutions has birthed multiple initiatives that promote innovation and entrepreneurship among aspiring innovators in Lebanon. One example is the "Smart Center" established through La Sagesse University's partnership with the Banque Libano-Francaise (BLF) back in 2015. The Smart Center boasts of coaching sessions that expose students and entrepreneurs to real-world financial simulations for excellent practice purposes (EBLF, 2019). The

MENA region has equally invested heavily in education for budding entrepreneurs, providing varying specializations across universities.

Through these academic endeavors, learners gain crucial knowledge and expertise necessary for launching commercial ventures into innovative products or services into regional markets successfully. Worth mentioning is HBMSU's Innovation and Change Management master's degree program alongside its Entrepreneurial Leadership master's degree course options offered by Dubai-based universities while AUB proposes an innovation-centered Bachelor of Business Administration.

Another important initiative in promoting innovation and entrepreneurship education in the MENA region is the provision of training and mentorship programs. These programs help to develop students' skills in innovation and entrepreneurship and provide them with the support they need to launch successful start-ups. For example, the MIT Enterprise Forum Arab Startup Competition offers training, mentorship, and funding opportunities to entrepreneurs in the MENA region.

According to Omoniyi et al. (2022), entrepreneurship education is a vital key that opens the door to the sustainable development of any nation, especially that sustainable education has been largely absent and not a priority in the MENA region. Some GCC countries have started to prioritize sustainable education, with the UAE leading the way by embedding sustainability in each of its pillars. For example, the Masdar Institute of Science and Technology in Khalifa University (KU), Abu Dhabi, offers degree programs in sustainable energy and sustainable infrastructure. Qatar Foundation's Education City campus in Doha is designed to be environmentally sustainable, incorporating features such as solar panels, rainwater harvesting, and energy-efficient lighting.

One of the key aspects of sustainable education in the MENA region is promoting environmental awareness and sustainability to incite the transition to sustainable societies that are in balance with nature, with social justice, and economic viability (Marouli, 2021). Sustainable education emphasizes the importance of interdisciplinary approaches, problem-solving, and constructivist learning spaces in interactive learning environments that address real environmental problems. The instructor's role is to organize the learning context and facilitate learning, while collaboration with the community and action research are also essential. The primary objective of these learning contexts is to inspire learners' action for environmental concern by promoting knowledge creation coupled with emotional engagement; thereby sustainable education aims at initiating transformative learning encouraging both individual and societal change through reflective environments that foster critical thinking and subsequent action fostering pedagogical tools achieving their objectives (Marouli, 2021).

Additionally, relevant mentalities supporting gender equality or ethnic diversity alongside necessary skill sets required for sustainable resource management are necessary. The Men's Education Network for Gender Equality Initiative (MENGEI) launched a comprehensive program in the MENA region focused on gender-equitable budgeting, planning, and education. Despite changes over the years, educational reforms seem insufficient to tackle problems such as political instability, financial scarcity, and persistence of large youth populations in the region.

Accordingly, e-education emerges as a viable alternative solution to bridging existing gaps; online courses or virtual classrooms akin to educational apps can bolster accessible and cost-effective education even in remote locations (Wong-Powell & Kusuma-Powell, 2020). Furthermore, this mode of delivery is essential to delivering innovative approaches that would lead to much-needed flexibility catering toward students with different learning curves. Hence, this segment aims at underscoring pertinent elements pertaining to e-education's integration for matching students' diverse needs while also highlighting potential challenges and implementing strategies.

An Overview of e-Education in the MENA Region: Challenges and Opportunities

E-Education—also known as digital or online learning—has become an indispensable part of the global education sector in today's world. The MENA region is not exempt from this trend either. Facing mounting requests for more flexible educational services to align with changing socioeconomic demands globally numerous digital learning models have emerged such as virtual classrooms; hybrid blended learning programs; Massive Open Online Courses (MOOCs) along with distance learning modules that have started showing tremendous potential across MENA countries (Fauzi, 2022). The advent of COVID-19 pandemic further underscored this shift toward remote learning approaches. Creating new realities that made students adopt innovative ways of immersive personal engagement through various e-learning platforms. This article examines the state of play about e-education across the MENA region; looking at challenges/opportunities presented and offering practical solutions on how stakeholders can better promote its uptake while enhancing its overall effectiveness within the rapidly evolving educational systems underway across MENA countries currently.

These advancements incorporate the availability of online materials and the flexibility to access them, opportunities for online interaction, quality online course design and structure, and proper guidance and facilitation provided by teachers. These factors have been identified as influential in positively enhancing the experience and outcomes of online learning (Alotaibi, 2022; Fan & Tian, 2022). Consequently, most higher education institutions in the MENA region (HEIs) have integrated e-learning modules and activities into their regular curricula and universities have expanded their campuses, labs, and educational facilities to accommodate online learning (Alotaibi, 2022).

There are several universities and institutions in the MENA region that have emerged in e-Education and offered online courses and degree programs. These include public universities, private universities, and specialized e-learning institutions. Some of the most well-known e-learning institutions in the region include Hamdan Bin Mohammed Smart University (HBMSU-UAE), King Saud University Online (KSU-Saudi Arabia), the Arab Open University (AOU-Bahrain, Kuwait, Lebanon, Oman, Saudi Arabia, and Jordan), Arab Academy for Science, Technology and Maritime Transport Online (AASTMT-Egypt), and the Mohammed VI Polytechnic University (UM6P-Morocco).

In Jordan, there are instances of online education being utilized to meet the educational requirements of refugees. Many of these refugees had been receiving education in Syria before being compelled to seek refuge in Jordan. Nevertheless, the government has mandated that all external organizations engaged in refugee education programs must ensure a minimum enrollment of 30% Jordanian students. It is expected that this percentage will rise to 50%, and some agencies, such as KIRON—a nongovernmental agency that offers free online learning opportunities to refugees and underserved communities in Jordan and Lebanon—are already working toward achieving that proportion (The Open University, 2018).

GCC governments have also been making great efforts to accelerate the use of innovation and technology in education, but the progress made by each country in the region varies significantly. The UAE was ranked highest in the region by the Global Innovation Index (GII) and 34th out of 134 countries in 2020, which considers innovation inputs and outputs. Similarly, the UAE was ranked 30th out of 134 countries in the 2020 Network Readiness Index (NRI), which is based on the pillars of Technology, People, Governance, and Impact. These rankings provide an overview of a country's ability to improve their innovation capabilities and build digital networks, as well as their readiness to support the education system with digital infrastructures. Due to the early investments in innovation and technology-enabled education system in the UAE, their education system was able to continue almost without interruption during the COVID-19 pandemic when lockdowns and campus closures forced higher education institutions (HEIs) in the MENA region to adopt online course delivery (UNESCO RCEP, 2022).

Saudi Arabia has also emerged as a leading nation in information and communication technology development, ranking 48th globally. The country's Vision 2030 emphasizes these technological advancements, positioning Saudi Arabia as one of the most digitally connected nations worldwide (Qureshi & Khan, 2022).

HEIs that had previously invested in online or blended learning programs, such as Hamdan Bin Mohamed Smart University and the Arab Open University, were better equipped to adapt, while those that had not made such investments had to rely on available technology to respond quickly. For example, the UAE's Higher Colleges of Technology (HCT) launched a two-day virtual-learning pilot program within days of in-person classes being canceled, while the UAE's Ministry of Education teamed up with the Abdulla Al Ghurair Foundation for Education to establish the University Consortium for Quality Online Learning. These institutions were able to leverage the growing investment in education technology start-ups in the years preceding the pandemic (Hall et al., 2022; UNESCO RCEP, 2022).

While most universities in the region did not anticipate the transition to distance learning, they have since adopted a range of online learning platforms to achieve scale. However, many countries faced challenges such as a lack of capability in technology-enabled approaches and constrained internet access, quality, and reliability. According to AlFallaj (2020), challenges can be categorized into four groups: technological, individual, cultural, and educational. Challenges of e-learning vary from country to country due to cultural differences, backgrounds, and developmental stages. Several primary difficulties exist within e-learning related mostly to informational awareness about information/communication technology commonly known as ICTs; poor network connections; substandard high-speed internet access within deprived areas; all of which can pose significant obstacles for individuals looking to take part in online education. For instance, according to Mulhanga and Lima (2017), social, political, and economic limitations affect Libya's e-learning program.

Furthermore, a considerable obstacle arises from the lack of trained and proficient instructors capable of effectively utilizing digital tools to facilitate learning (Putri et al., 2020).

Transitioning traditional teaching methods into online learning methodologies can create various problems for educators. According to Putri et al., teachers face challenges that include a restricted curriculum coverage, substandard technological skills that hinder effective online teaching, the time-consuming activity of developing e-content/presentations, more screen time while creating content and appraising student work resulting in an increase in expenses related to internet use especially in regions with low-income earners.

Funding difficulties are also commonplace when it comes to e-education. While some governments have invested substantially into e-education solutions, many institutions across the MENA region still face inadequate resources for developing and maintaining interconnected online courses and virtual degree programs (Karsh, 2021).

Quality assurance remains another persistent problem with e-education across most regional educational institutions worldwide; evidence includes extensive reporting highlighting these concerns arising as a result we must continually question their legitimacy particularly in the MENA region as reported by Naciri et al. (2020).

In response to COVID-19 pandemic outbreaks worldwide, global institutions had no practical options but switching swiftly toward online learning as their principal means of providing continuity in education during such uncertain times; regrettably this transition was not without its difficulties including little preparation time available for instructors or students. As a result, institutions and students had to quickly adapt to new teaching and learning methods, relying on learning management systems, course websites, and interactive resources for online education (Ferri et al., 2020). Ensuring quality standards and developing a comprehensive assessment and accreditation system for online programs is essential to ensuring that students receive a high-quality education.

Despite the challenges, the forced experiment of the past three years presents a unique opportunity for HEIs to make strategic choices about the mix of remote and in-person learning to optimize the quality and equity of their education and reconfigure their use of physical and virtual space accordingly. The region has a large and growing population, with a high demand for education and a strong emphasis on academic achievement. E-education provides a way to meet this demand without the need for extensive physical infrastructure. Governments and institutions in the region can play a key role in promoting e-education by investing in technology and infrastructure, supporting quality standards and accreditation, and promoting cultural change toward online learning. There is also potential for international partnerships and collaborations to support the development of e-education in the region. An instance in Tunisia illustrates how the number of instructors providing online courses rose significantly from 1,600 to over 13,000 between February and July 2020. Moreover, the quantity of courses provided increased from 2,400 to more than 34,000, and the number of students participating in these courses tripled from 40,000 to over 121,000.21 (Hall et al., 2022).

Alotaibi (2022) stresses the importance of paying attention to the social contexts and ideological commitments that support and shape the adoption and use of e-education technologies in higher education. Scaling e-education requires a student-centered approach, early involvement of faculty, and innovative and interactive learning and assessment methods (Fauzi, 2022). Long-term benefits of successful digital learning include more individualized, adaptive learning paths, and expanding higher education access to traditionally underserved populations (AlFallaj, 2020). These technologies constantly evolve, enabling educational institutions and educators to better monitor students' academic progress and assess them (Alotaibi, 2022). The next section will explore the types of assessments in e-education and the strategies that can be employed to maximize the quality of e-education in the region.

Assessments in e-Education

There are various types of assessments used in e-education to measure student learning and progress. The type of assessment used may depend on the learning objectives, the level of the students, the subject matter, the requirement by the accrediting or regulatory body, the preferences of the instructor or institution, among other factors. Some of the most common types of assessments include:

Continuous Assessment: Continuous assessment is used to evaluate student learning during the learning process. It provides ongoing feedback to both teachers and students to identify areas of strength and weakness, adjust teaching strategies, and improve student learning. It can be used to assess students' skills. Forms of continuous assessments in e-education include online quizzes and tests. They may include multiple-choice questions, true/false questions, and short-answer questions. Another form is online discussions or discussion boards/forums. They are used to evaluate students' ability to engage in meaningful conversations related to the course content. These discussions may be graded based on the quality of students' contributions, the depth of their critical and analytical analysis, and their ability to interact with their peers and the instructor (Craig & Kay, 2021; Perera-Diltz & Moe, 2014).

Summative Assessment: Summative assessment is used to evaluate student learning at the end of a learning unit or course. It typically takes the form of a final exam or project and is used to determine a student's overall performance in the course. This type of assessment can be given as online assignments and can take various forms, such as essays, research papers, projects, and other written work. They are used to evaluate students' knowledge and understanding of the subject matter rather than skills. These assignments may be submitted online and evaluated by instructors using digital tools to detect plagiarism and AI-generated work (Craig & Kay, 2021; Perera-Diltz & Moe, 2014).

Diagnostic Assessment: Diagnostic assessment is used to identify areas of strength and weakness in student learning. It is typically used at the beginning of a course or unit to assess students' prior knowledge and understanding of the subject matter (Ahmed et al., 2010).

Competency-Based Performance Assessment: Competency-based performance assessment evaluates a student's ability to perform a specific task or demonstrate a specific skill. It typically involves real-world scenarios or projects that require students to apply their knowledge and skills in a practical context (Sluijsmans et al., 2006).

Portfolio Assessment: Portfolio assessment involves the collection of a student's work over a period of time to demonstrate their progress and achievement. It may include written work, projects, and other assignments (Bhattacharya & Hartnett, 2007).

Self-Assessment: Self-assessment is used in e-education to encourage students to reflect on their own learning and progress. It can be used to help students identify their strengths and weaknesses and set goals for improvement (e.g., self-reflection exercises, think papers, or self-evaluation of assignments) (Craig & Kay, 2021; Yan et al., 2022).

Peer Assessment: Peer assessment involves students evaluating the work of their peers. It can be used in e-education to evaluate students' work, provide feedback, promote collaboration, and develop critical thinking skills. Examples of this type of assessment include peer review of essays, research papers, and other assignments (Yan et al., 2022).

Digital Badges and Certificates: Digital badges and certificates are used in e-education to recognize students' achievements and skills. These badges and certificates may be awarded based on completion of specific tasks or the mastery of specific skills (Flynn et al., 2023).

Online Simulations: Online simulations are used to evaluate students' ability to apply their knowledge and skills in real-world scenarios. These simulations may be used to assess critical thinking, problem-solving, and decision-making skills. This method is increasingly popular and effective in skill building setups. It is very convenient to be used in e-education environments as it can be used in continuous assessments (on weekly basis, where each round could be equivalent to one year in real life), as well as in summative assessment as the cumulative total rounds (final game), final debriefing report, and/or final presentation (Campos et al., 2020).

Different types of assessments, especially continuous ones, including online simulations, can be mostly used to evaluate various forms of skills, including cross-functional teams (cross-skilling), lifelong learning (re-skilling), professional development (up-skilling), and long-term committed learning (deep skilling). For instance, they can promote the learning process of cross-functional teams through introducing a hands-on approach of the symbiotic impacts of the various functions of the team. Furthermore, they can properly evaluate re-skilling of continuing learners (i.e., lifelong learning process) through credit-bearing skill-based courses, such as micro-certificates, industry-specific workshops and seminars, self-paced online courses (e.g., Coursera, edX, Udemy), podcasts and webinars, and Web Badges. Similarly, deep skilling can be assessed for long-term structured and devoted approach of students toward set of goals (e.g., Bachelor, Master, and Doctoral degrees; Micro/Nano Bachelor and Micro/Nano master's degrees). Finally, up-skilling can also be evaluated through these types of continuous assessments, including online simulations, where compressed programs, professional courses/ programs, and certificates (e.g., six sigma, ISO, LEED, Lean, etc.).

The type of assessment used in e-education may depend on various factors, including the learning objectives, the level of the students, and the subject matter. A variety of assessment methods should be used to provide a comprehensive picture of student learning and progress in e-education.

Grading assessments in e-education is a crucial element in promoting higher quality online learning experiences, particularly in the MENA region. Educators in this region are faced with the challenge of establishing grading systems that strike a balance between being strict enough to maintain academic standards and being lenient enough to accommodate the unique circumstances of remote learning. Stricter grading systems can ensure that students meet rigorous academic requirements, fostering a culture of excellence and accountability in e-education. On the other hand, lenient grading systems can recognize the inherent challenges and limitations of online learning, considering factors such as technical difficulties, limited resources, and the need for flexibility. The next section will explore grading systems that can promote academic achievement while addressing the unique needs and circumstances of students in online learning environments.

Grading Systems for Promoting Higher Quality e-Education

Grading e-education assessments has emerged as an essential component within the dynamic realm of digital learning. Grading encompasses the process through which teachers evaluate student learning by means of classroom tests and assignments, the establishment of this process within the educational context, and the ensuing discussions that define the significance of grades to different audiences. According to Anderson and Walvoord (1998), the act of grading fulfills several key roles: (1) it *evaluates* the quality of a student's work; (2) it *communicates* with the student, employers, graduate schools, and other relevant parties; (3) it *motivates* how students study, what they prioritize, and their engagement in the course; and (4) it *organizes* by marking transitions, concluding activities, and guiding efforts for both students and teachers.

Within this landscape, higher education institutions and educators face a formidable challenge: to evaluate and grade these digital assessments effectively and equitably. Grading in the online learning environment presents a distinctive array of considerations and complexities when compared to traditional face-to-face settings. Therefore, it is of great importance to cultivate assessment practices that are both reliable and valid within the virtual classroom (Cain et al., 2022). Validity means the accuracy of a grade's reflection of student learning and achievement while reliability concerns the degree of random error that might be present and affect validity (Haladyna, 2019).

According to Cain et al. (2022), some educators are now questioning the validity and assumptions of traditional practices, including the determination of grades and their impact on learner behavior. A study conducted by Schinske and Tanner (2014) on grading and feedback points out that feedback can be categorized into two main types: evaluative feedback and descriptive feedback. Evaluative feedback involves judgments of student work, such as letter grades or written praise/criticism, while descriptive feedback provides information on how students can improve their competence. However, there is anecdotal evidence and research suggesting that a significant number of students not only neglect to read the written feedback provided but also fail to utilize it to improve their subsequent work.

Grades seem to tap into students' fears of punishment or shame, as well as their desire to outperform their peers, rather than igniting motivation and enjoyment for the learning process (Cain et al., 2022; Pulfrey et al., 2011). Motivation in learning can be categorized as either intrinsic or extrinsic. Intrinsic motivation refers to students' natural curiosity and desire to gain knowledge and skills, leading them to engage in learning activities. On the other hand, extrinsic motivation drives students to participate in activities for external rewards, such as earning a good grade or pleasing the instructor, rather than an internal desire to learn (Cain et al., 2022). When students seek credit points, they demonstrate extrinsic motivation, whereas intrinsic motivation prompts students to learn for the sake of learning, without any specific rewards in mind. Although students may still learn and allocate appropriate attention to their studies if they personally endorse the value of the activities beyond the grade, decades of research have consistently shown that using external rewards to motivate learning is less effective compared to intrinsic motivation (Yahiaoui et al., 2022). The implications of grades extend beyond merely dampening intrinsic motivation; they also give rise to extrinsic motivation, intensify the fear of failure, diminish interest, reduce enjoyment in class activities, increase anxiety, impede performance in subsequent tasks, foster avoidance of challenging assignments, and heighten competitiveness (Pulfrey et al., 2011; Schinske & Tanner, 2014). Rather than perceiving low grades as an opportunity for self-improvement, students who receive low scores tend to disengage from their classwork. While students often express a desire for grading, surveys indicate that they prefer descriptive comments over grades as a form of feedback (Schinske & Tanner, 2014).

In a study conducted by Swinton (2010), it was discovered that a grading system that rewarded knowledge while acknowledging effort had a positive impact on stimulating student interest in self-improvement. This suggests that a balanced approach, combining accurate grading with meaningful feedback and recognition of student effort, could help mitigate some of the adverse effects of grading.

Multiple-choice assessments, that are widely used in e-assessments, typically allow for objective grading, as they do not require the use of professional judgment from one paper to another. However, despite the advantages of objective grading in multiple-choice assessments, concerns have been raised about their widespread use. These concerns include the potential for false indications of student understanding, limitations in promoting critical thinking, and the potential for bias against specific student groups (Schinske & Tanner, 2014; Stanger-Hall, 2012).

Grading student writing, such as essays, reports, or constructed-response test items, introduces more opportunities for subjectivity. However, these assessments depend largely on the subjective estimation of the faculty rather than the actual quality of the work (Schinske & Tanner, 2014). According to Meadows and Billington (2005), marking reliability varies significantly due to differences in instructor training, assessment type, grading system, and the specific topic assessed.

Using rubrics to grade assignments or tests can help reduce inconsistencies and make the grading of written work more objective. Sharing rubrics with students can enhance learning by providing feedback and opportunities for self-assessment (Reddy & Andrade, 2010). Improving consistency in grading tests can also be achieved by designing longer tests with narrower focused questions, although this may limit the variety of question types that can be included on an exam (Meadows & Billington, 2005).

Accomplishing this necessitates educators to skillfully navigate a multitude of factors, including protecting academic integrity, delivering timely feedback, and maintaining consistent standards across a diverse array of digital platforms. Additionally, educators must consider the impact of automated grading systems, adaptive learning algorithms, and the use of rubrics tailored to online assessments. In addition, alternative grading methods, such as competency-based assessment, specifications grading, and "ungrading," have gained popularity as educators recognize the drawbacks of conventional grading systems. By understanding the unique characteristics and intricacies of grading e-education assessments, educators can adapt their practices to effectively evaluate student learning and provide meaningful feedback (Cain et al., 2022).

Recently, computer-assisted assessments, also known as automated grading systems, are gaining popularity in higher education institutions due to their ability to greatly enhance the learning process. These systems include (a) Case-Based Auto Graders, such as CASEGRADER by Thomson Course Technology, (b) Procedural-Based Grading, systems such as SAM2007 by Thomson Course Technology or SNAP by EMC Paradigm Publishing, and (c) test-bank systems that normally exist within other systems such as Blackboard (Matthews et al., 2012). While these systems are very efficient and offer challenging, multi-step, realistic problems, they have some limitations like the inability of instructors to create their own cases and do not allow for instant changes by the instructor.

Smarter systems were proposed and tested such as the Adaptive Grading/Learning System (AGLS) by Matthews et al. (2012). This system enables instructors to efficiently grade assignments while providing valuable feedback to students, thus promoting effective learning. It ensures consistency in grading by employing a standardized rubric for each assignment. One noteworthy aspect is that it has the capacity to "learn" correct and incorrect responses, incorporating them into the grading rubric.

AI engines such as Chat GPT, Murf, Synthesia, and Stock AI, also have a significant impact on education and assessments, transforming the way students learn and teachers assess their progress. These technologies have the potential to enhance educational experiences, provide personalized learning opportunities, and streamline assessment processes. These tools can analyze students' learning patterns, identify knowledge gaps, and deliver tailored content and resources to address their specific needs. By offering adaptive and customized learning paths, AI tools can improve engagement and help students achieve better learning outcomes. They can also automate the assessment process, saving instructors time and effort. By leveraging natural language processing and machine learning algorithms, these tools can analyze and evaluate students' written responses, essays, or assignments. They can provide objective scoring and feedback based on predefined criteria, ensuring consistency and reducing subjectivity in grading. These automated assessments enable educators to focus more on instructional tasks and personalized student support (AlAfnan et al., 2023; UNESCO IESALC, 2023). The speed in generating responses by AI tools is an added advantage as it saves time on generating authentic workshop or discussion material. Hence, the use of AI tools can be encouraged by professors as part of the formal and informal learning in case students need a definition of a concept or insights or information regarding a term, but its use shall be discouraged for writing assessments or official submissions (AlAfnan et al., 2023; UNESCO IESALC, 2023). To avoid any cheating or copying practices, instructors are encouraged to use plagiarism detection software such as Turnitin as a platform to authenticate students' work.

Another critical question arises as to which grading system, strict or lenient, is most suitable for e-education. A strict grading system may motivate students to work harder and produce higher quality work, as they know that they will be held to high standards and receive lower grades for poor quality work. However, a strict grading system may also create a high-pressure environment that can lead to anxiety and discourage experimentation and creativity. In some cases, a strict grading system can lead to students focusing solely on memorizing information rather than understanding and applying it (Mozenter, 2019). On the other hand, a lenient grading system may encourage students to take risks and explore new ideas, as they feel more comfortable making mistakes and learning from them. However, a lenient grading system may also lead to lower quality work, as students may not feel the same level of motivation to produce high-quality work if they know that they will receive a good grade regardless (Mozenter, 2019).

The decision to adhere to a lenient or strict grading system is determined by several factors. According to Brookhart et al. (2016), grades and their interpretation are shaped by multiple factors, including different sources of evidence (such as achievement and non-achievement data), contextual and external factors, and the personal values and beliefs held by instructors. Many contextual factors affect the instructor's grading practices, such as study levels, subject matter, state and district-wide grading policy, and large-scale assessment (Cheng et al., 2020). Additional studies pointed out by Cheng et al. (2020) indicate that the underlying values and philosophies of instructors have a major effect on grading practices. The purpose of grading, conceptions of fairness, and the consequences of grades influence grading decisions.

Influencers of Grading e-Education Assessments in the MENA Region

In the MENA region, several factors influence the grading system in e-education. These factors can vary based on the specific country, institution, and educational context (Cheng et al., 2020). Here are some key influencers of the grading system in MENA online education:

1. *Cultural and Social Norms*: The MENA region has a diverse cultural context and educational norms that may impact grading systems. Cultural values, societal expectations, and educational traditions influence the approach to assessments and grading. These factors must be considered to ensure relevance, fairness, and acceptance among students and educators in the region. In the UAE and Kuwait for example, cultural and social values, like other Middle Eastern countries, encompass specific norms of interaction and communication for females. This aspect, as highlighted by Al-Fadhli (2008) and Gokah et al. (2015), leads to shyness in interaction and a lack of confidence in communication especially with the opposite gender. Hence, e-education provides an opportunity for them to learn and be assessed with limited barriers and more confidence (AlFallaj, 2020; Meehy, 2015). In addition to that, the MENA region is known for its collectivist cultural values, where the well-being and harmony of the group are emphasized over individual achievements. This can impact grading systems by placing less emphasis on individual competition and more on collaborative learning. Grading criteria may focus on teamwork, cooperation, and group projects, rather than solely on individual performance which leads to a more lenient grading system (Brignardello-Petersen et al., 2020).

   In Jordan, a certain level of cultural resistance toward online learning exists due to its lack of face-to-face interaction because the country has a strong tradition of knowledge transmission through oral means, where information and wisdom are passed from person to person through in-person interaction, which gives higher value to face-to-face education. Although this perspective is gradually changing with the adoption of new technologies, it remains a significant factor when students (and their families) contemplate their study options (The Open University, 2018).

2. *Technology Infrastructure and Advancements*: The MENA region has witnessed significant advancements in technology infrastructure, with increased access to online education platforms and AI tools. Yet, countries vary in terms of technological advancements and internet connectivity. The availability and capabilities of the technological infrastructure influence the design and implementation of grading

systems in online education. The grading system should align with the online learning platforms used in the region, ensuring seamless integration with assessment tools and data management systems. Considerations such as scalability, security, authentication, and accessibility are vital when selecting or developing an online grading system in the MENA region (Ahmad et al., 2018; Gokah et al., 2015). The grading system needs to consider the ability of students to submit assignments online or access online assessment platforms, the originality of students' work, and the security and verification of submissions, and the clarity of guidelines and rubrics.

In Egypt, for example, landline connections and broadband services are not widely available. In cases where broadband via landline exists, it is both costly and an unreliable option, making it unappealing to users. Students frequently encounter issues such as slow download speeds that are inadequate for the materials they need, such as videos and animations, as well as server problems. Current estimates suggest that internet penetration has reached nearly 50%, mainly driven by mobile internet usage in urban areas while in many parts of the country, internet access is still nonexistent (The Open University, 2018).

3. *Government Policies and Regulations*: Government policies and regulations have a direct impact on the grading system in online education. Education authorities and regulatory bodies set guidelines and standards for grading practices, including assessment methods, grading scales, and criteria for evaluating student work. For instance, the UAE, Saudi Arabia, and Egypt governments establish standardized assessment frameworks and guidelines for e-education. These frameworks provide a basis for grading practices by defining assessment criteria, grading scales, and performance indicators. They ensure consistency and comparability of grades across different educational institutions and programs and emphasize the alignment of e-education with national curricula in accordance with the prescribed learning outcomes and content standards defined by the government (CAA, 2021; Meehy, 2015; MOE-KSA, 2023). Governments usually conduct regular assessments and audits to ensure that grading systems

are fair, transparent, and reliable. Feedback from these evaluations informs policy revisions and improvements in grading methodologies.

With the rise of AI tools and engines which have a significant impact on education and assessments, governments in the MENA region varied in their responses and regulations governing the use of such tools. The UAE has been at the forefront of embracing emerging technologies in education. The Ministry of Education has been actively promoting the integration of AI in education, and they have set specific guidelines and frameworks along with the Ministry of State for Artificial Intelligence that address the use of AI-powered systems like Chat GPT in educational institutions (MoAI, 2023). In Saudi Arabia, significant investments in AI and education have been made lately. The Saudi Ministry of Education may have guidelines in place for the use of AI technologies in higher education considering critical factors such as privacy, ethics, and the impact on learning outcomes (MOE-KSA, 2023). It's important to note that the MENA region encompasses various countries, each with its own regulatory landscape affecting the way students learn and educators assess their progress. These technologies have the potential to enhance educational experiences, provide personalized learning opportunities, and streamline assessment processes.

4. ***Quality Assurance and Accreditation Requirements***: Grading systems in online higher education in the MENA region should adhere to quality assurance standards and accreditation requirements (Aburizaizah, 2022). Aligning grading practices with established educational standards ensures consistency, transparency, and credibility. Accreditation agencies and regulatory bodies such as the UAE's Commission for Academic Accreditation (CAA), the Saudi Arabia's National Center for Academic Accreditation and Evaluation (NCAAA), and the Qatar National Accreditation System (QNAS) have set specific guidelines that need to be followed to maintain the quality and integrity of grading systems. These bodies evaluate various aspects, including grading systems, to ensure compliance with quality standards. They review the design, implementation, and assessment

methods of grading systems to assess their validity, fairness, and alignment with learning outcomes. In addition to that, educational institutions in the MENA region implement internal quality assurance processes to monitor and enhance grading practices. These processes may include the establishment of grading committees or quality assurance units responsible for reviewing and ensuring the fairness and consistency of grading across programs and courses. Internal audits and evaluations help identify areas for improvement and promote the continuous enhancement of grading practices (Aburizaizah, 2022; Al Helih & Nasereddin, 2019).

5. *Pedagogical Approaches*: Pedagogical approaches play a significant role in shaping the grading practices of e-education in the MENA region. A diverse range of approaches influences how assessments are conducted and grades are assigned, providing a comprehensive framework for evaluating student performance. Some prominent examples include competency-based assessment, project-based learning, formative assessment, simulations, and peer assessment (Campos et al., 2020; Craig & Kay, 2021; Perera-Diltz & Moe, 2014; Sluijsmans et al., 2006; Yan et al., 2022). Some of these assessments follow a more lenient approach than the others, for example, open-ended assignments, project-based assessments, and peer assessments are more lenient than formative assessments.

6. *Educational Goals and Expectations*: Different educational systems and institutions in the MENA region may have different goals and expectations for student performance. If the focus is on mastery of content or skills, a lenient grading system may be preferred to encourage students to take risks and learn from their mistakes. On the other hand, if the focus is on achievement and competition, a stricter grading system may be preferred (Campos et al., 2020; Kayan-Fadlelmula et al., 2022; Omoniyi et al., 2022).

7. *Faculty Perspectives and Beliefs*: Faculty members play a crucial role in shaping the grading system. Their perspectives, beliefs, and teaching philosophies influence how they design assessments, evaluate student work, and assign grades. Faculty members' understanding of online education and their beliefs about grading practices impact the grading system (Cheng et al., 2020).

It is important to note that these influencers are interconnected and can vary across different countries and educational contexts within the MENA region. The grading system and whether it should be strict or lenient should consider these factors to ensure fairness, consistency, and alignment with the educational goals and values of the region.

Strict or Lenient Grading Systems in the MENA Region?

Strict Grading Systems

The strict grading system is an approach to evaluating student performance that adheres to rigorous standards and imposes high expectations for achievement. It is characterized by several key principles, such as high standards, objective evaluation, limited flexibility, and emphasis on mastery. It places importance on deep comprehension, comprehensive knowledge, and high levels of competency. Students are expected to meet specific learning objectives and demonstrate a comprehensive understanding of the concepts covered. While this system has many advantages like setting clear expectations, promoting high academic rigor, teaches accountability and high standards, it also has many disadvantages like creating additional stress and pressure on students, may not adequately recognize incremental improvements or personal development, and it may discourage students from taking risks or exploring creative approaches, as it primarily rewards adherence to predefined standards. This can stifle innovation and limit students' ability to think outside the box (Gray & Bunte, 2022; Mozenter, 2019; Schinske & Tanner, 2014).

The MENA region places a strong emphasis on academic achievement and excellence. The strict grading system aligns with this cultural value, as it sets high standards and encourages students to strive for academic excellence. It also aligns with the preparation for the competitive job market; the strict grading system can prepare students for the challenges they will face and instills a strong work ethic, discipline, and a drive for excellence that are highly valued by employers. While the strict grading system aligns with cultural values and expectations, it may also contribute to increased stress and pressure on students in the MENA region. It is essential for educators and policymakers in the MENA region to strike a balance between maintaining high standards and promoting a supportive and inclusive learning environment that nurtures students' overall growth and development.

Lenient Grading Systems

The lenient grading system is characterized by a more forgiving approach to grading student work. It is based on the principle that the focus should be on students' progress and learning rather than their final grades. In this system, grades are not necessarily a measure of mastery but rather a representation of effort and improvement. The lenient grading system typically focuses on promoting and supporting learning. Grades are viewed as a tool to help students improve their skills and knowledge. It values effort over final outcomes. Students are rewarded for their hard work and dedication, even if they do not achieve the highest grades. The system is also designed to be flexible, with opportunities for students to improve their grades through extra credit, revisions, or retakes. Hence, this grading system is inclusive and acknowledges the diversity of student backgrounds and learning styles. Students are not penalized for factors beyond their control, such as language barriers or disabilities.

Due to all these factors, a lenient grading system can reduce stress and anxiety among students, who may feel more comfortable taking risks and making mistakes without fear of failing. It also increases engagement in the learning process as they feel that their effort and progress are valued (Cain et al., 2022; Schinske & Tanner, 2014).

A drawback to the lenient grading system is that it may not accurately reflect students' mastery of the subject matter. In some cases, students may receive high grades even if they have not fully grasped the material. It can also be subjective, with grades reflecting the instructor's personal biases or preferences. Employers or other institutions may also misinterpret lenient grades as evidence of lower academic standards (Cain et al., 2022; Schinske & Tanner, 2014).

The lenient grading system has several implications for the MENA region, where traditional teaching methods have emphasized rote learning and memorization over critical thinking and creativity. A shift toward a more lenient grading system could encourage students to focus on the learning process rather than memorization, promoting a more dynamic and innovative approach to education. Furthermore, the lenient grading system can promote equity and inclusivity, which is particularly relevant in the MENA region, where disparities in education and socioeconomic status are prevalent. By accounting for factors such as language barriers and learning disabilities, the lenient grading system can ensure that all students have equal opportunities to succeed.

However, implementing a lenient grading system in the MENA region may face resistance from traditionalists who view grades as the primary measure of academic achievement. There may also be concerns about the credibility of lenient grades and their impact on students' preparedness for the job market or higher education institutions (Gokah et al., 2015; UNESCO RCEP, 2022).

Considerations

In the MENA region's evolving landscape of online higher education, the debate surrounding strict and lenient grading systems requires careful consideration. While a strict approach may uphold academic rigor and maintain consistency, a lenient approach can provide a more comprehensive and inclusive assessment of students' abilities. Striking a balance between these two approaches, tailored to the MENA context, is crucial.

It is vital for institutions in the MENA region to assess their unique educational goals, cultural values, and technological capabilities when making decisions about grading systems in online higher education. Ultimately, the adoption of a grading system should align with the region's aspirations for educational quality, equity, and student success, ensuring that assessment practices promote meaningful learning experiences and support the diverse needs of students in the MENA.

Effective grading and evaluation of student work in e-education requires careful planning, clear communication, and a focus on student learning. Here are some critical considerations.

Establish Clear Learning Objectives: Before grading and evaluating student work, it is essential to have a precise understanding of the learning objectives for the course or assignment. These objectives should be clearly communicated to students at the beginning of the course or assignment, guiding the development of assessment tools.

Utilize a Variety of Assessment Methods: In e-education, there exists a range of assessment methods to evaluate student work, such as quizzes, essays, discussion boards, presentations, and projects. Employing diverse assessment methods ensures that students demonstrate their knowledge and skills in different ways, providing a comprehensive view of their learning.

Integrate and Regulate the Use of AI: Set clear objectives for integrating AI in the course, identifying specific areas where AI can enhance learning experiences, such as personalized learning, automated assessments, or intelligent tutoring systems. Clearly define desired outcomes and benefits to guide the implementation process. Additionally, incorporate AI-related concepts and skills into the curriculum, preparing students for an AI-driven future and fostering critical thinking and digital literacy skills to understand and navigate AI technologies.

One can argue that the best approach to deal with the emergence of disruptive technology such as ChatGPT is to constructively use it rather than banning it. What matters is the design of the assessment to focus on the learning process and the critical thinking rather than just the outcome. There are growing interests today in few approaches that emphasize on "how" things are being done instead of "what" is being done. The concept of "Proof of Work" (POW) as coined by Jakobsson and Juels (1999) a technique used today by cryptocurrencies to verify the accuracy of new transactions that are added to a blockchain—may also be borrowed to assess and validate the learning process and critical analysis.

Another rising assessment strategy is "Prompt Engineering," which basically examines a systematic way for querying (or prompting) ChatGPT to get certain required information. In fact, ChatGPT will give different answers to the same question based on the user's deep understanding of the subject, knowledge of the specific information, and the adequate context. Methods such as Prompt Engineering and Proof of Work would disable high levels of plagiarism, boost critical thinking skills, foster deep knowledge of the subject, while making use of AI tools in the new smart learning paradigm.

Provide Explicit Guidelines and Rubrics: To ensure consistent grading and evaluation, it is vital to furnish clear guidelines and rubrics that articulate expectations for each assignment or assessment. These guidelines should be communicated to students in advance, aligning them with the learning objectives.

Deliver Timely Feedback: Timely feedback is essential for facilitating student learning and improvement. In e-education, feedback can be provided through various means, such as written comments, video feedback, or live discussions. Feedback should be specific, constructive, and aligned with the learning objectives.

Foster Self-assessment and Reflection: Encourage students to engage in self-assessment and reflection to foster ownership of their learning and identify areas for improvement. Integrating self-assessment into assignments and assessments promotes deeper learning and metacognition.

Evaluate the Effectiveness of the Grading and Evaluation Process: Regularly assessing the effectiveness of the grading and evaluation process is crucial for making improvements and ensuring alignment with the learning objectives. This evaluation can be conducted through surveys, focus groups, or other feedback mechanisms involving students.

Conclusion: The Need for a Balanced Grading System for Higher Quality e-Education in MENA Region

In the MENA region, e-education has emerged as a transformative force, revolutionizing the way education is delivered and assessments are conducted. The adoption of online learning platforms and digital tools has brought numerous advantages, such as increased access, flexibility, and personalized learning experiences. However, to ensure higher quality e-education, it is crucial to establish an assessment and a grading system that aligns with the unique characteristics of the region and addresses its specific challenges.

One of the key elements to consider while developing assessments is the clear definition of learning objectives. By establishing well-defined and measurable outcomes, educators can design assessments that accurately assess students' knowledge and skills. This promotes a sense of purpose and direction, enabling learners to track their progress and understand the expectations. Adopting a balanced grading system can incorporate a variety of assessment methods that cater to different learning styles and objectives. By using a combination of assessment strategies, educators can evaluate students' holistic understanding and application of concepts. This multifaceted approach provides a comprehensive view of students' abilities, allowing for a more accurate and fair assessment.

The integration of technology, including AI tools, offers significant opportunities for enhancing assessments in e-education. AI can automate the grading process, provide timely feedback, and assist in data analysis, freeing up educators' time for more personalized interactions. However, a balanced grading system strikes a harmony between AI-driven automation and human judgment, ensuring that the assessment process remains transparent, ethical, and inclusive.

To achieve higher quality e-education, it is also essential to recognize the importance of student engagement and motivation. By utilizing a balanced grading system with interactive and collaborative learning experiences, active participation, critical thinking, and the development of essential twenty-first-century skills can be nurtured and fostered.

In conclusion, fostering collaboration among various stakeholders is crucial for the successful implementation of a balanced grading system in e-education. Educators, policymakers, institutions, and technology providers need to join forces and establish clear guidelines, standards, and regulations that promote fair and reliable assessment practices. Furthermore, ongoing professional development programs should be prioritized to equip educators with the essential skills and knowledge to design and implement effective assessments in the digital realm. By working together, these stakeholders can ensure that students receive a high-quality and equitable educational experience, with assessments that accurately measure their learning outcomes and support their academic growth in the digital learning era.

References

AARU. The Association of Arab Universities. https://www.chea.org/internati onal-directory/association-arab-universities. Accessed on June 1, 2023.

AASTMT. Arab Academy for Science, Technology and Maritime Transport, Egypt. https://aast.edu/en/. Accessed on June 1, 2023.

Aburizaizah, S. J. (2022). The role of quality assurance in Saudi higher education institutions. *International Journal of Educational Research Open, 3,* 100127. https://doi.org/10.1016/j.ijedro.2022.100127

Ahmad, A., Nemeah, A., & Mohammed, H. (2018). A review of adoption of e-learning in Middle East countries. *Journal of Software Engineering & Intelligence Systems, 3*(1), 61–66.

Ahmed, A., Al-Mashari, A., & Al-Lawati, A. (2010). On the development of a computer based diagnostic assessment tool to help in teaching and learning process. *International Journal of Education and Development Using ICT, 6*(1), 76–87.

Alafnan, M., Dishari, S., Jovic, M., & Lomidze, K. (2023). ChatGPT as an educational tool: Opportunities, challenges, and recommendations for communication, business writing, and composition courses. *Journal of Artificial Intelligence and Technology, 3,* 60–68. https://doi.org/10.37965/jait. 2023.0184

Al-Fadhli, S. (2008). Students' perceptions of e-learning in Arab society: Kuwait University as a case study. *E-Learning and Digital Media, 5*(4), 418–428. https://doi.org/10.2304/elea.2008.5.4.418

AlFallaj, F. S. S. (2020). E-learning challenges in Saudi Arabia: Exploration of factors with special reference to EFL. *TESOL International Journal, 15*(3), 20–40.

AlHarmoodi, S., & Awofeso, A. (2023). Optimizing self-regulation for youth development in the United Arab Emirates. *Youth Voice Journal, 3*, 68–81. ISBN (ONLINE): 978-1-911634-80-5.

Al Helih, M. M., & Nasereddin, T. Y. (2019). The application of quality assurance criteria in light of governance principles (the Middle East University as a model). *Technology, 10*(6), 66–79.

Alotaibi, N. S. (2022). The significance of digital learning for sustainable development in the post-COVID19 world in Saudi Arabia's higher education institutions. *Sustainability, 14*(23), 16219. https://doi.org/10.3390/su1423 16219

Anderson, V., & Walvoord, B. (1998). *Effective grading: A tool for learning and assessment*. Jossey-Bass.

ANQAHE. The Arab Network for Quality Assurance in Higher Education. http://www.anqahe.org/. Accessed on June 1, 2023.

AOU. Arab Open University. https://www.arabou.edu.kw/Pages/default.aspx. Accessed on June 1, 2023.

AQACHEI. Accreditation and Quality Assurance Commission for Higher Education Institutions, Jordan. http://en.heac.org.jo/?p=7175. Accessed on June 1, 2023.

AUB. American University of Beirut, Lebanon. https://www.aub.edu.lb/. Accessed on June 1, 2023.

AUC. American University in Cairo, Egypt. https://www.aucegypt.edu/. Accessed on June 1, 2023.

BAU. Beirut Arab University. https://www.bau.edu.lb/. Accessed on June 1, 2023.

Bhattacharya, M., & Hartnett, M. (2007, October). *E-portfolio assessment in higher education*. 2007 37th Annual Frontiers in Education Conference-Global Engineering: Knowledge Without Borders, Opportunities Without Passports, T1G-19. IEEE. https://doi.org/10.1109/FIE.2007.4418182

Brignardello-Petersen, R., Izcovich, A., Rochwerg, B., Florez, I. D., Hazlewood, G., Alhazanni, W., Yepes-Nuñez, J., Santesso, N., Guyatt, G. H., & Schünemann, H. J. (2020). GRADE approach to drawing conclusions from a network meta-analysis using a partially contextualised framework. *The BMJ, 371.* https://doi.org/10.1136/bmj.m3900

Brookhart, S. M., Guskey, T. R., Bowers, A. J., McMillan, J. H., Smith, J. K., Smith, L. F., Stevens, M. T., & Welsh, M. E. (2016). A century of grading research: Meaning and value in the most common educational measure. *Review of Educational Research, 86* (4), 803–848. http://www.jstor.org/stable/44668237

CAA. (2021). Standards. https://www.caa.ae/Pages/Guidelines/Standards.aspx. Accessed on 16 May 2023.

Cain, J., Medina, M., Romanelli, F., & Persky, A. (2022). Deficiencies of traditional grading systems and recommendations for the future. *American Journal of Pharmaceutical Education, 86* (7), 8850. https://doi.org/10.5688/ajpe8850

Campos, N., Nogal, M., Caliz, C., & Juan, A. A. (2020). Simulation-based education involving online and on-campus models in different European universities. *International Journal of Educational Technology in Higher Education, 17,* 1–15. https://doi.org/10.1186/s41239-020-0181-y

Cheng, L., DeLuca, C., Braund, H., Yan, W., & Rasooli, A. (2020). Teachers' grading decisions and practices across cultures: Exploring the value, consistency, and construction of grades across Canadian and Chinese secondary schools. *Studies in Educational Evaluation, 67,* 100928. https://doi.org/10.1016/j.stueduc.2020.100928

Commission of Academic Affairs, UAE. https://www.caa.ae/. Accessed on June 1, 2023.

Craig, C. D., & Kay, R. (2021). *Examining peer assessment in online learning for higher education—A systematic review of the literature.* ICERI2021 Proceedings, 1832–1841. https://doi.org/10.21125/iceri.2021.0488

Dalbani, H., Eissa, S., Syed-Ahmad, S. F., & Almusharraf, N. (2022). Transitioning to flipped classrooms: Instructors' perspectives. *Sustainability, 14,* 13426. https://doi.org/10.3390/su142013426

David, S. (2023). Pillar of internationalization in higher education: The contribution of international collaborations and online delivery approaches to internationalization in HEIS. *SHS Web of Conferences, 156.* https://doi.org/10.1051/shsconf/202315605004

EBLF. (2019). *Inauguration of "BLF Sagesse Smart Center" at La Sagesse University in partnership with Banque Libano-Française.* https://www.eblf.com/english/news/sagesse-smart-center. Accessed on June 1, 2023.

Elbyaly, M., & Elfeky, A. (2023). The impact of blended learning in enhancing the skill performance of producing digital content among students of optimal investment. *Annals of Forest Research, 66*(1), 2031–2043.

EQUIS. European Quality Improvement System. https://www.efmdglobal.org/accreditations/business-schools/equis/. Accessed on June 1, 2023.

Fan, J., & Tian, M. (2022). Influence of online learning environment and student engagement on international students' sustainable Chinese learning. *Sustainability, 14*(17), 11106. https://doi.org/10.3390/su141711106

Fauzi, M. A. (2022). E-learning in higher education institutions during COVID-19 pandemic: Current and future trends through bibliometric analysis. *Heliyon, 8*(5), e09433. https://doi.org/10.1016/j.heliyon.2022.e09433

Ferri, F., Grifoni, P., & Guzzo, T. (2020). Online learning and emergency remote teaching: Opportunities and challenges in emergency situations. *Societies, 10*(4), 86.

Flynn, S., Cullinane, E., Murphy, H., & Wylie, N. (2023). Micro-credentials & digital badges: Definitions, affordances and design considerations for application in higher education institutions. *AISHE-J: The All Ireland Journal of Teaching & Learning in Higher Education, 15*(1), 1–18.

Gokah, T. K., Gupta, N., & Ndiweni, E. (2015). E-learning in higher education—Opportunities & challenges for Dubai. *International Journal on E-Learning, 14*(4), 443–470.

Gray, T., & Bunte, J. (2022). The effect of grades on student performance: Evidence from a quasi-experiment. *College Teaching, 70*(1), 15–28. https://doi.org/10.1080/87567555.2020.1865865

Haladyna, T. M. (2019). *Assigning a valid and reliable grade in a course* (IDEA Paper #79). IDEA Center, Inc. https://files.eric.ed.gov/fulltext/ED598950.pdf. Accessed on 16 May 2023.

Hall, S., Schmautzer, D., Tmiri, S., & Tschupp, R. (2022). *Reimagining higher education in MENAP.* McKinsey & Company Global Publishing. https://www.mckinsey.com/industries/education/our-insights/reimagining-higher-education-in-menap. Accessed on 16 May 2023.

HBMSU. Hamdan Bin Mohamed Smart University, UAE. https://www.hbmsu.ac.ae/. Accessed on June 1, 2023.

HBMSU. (2022, October 3). *HBMSU launches 'H-Preneurs' platform to support learners' entrepreneurial ambitions.* https://www.hbmsu.ac.ae/news/hbmsu-launches-%E2%80%98h-preneurs%E2%80%99-platform-support-learners%E2%80%99-entrepreneurial-ambitions. Accessed on June 1, 2023.

HCT. Higher Colleges of Technology, UAE. https://hct.ac.ae/en/. Accessed on

June 1, 2023.

Jakobsson, M., & Juels, A. (1999). Proofs of work and bread pudding protocols. In *Secure information networks: Communication and multimedia security* (pp. 258–272). Kluwer Academic. https://doi.org/10.1007/978-0-387-35568-9_18

Karsh, S. A. (2021). E-learning: Boon or bane to higher education during COVID-19 at MENA region. *E-Learning, 8*(2), 91–95. https://doi.org/10.30726/ijmrss/v8.i2.2021.82012

KAUST. King Abdullah University of Science and Technology, Saudi Arabia. https://www.kaust.edu.sa/. Accessed on June 1, 2023.

Kayan-Fadlelmula, F., Sellami, A., Abdelkader, N., & Umer, S. (2022). A systematic review of STEM education research in the GCC countries: Trends, gaps and barriers. *International Journal of STEM Education, 9*(1), 1–24. https://doi.org/10.1186/s40594-021-00319-7

Khaldi, A., Bouzidi, R., & Nader, F. (2023). Gamification of e-learning in higher education: A systematic literature review. *Smart Learning Environments, 10*(1), 10. https://doi.org/10.1186/s40561-023-00227-z

KSU. King Saud University, Saudi Arabia. https://ksu.edu.sa/en/. Accessed on June 1, 2023.

KU. Khalifa University-Masdar Institute of Science and Technology, UAE. https://www.ku.ac.ae/masdar-institute-of-science-and-technology-board-of-trustees-convenes. Accessed on June 1, 2023.

LAU. Lebanese American University, Lebanon. https://www.lau.edu.lb/. Accessed on June 1, 2023.

Lebanese Ministry of Education and Higher Education, Lebanon. https://www.higheredu.gov.lb

Marchesini, G. (2020). COVID-19 and internationalization in the MENA region. *International Higher Education, 104*, 22–23.

Marouli, C. (2021). Sustainability education for the future? Challenges and implications for education and pedagogy in the 21st century. *Sustainability, 13*(5), 2901. https://doi.org/10.3390/su13052901

Matthews, K., Janicki, T., He, L., & Patterson, L. (2012). Implementation of an automated grading system with an adaptive learning component to affect student feedback and response time. *Journal of Information Systems Education, 23*(1), 71–84.

Meadows, M., & Billington, L. (2005). *A review of the literature on marking reliability*. AQA.

Meehy, A. (2015). *Higher education policies and welfare regimes in Egypt and Tunisia*. University of California at Berkeley. https://doi.org/10.13140/RG.2.2.12332.62089

MIT Arab Startup Competition. https://www.mitarabcompetition.com/. Accessed on June 1, 2023.

MoAI. (2023). *United Arab Emirates Minister of State for Artificial Intelligence, Digital Economy, and Remote Work*. https://ai.gov.ae/. Accessed on May 30, 2023.

MOE-KSA. (2023). *Rules, regulations, and policies*. https://moe.gov.sa/en/abo utus/nationaltransformation/Pages/rpr.aspx. Accessed on May 15, 2023.

Mohamed, M., & Morris, P. (2021). Buying, selling and outsourcing educational reform: The Global Education Industry and 'policy borrowing' in the Gulf. *Compare: A Journal of Comparative and International Education, 51*(2), 181–201. https://doi.org/10.1080/03057925.2019.1607255

Moritz, R., & Zahidi, S. (2023). *Putting skills first: A framework for action*. World Economic Forum. https://www3.weforum.org/docs/WEF_CNES_P utting_Skills_First_2023.pdf. Accessed on 16 May 2023.

Mozenter, Z. D. (2019). *Essays on the effects of teacher grading standards and other teaching practices* (PhD thesis). University of North Carolina, Chapel Hill.

Mulhanga, M., & Lima, R. S. (2017). *Podcast as e-Learning enabler for developing countries: Current initiatives, challenges and trends*. Proceedings of the 2017 9th International Conference on Education Technology and Computers, 126–130. https://doi.org/10.1145/3175536.3175581

Naciri, A., Baba, M. A., Achbani, A., & Kharbach, A. (2020). Mobile learning in higher education: Unavoidable alternative during COVID-19. *Aquademia, 4*(1), ep20016.

Nagodavithana, S., & Premarathne, P. B. T. K. (2022). Learner perspectives of synchronous and asynchronous online education: A comparative study. *International Journal of Scientific and Research Publications, 12*(7), 126–132. https://doi.org/10.29322/IJSRP.12.07.2022.p12717

NAQAAE. National Authority for Quality Assurance and Accreditation of Education, Egypt. https://naqaae.eg/ar/. Accessed on June 1, 2023.

NCAAA. National Commission for Academic Accreditation and Assessment, KSA. https://etec.gov.sa/ncaaa. Accessed on June 1, 2023.

NDU. Notre Dame University. https://www.ndu.edu.lb/home. Accessed on June 1, 2023.

Omoniyi, I., Gamede, B., & Olaniran, S. (2022). Amplifying entrepreneurship development in the knowledge economy: The role of entrepreneurship education. *International Journal of Innovation, Creativity and Change, 16*(2), 432–449.

Papadakis, S. (2023). MOOCs 2012–2022: An overview. *Advances in Mobile Learning Educational Research, 3*(1), 682–693. https://doi.org/10.25082/AMLER.2023.01.017

Peddada, K., & Alhuthaifi, W. (2021). Role of private sector in G.C.C. education. *Journal of Advances in Education and Philosophy, 5*(7), 170–175.

Perera-Diltz, D., & Moe, J. (2014). Formative and summative assessment in online education. *Journal of Research in Innovative Teaching, 7*(1), 130–142.

Pulfrey, C., Buchs, C., & Butera, F. (2011). Why grades engender performance-avoidance goals: The mediating role of autonomous motivation. *Journal of Educational Psychology, 103*(3), 683.

Putri, R. S., Purwanto, A., Pramono, R., Asbari, M., Wijayanti, L. M., & Hyun, C. C. (2020). Impact of the COVID-19 pandemic on online home learning: An explorative study of primary schools in Indonesia. *International Journal of Advanced Science and Technology, 29*(5), 4809–4818.

QBIC. Qatar Business Incubation Center, Qatar. https://qbic.qa/. Accessed on June 1, 2023.

Quality Assurance Commission for Higher Education Institutions, Jordan. http://en.heac.org.jo/?p=7175

Qureshi, M. I., & Khan, N. (2022). Business disruptions and innovations beyond COVID-19. *Foresight, 24*(3/4), 297–300.

Reddy, Y. M., & Andrade, H. (2010). A review of rubric use in higher education. *Assessment & Evaluation in Higher Education, 35*(4), 435–448.

Schinske, J., & Tanner, K. (2014). Teaching more by grading less (or differently). *CBE—Life Sciences Education, 13*(2), 159–166. https://doi.org/10.1187/cbe.cbe-14-03-0054

Sharma, R. (2023, February 08). *TAP growth prospects in MENA education market*. World Education Summit. https://wes.eletsonline.com/tap-growth-prospects-in-mena-education-market/. Accessed on 16 May 2023.

Sluijsmans, D. M., Prins, F. J., & Martens, R. L. (2006). The design of competency-based performance assessment in e-learning. *Learning Environments Research, 9*, 45–66. https://doi.org/10.1007/s10984-005-9003-3

Stanger-Hall, K. F. (2012). Multiple-choice exams: An obstacle for higher-level thinking in introductory science classes. *CBE—Life Sciences Education, 11*(3), 294–306.

Swinton, O. H. (2010). The effect of effort grading on learning. *Economics of Education Review, 29*(6), 1176–1182.

The Open University. (2018, November). *Online education in tertiary educa-tion in The Middle East and North Africa*. https://www.open.ac.uk/res earch/sites/www.open.ac.uk.research/files/files/Documents/Online%20lear ning%20in%20tertiary%20education%20in%20the%20Middle%20East% 20and%20North%20Africa%20.pdf. Accessed on 16 May 2023.

UL. Lebanese University, Lebanon. https://www.ul.edu.lb/. Accessed on June 1, 2023.

UM6P. Mohammed VI Polytechnic Universit, Morocco. https://um6p.ma/en. Accessed on June 1, 2023.

UNESCO. (2007). *Third global forum on international quality assurance, accred-itation, and the recognition of qualifications in higher education final report*. UNESCO.

UNESCO IESALC. (2023). *ChatGPT and Artificial Intelligence in higher education: Quick start guide*. UNESCO.

UNESCO RCEP. (2022, February). *Future scenarios for education in the GCC countries*. https://rcepunesco.ae/en/KnowledgeCorner/ReportsandStudies/ ReportsandStudies/Future%20Scenarios%20for%20Education%20FULL% 20REPORT%20FINAL.pdf. Accessed on 16 May 2023.

USEK. Holy Spirit University of Kaslik, Lebanon. https://www.usek.edu.lb/en/ home. Accessed on June 1, 2023.

USJ. Université Saint-Joseph de Beyrouth, Lebanon. https://www.usj.edu.lb/. Accessed on June 1, 2023.

Wong-Powell, J., & Kusuma-Powell, O. (2020). *Knowing our students in the virtual environment*. ICERI2020 Proceedings (pp. 1405–1410). IATED.

Yahiaoui, F., Aichouche, R., Chergui, K., Brika, S. K. M., Almezher, M., Musa, A. A., & Lamari, I. A. (2022). The impact of e-learning systems on motivating students and enhancing their outcomes during COVID-19: A mixed-method approach. *Frontiers in Psychology, 13*, 874181. https://doi. org/10.3389/fpsyg.2022.874181

Yan, Z., Lao, H., Panadero, E., Fernández-Castilla, B., Yang, L., & Yang, M. (2022). Effects of self-assessment and peer-assessment interventions on academic performance: A pairwise and network meta-analysis. *Educational Research Review, 37*. https://doi.org/10.1016/j.edurev.2022.100484

12

Reforming Higher Education Through AI

Johny Karam

Introduction

In every historical epoch, society has recognized the critical role of education. Yet, in our modern world, it is higher education that has emerged as a pivotal driver of progress and prosperity. It's an irreplaceable asset, an institution that functions not just to equip individuals with practical skills for the workforce, but as the bedrock of societal development and democratization.

The worth of higher education is multifaceted, shaping lives and societies in ways that are both profound and enduring. Higher education nurtures intellectual curiosity and critical thinking, forging minds that can navigate complexity, appreciate diversity, and foster innovation. In these hallowed halls, young minds learn not just to make a living, but to live a thoughtful and responsible life.

J. Karam (✉)
Tabarja Beach Resort, Tabarja, Lebanon
e-mail: johnnykkaram@outlook.com

N. Azoury and G. Yahchouchi (eds.), *Governance in Higher Education*, https://doi.org/10.1007/978-3-031-40586-0_12

In our economies, the importance of higher education is particularly striking. It cultivates a skilled workforce capable of driving technological advancement and economic growth.[1] The value of a college degree is clear: individuals with higher education levels tend to have higher earnings and better job prospects. As the economic divide widens in many societies, higher education can act as a powerful engine of social mobility, providing opportunities for individuals, particularly those in vulnerable circumstances, to break the cycle of poverty and stride toward a stable future.

Yet, the impacts of higher education extend beyond the economic realm. Higher education equips individuals with the knowledge and analytical skills to actively participate in and contribute to a democratic society. These are the citizens who vote, voice their opinions, challenge injustices, and strive for a better world.

Moreover, higher education has broader societal benefits. College-educated adults are more likely to lead healthier lifestyles, which not only improves their quality of life but also reduces healthcare costs for society. They are also more likely to receive health insurance and pension benefits from their employers, thus enhancing their personal security while also relieving the public purse.

In families, the benefits of higher education resonate profoundly. College-educated mothers, for instance, tend to spend more quality time with their children, adapting their interactions to cater to the developmental needs of their offspring. This nurturing environment is fundamental for the growth of future generations, thereby perpetuating a virtuous cycle of education and societal progress.[2]

Ultimately, the value of higher education permeates every aspect of our society. It is an investment with immeasurable returns—for the individual, the economy, and society. As we stand at the verge of unprecedented global challenges yet exceptional advancements, the need for higher education has never been greater. But it is equally true that higher education itself is facing considerable challenges, and it must evolve and innovate to fulfill its promise in the modern world.

---

[1] UNESCO (2023).

[2] Baum et al. (2013).

This chapter delves into the intricate dynamics of higher education, particularly focusing on the pressing challenges that need urgent attention. Our exploration will take a two-pronged approach, considering both institutional hurdles and teaching–learning conundrums. With a global perspective as our vantage point, we will specifically spotlight the Middle East and North Africa (MENA) region, assessing its unique characteristics and obstacles within the higher education sector.

We will attempt to unravel the profound potential that Artificial Intelligence (AI) offers as a game-changer in higher education. By demystifying what AI truly is, we aim to shed light on how this powerful technology could ameliorate a spectrum of higher education challenges. From making education more equitable and accessible, to aiding students in making informed academic decisions, and liberating educators from non-educational tasks—the promise of AI seems limitless.

However, like every transformative technology, AI also poses its own threats and ethical quandaries. Without careful oversight and governance, the tools meant to elevate higher education could undermine it, creating new disparities and perpetuating existing ones. Thus, a part of our exploration will be dedicated to outlining the potential perils of unregulated AI use in education, underlining the need for a robust ethical framework and judicious governance.

The journey through this chapter will offer an in-depth analysis of the contemporary challenges of higher education, the role of AI as a potential problem-solver, and the precautions we must take to ensure this powerful technology serves as an aid, not an adversary. Through this comprehensive exploration, we aspire to contribute to the ongoing global dialogue on reimagining and revolutionizing higher education for a brighter, more equitable future.

Global Challenges of Higher Education

As we delve deeper into the realm of higher education, it becomes apparent that despite its inherent value, it is facing an array of global challenges that necessitate urgent attention and creative solutions. In this vein, we find ourselves at a crossroads where we must either adapt and innovate or risk falling behind in a rapidly evolving world. Let's dissect some of these challenges.

The advent of the Fourth Industrial Revolution has undeniably left profound imprints across our global landscape, causing a cascade of disruption across diverse industries, and ushering in a transformative overhaul of our traditional understanding of work. Emerging technologies, such as artificial intelligence, robotics, blockchain, and more, are steering the direction of this revolution, sculpting an uncharted, new-age professional landscape that is both intriguing and intimidating.

This sea of change is now beckoning higher education institutions to respond to a unique and daunting challenge. They are shouldered with the responsibility of preparing students for a future of work that is veiled in ambiguity—careers that are in the throes of evolution or perhaps, not yet conceived.

This necessitates a drastic shift in the perspective of these institutions. It demands that they go beyond the conventional academic approach of regarding curricula as mere vessels for transferring knowledge. Instead, they must reimagine them as dynamic, transformative platforms that enable students to sharpen a range of skills crucial for the unpredictable professional world that awaits them.

Skills, such as critical thinking and problem-solving, adaptability and resilience in the face of change, creativity, and innovation, and not to mention, digital literacy, are becoming increasingly important. It's these abilities that would allow future professionals to navigate the complexities of their jobs, fuel innovation, and ultimately, thrive in their careers.[3]

Then comes the issue of access and affordability in higher education as a multifaceted challenge and an acute concern that demands our attention. Higher education, historically revered as the great equalizer, a ladder to social mobility, and a catalyst for economic stability, is witnessing an escalating crisis of accessibility.

The costs associated with higher education have skyrocketed over the years. What was once considered a right, available to all who sought it, has now become a privilege, accessible primarily to those who can afford

---

[3] Østergaard and Nordlund (2019).

it. This escalating cost has created a chasm, a stark divide between those who can access higher education and those who cannot. For many, the dream of higher education remains just that—a dream, tantalizingly out of reach, eclipsed by financial constraints.

This issue is not limited to the costs of tuition alone. It extends to include the costs of living, textbooks, and other resources essential for the successful pursuit of higher education. This financial burden can be debilitating, forcing students to take on jobs alongside their studies, accruing debt, and in many cases, leading them to abandon their educational pursuits altogether.

Beyond financial constraints, a labyrinth of other barriers often stands between students and their academic aspirations. A lack of information about the opportunities available, the process of admission, and the availability of financial aid often leaves prospective students feeling lost and overwhelmed. This is particularly true for first-generation students who may not have familial experience or guidance to navigate this complex landscape.

Moreover, students from disadvantaged backgrounds face an uphill battle to academic success. The challenges they confront are not only financial but also systemic and deeply entrenched in societal structures. These students may lack access to quality pre-college education, making the transition to higher education more strenuous. They may also face cultural and language barriers, struggle with feelings of belonging and inclusivity, and lack the support networks that are vital to persist in the face of challenges.[4]

In this scenario, the quest for higher education becomes less about intellectual curiosity and personal growth, and more about overcoming hurdles. It becomes less about the promise of a brighter future, and more about the struggle for survival in the present. The narrative around higher education shifts from being an empowering journey to a daunting obstacle course.

Pivotal among those challenges is the imperative to maintain and elevate the quality and relevance of higher education. Universities and colleges worldwide bear the formidable duty of delivering high-caliber

---

[4] World Bank (2014).

programs that not only resonate with the evolving needs of their students but also serve the broader societal aspirations. Yet, this task is far from static. The definitions of quality and relevance are fluid, constantly reshaped by global currents, technological innovations, and the fluctuating demands of the labor market. Consequently, the burden is on these institutions to continually reassess and refine their curricula, teaching methodologies, and engagement with the labor market, thus ensuring their value proposition remains robust and compelling.

In line with that, we find that the issues of governance and management have assumed a prominent position in the discourse surrounding higher education. The seamless operation and ultimate success of higher education institutions pivot significantly on effective leadership, strategic foresight, prudent financial management, and a culture of accountability. As these institutions burgeon in size and complexity, they face the paradox of coping with escalating demands while contending with shrinking resources. This scenario underscores the criticality of wise governance and management in steering these institutions through turbulent waters.

Notwithstanding these complexities, higher education institutions must shoulder another substantial responsibility: kindling the flame of research and innovation. These institutions serve as epicenters of intellectual inquiry, ceaselessly pushing the boundaries of human knowledge, fostering a culture of innovation, and sculpting the future. Yet, the reality is often more complex and fraught with challenges. Despite their central role in this domain, many institutions wrestle with the arduous task of cultivating effective research programs and transforming the fruits of research into practical, market-ready applications.

Challenges such as inadequate funding, the scarcity of collaborative opportunities, and the daunting gaps in translating research into viable commercial products often beset this domain. Moreover, research programs, particularly those in advanced and emerging fields, demand significant financial investment, collaborative networks, high computing infrastructure, and the continuous upskilling of faculty and researchers. The lack of these resources can stagnate research initiatives and dilute the quality of research output, thereby undermining the institution's role as a catalyst for innovation.

With this expansive set of challenges laid bare, it's clear that the higher education sector stands at a significant juncture. The labyrinthine landscape necessitates reform and transformation at a scale previously unseen. As we chart our course forward, the pressure to reinvent, revitalize, and reimagine higher education is palpable. However, it's important to understand that these challenges aren't evenly distributed across the globe; distinct regions face unique issues. This observation grows increasingly critical as we turn our focus to one such region—the Middle East and North Africa. The path forward promises a deeper understanding of the region-specific intricacies in the higher education sector.

Higher Education Challenges in the MENA Region

The Middle East and North Africa (MENA) region, a historical cradle of higher education, grapples with a unique set of challenges in this sector today. Institutions, such as Al-Qarawiyyin University in Morocco, Al-Azhar University in Egypt, and University of Bologna in Italy, counted among the world's oldest, remain testaments to the region's rich past. However, the current landscape of higher education in the region presents a more complex narrative.

The MENA region is under significant demographic pressure, with approximately 127 million young individuals anticipated to join the labor market by 2040. This situation poses a formidable job-creation challenge, further amplified by the need to increase women's participation in the labor market.

As this surge in labor demand unfolds, the region's Higher Education Institutions (HEIs) are also navigating the accelerated pace of the Fourth Industrial Revolution, catalyzed further by the COVID-19 pandemic. They must equip students with new skills and higher qualifications in response to digitization and automation trends, a challenging prospect amidst the financial constraints inflicted by the pandemic.[5]

---

5 Hall et al. (2022).

The economic conditions in the region add another layer of complexity. The combined impact of an oil downturn and a global health crisis led to an average 3 percent regional GDP decrease across MENAP and Afghanistan in 2020. The repercussions are felt more acutely by private universities, such as those in Lebanon, where reduced tuition fee income and the need to maintain quality in an increasingly digital educational context intensify their challenges.

The challenge matrix further expands when considering the political instability and conflicts that significantly impact higher education accessibility for this youthful demographic. Disparities stemming from socio-economic factors, geographic location, and the aftermath of military conflicts and civil unrest disenfranchise many potential students. Their aspirations for academic achievement are compromised by these turbulent circumstances, leading to a substantial gap in access to higher education, particularly among disadvantaged and conflict-affected individuals.

Despite these multifaceted challenges, another issue to address is the perceived low quality of higher education in the MENA region. Employers often critique that while university graduates may be academically proficient, they lack the practical skills needed in the global marketplace. This concern is especially pronounced in technical fields such as science, engineering, and mathematics, where job opportunities abound.

Another area that warrants attention is the deficiency in "soft skills"—creativity, teamwork, critical thinking, among others—among graduates. This gap is partly attributed to an education system that emphasizes memorization and rote learning, hindering the development of these critical abilities.[6]

Interestingly, the prevalence of free higher education in the region unintentionally contributes to this quality challenge. Without the financial motivation from tuition fees, universities might overlook the importance of investing in curriculum enhancement. Similarly, students not bearing the cost of their education might demand less of their educational quality.

---

[6] Devarajan (2016).

Given these intricate challenges, the MENA region's higher education sector is undoubtedly navigating complex terrain. By shifting the focus of higher education from solely catering to public-sector jobs toward a financing system that aligns incentives with quality, the region could initiate a transformative journey. Such a journey aims to restore the grandeur of higher education in the MENA region while preparing its youth for future demands.

The Global Teaching and Learning Dilemma

The Standardized Approach to Learning

Our current education system, deeply rooted in the efficiency-centric principles of the Industrial Revolution, still bears distinct relics of this bygone era. The use of letter grades to evaluate students, the unidimensional focus on rote learning, and the regimented model of disseminating knowledge to a supposedly 'uniform' group of students—these practices are eerily reminiscent of the factory-model schooling conceived during the height of industrialization. This system, though historically significant, is glaringly ill-equipped to cater to the rapidly changing needs of our contemporary world, particularly in the higher education sector.

A critical examination of this standardized approach of teaching and learning brings to light its numerous inherent shortcomings. The emphasis on uniformity and rote memorization effectively overlooks the profound range of individual differences, potential, and learning styles among students. As a result, our higher education institutions, operating within this antiquated framework, may inadvertently stifle creativity and curb the innovative spirit of their students.

Furthermore, this archaic system does not merely inhibit the development of critical and creative skills; it undermines students' ability to adapt to a rapidly evolving global context. Our era, characterized by constant technological advancements, shifting labor market needs, and continuous knowledge expansion, calls for a more flexible, individual-centric educational model. Yet, our education system's monolithic approach falls short of preparing students for this reality.

The Time Allocation of University Instructors

Educators form the backbone of any higher education institution, their roles often extending beyond mere instruction. Their commitment to shaping the minds of tomorrow is unquestionable, yet their efforts are often stretched thin by an array of non-teaching tasks. A study conducted by Boise State University helps shine a light on the extent of this predicament.

According to the study, faculty participants reported working an average of 61 hours per week, a significant increase over the standard 40-hour workweek. Such an increase indicates an overwhelming workload that extends well into personal time, potentially impacting overall productivity and well-being. This extended workweek is not filled with direct instruction or student engagement, as one might assume.

In fact, the faculty members in the study reportedly spent only 35% of their workweek on teaching-related tasks. This encompasses 12% on actual instruction and 11% on course administration tasks such as grading and updating course webpages. In effect, only a third of their extensive workweek directly contributes to the principal function of an educator: imparting knowledge.

Meanwhile, a substantial portion of their time, about 17% of their workweek, is claimed by meetings, some of which involve students. Furthermore, they devote an additional 13% of their day to managing emails related to both research and student communication. In total, 30% of their workweek is swallowed up by administrative tasks, reflecting a substantial diversion from their core roles.

Most strikingly, the study found that only a minuscule 3% of their work-week day was dedicated to primary research, with an even smaller 2% spent on manuscript writing. These figures underline a stark reality: the excessive administrative and preparatory demands placed on university instructors significantly curtail their capacity to conduct research. This imbalance potentially inhibits the production of innovative ideas and high-quality research that universities are traditionally known to foster.[7]

---

[7] Flaherty (2014).

The pressing need for a reallocation of faculty time within higher education institutions is evident. The current imbalance, focusing disproportionately on administrative tasks and extending work hours, negatively impacts both teaching quality and research progress. By redistributing responsibilities, we can empower educators to focus on student engagement and research, thereby elevating the overall standard of higher education.

The Two Sigma Problem

The challenges in the higher education sector are further compounded by what has been termed as "The Two Sigma Problem." Coined by renowned educational psychologist Dr. Benjamin Bloom in 1984, this concept hinges on the significant differential in learning outcomes between group instruction and one-to-one tutoring.

According to Bloom, one-to-one tutoring using mastery learning techniques results in an average student performance improvement of two standard deviations above the mean achieved through conventional classroom instruction. This indicates a remarkable shift in academic performance that can significantly enhance a student's understanding and mastery of a given subject. Essentially, the "two sigma" refers to this remarkable increase in performance, underscoring the effectiveness of personalized learning.[8]

However, the adoption of this highly effective method on a large scale presents formidable logistical and economic challenges. The costs associated with providing individual tutoring are steep, placing a significant burden on education budgets, and making it unaffordable for a vast number of students. Consequently, the superior learning outcomes achieved through this method remain largely inaccessible for most students, barring a privileged few.

This scenario underscores the stark inequity inherent in our current educational system. As Bloom's research indicates, personalized, one-on-one tutoring can significantly boost learning outcomes. Yet, the high

---

[8] Bloom (1984).

costs associated with this teaching model limit its accessibility, making it a privilege enjoyed by only a select few. This effectively widens the existing learning and opportunity gap, where only those with the means to afford personalized tutoring can fully exploit their learning potential.

In this context, the challenge is to find ways of achieving the learning outcomes of one-on-one tutoring in a more cost-effective, scalable manner. The resolution of this issue is crucial for ensuring equitable access to high-quality education and unlocking the full learning potential of all students. This problem poses a formidable challenge, yet it also provides a significant opportunity to transform the higher education sector, making learning a more personalized and effective experience for all.

Classification of Challenges

In the journey to dissect the challenges facing higher education, we have encountered diverse issues, each with unique implications and potential solutions. To facilitate a more nuanced understanding, we have synthesized these challenges into a multidimensional classification, visually represented through a spider chart. This spider chart enables a comparative analysis of the different challenges based on their impact on the quality of education, the institutional difficulty in addressing them, and the urgency with which they need to be resolved.

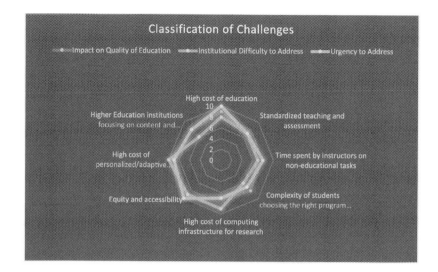

Examining the spider chart reveals some crucial insights. For instance, 'Equity and Accessibility' and 'High Cost of Education' are identified as the most urgent and impactful challenges. Addressing these is not only critical for enhancing learning outcomes, but also for cultivating a more equitable and accessible educational landscape.

Challenges such as 'Standardized Teaching and Assessment' and 'Higher Education Institutions Focusing on Content and Not Skills' pose significant difficulties for institutions aiming to reform their educational practices. They necessitate systemic changes in educational philosophy and require substantial time and resources to effectively address.

The 'High Cost of Personalized/Adaptive Learning', while demonstrating immense benefits for the quality of education, is somewhat lower on the urgency scale. This is primarily due to the prohibitive costs and logistical challenges associated with implementing personalized learning on a large scale.

Meanwhile, the 'High Cost of Computing Infrastructure for Research' is an institutional challenge that can greatly impact the quality and output of academic research. This underlines the need for significant investment in digital infrastructure to foster a culture of research and innovation within higher education institutions.

In the end, the purpose of this classification is not to rank the challenges, but to provide a comprehensive understanding of the multi-faceted issues facing higher education. As we transition to discuss the potential role of AI in addressing these challenges, this classification will serve as an essential guiding framework for our exploration.

A Brief History of AI

The Social History of AI

Artificial Intelligence (AI) and robotics are not novel concepts; in fact, they trace their roots deep into human history, embodying the dichotomy of fear and fascination that humanity has had for the concept of self-operating machines. Their historical presence highlights that, as a society, our curiosity, hopes, and anxieties surrounding cutting-edge technologies have remained constant over the years, even as the context of these technologies has radically evolved. Thus, understanding the history of AI provides valuable insights into our complex relationship with it and can shed light on the course it might chart in the future.

The notion of artificial beings—autonomous entities capable of performing tasks independently—has captivated human imagination for centuries. Ancient Greek mythology tells the tale of Pygmalion, a sculptor who falls in love with his own creation that comes to life. This archetype of a man-made, animate object, capable of replicating human behavior, spans across diverse cultures and times, underscoring a universal longing to bring forth life from inanimate matter. Whether as artificial servants, self-governing war machines, or companions, these early conceptualizations of 'robots' reflect the timeless human aspiration for mastery and control—an aspiration that continues to shape our engagement with modern-day AI and robotics.[9]

However, it was in the early twentieth century that AI began to transition from myth to a conceivable reality. This period saw the advent of

---

[9] Truitt (2021).

science fiction as a genre, which, with its portrayals of artificially intelligent beings, acted as a critical catalyst in popularizing the concept of AI. Early science fiction narratives, such as the "heartless" Tin Man from the Wizard of Oz or the humanoid robot in Fritz Lang's Metropolis, presented audiences with an image of AI entities that were remarkably similar to humans. These anthropomorphic depictions sparked public interest and curiosity, effectively laying the groundwork for the scientific pursuit of AI in the latter half of the twentieth century.

Thus, from the annals of ancient mythologies to the frames of early twentieth-century cinema, the history of AI is intricately woven into the fabric of human culture. These historical narratives remind us that AI is not just a scientific or technological pursuit, but also a socio-cultural phenomenon, embodying deep-seated human desires and fears. As we continue to advance in AI technology, it's essential to remember this history and consider its implications for the future.

From Speculation to Reality: Tracing the Origins of AI

The roots of artificial intelligence (AI) lie entwined in the tapestry of human imagination, with the quest for intelligent machines dating back centuries. This enduring vision took a definitive shape in the mid-twentieth century, when British polymath Alan Turing ventured into uncharted territory. Turing's proposition is that if humans could utilize available information to reason and solve problems, machines should potentially possess similar capabilities. Turing's groundbreaking 1950 paper, "Computing Machinery and Intelligence," was the first to bring AI into the realm of scientific exploration.

Alan Turing's torch was carried forward by visionaries such as Allen Newell, Cliff Shaw, and Herbert Simon, who created the Logic Theorist in the 1950s. This program, simple in its construction by modern standards, was a groundbreaking development that simulated human problem-solving capabilities. Its presentation at the Dartmouth Summer Research Project on Artificial Intelligence in 1956 was a pivotal moment in AI history.

The golden age of AI, extending from 1957 to 1974, witnessed rapid advancements and heightened aspirations. As computing technology evolved, becoming faster, more affordable, and widely available, AI grew symbiotically. The development of enhanced machine learning algorithms provided the framework for advanced AI systems. However, the journey was far from smooth. Although AI research enjoyed significant government funding, the initial euphoria receded as the limitations of computational power became evident.

Yet, the pursuit of AI continued undeterred. The 1980s saw a resurgence of enthusiasm for AI, marked by the introduction of "deep learning" techniques and the creation of expert systems. These novel approaches, spearheaded by John Hopfield and David Rumelhart, rejuvenated AI research. At the same time, Edward Feigenbaum's expert systems, designed to mimic human decision-making processes, offered fresh directions for exploration.

The path to realizing AI was neither straightforward nor easy. The lofty ambitions of the 1980s met with mixed outcomes. However, in the quiet recesses of the 1990s and 2000s, AI blossomed steadily. A watershed moment arrived in 1997 when IBM's Deep Blue defeated world chess champion Gary Kasparov. This victory underscored the considerable progress made in AI. That same year, the implementation of Dragon Systems' speech recognition software on Windows marked another critical milestone.

The evolution of AI from its early conceptual stages to its present stature is a testament to human resilience, creativity, and the relentless pursuit of knowledge. It is a narrative of both setbacks and triumphs, illuminating our evolving perception of what machines can achieve. As we look to the future, the transformative potential of AI looms large, promising to redefine our world in unimaginable ways.

As the narrative of AI has unfolded over the decades, there have been significant milestones and innovations that have left profound imprints on its course. Among these innovations, the advent and evolution of machine learning have been a turning point. By teaching machines to learn from data and improve over time, machine learning has allowed AI to take on increasingly complex tasks and to do so with growing efficacy.

Yet, even among the many types of machine learning, one particular category has emerged to play a pivotal role in the story of AI: Large Language Models.

The Story of Large Language Models

Imagine stepping into the world's largest library, where every written work across time, language, and culture resides. As you meander through the vast aisles, your task is not merely to read and comprehend every book, article, and manuscript but also to draw connections between the ideas, themes, and patterns they present. Moreover, you are expected to articulate new, meaningful sentences based on this colossal repertoire of knowledge. This, in essence, is the metaphorical equivalent of the role played by Large Language Models (LLMs) in the realm of artificial intelligence.

Large Language Models (LLMs) stand at the intersection of AI and linguistics, marrying the predictive power of machine learning with the vast complexities of human language. These models have reshaped our understanding of what is possible in AI, enabling computers to understand and generate human language with impressive accuracy. It is best to describe LLMs as computational juggernauts characterized by neural networks consisting of billions of parameters, trained on an enormous amount of text. Picture these models as gigantic, adaptable minds capable of learning almost anything, provided they are supplied with ample data and processing power. Despite being trained on ostensibly simple tasks like predicting the next word in a sentence, LLMs' proficiency in mimicking human language's structure and semantics is extraordinarily advanced. These models act as a receptacle for a treasure trove of worldly knowledge, effectively 'memorizing' an astronomical quantity of facts during their training phase.

Among the constellation of LLMs, the GPT series, short for Generative Pre-trained Transformer, developed by OpenAI, shines the brightest. These deep learning models harness unsupervised learning to generate human-like text. GPT models train on enormous volumes of text data, thereby learning patterns and relationships between words and phrases.

This enables them to generate coherent, meaningful text without explicit programming to do so.

The groundwork for this odyssey was laid in 2016, when OpenAI published seminal research on generative models. These models, by design, learn from an enormous corpus of data within a specific domain—such as images, sentences, or sounds—and are subsequently trained to generate similar data. The underpinnings of this research would later serve as the foundational bricks for the construction of the GPT edifice.

A pivotal step in this journey came three years later in 2019, when OpenAI finessed the training of GPT-2, fine-tuning it with human preferences and feedback. This breakthrough hinted at the unfolding potential of large language models, heralding a future where AI was not only capable of understanding and generating human-like text but also of calibrating its output based on human interaction and input. It was a harbinger of things to come, paving the way for the GPT series' most defining chapters.

The year 2022 witnessed significant strides in the development of the GPT series. Building upon their existing accomplishments, OpenAI introduced the world to InstructGPT models, siblings of ChatGPT. This new breed of models exhibited an enhanced ability to follow instructions, reduce the fabrication of facts, and limit toxic output. The revolutionary shift these models represented was not just in their technological sophistication but also in the manner they underscored AI's growing cognizance and sensitivity toward its users' needs and societal concerns.

The latter part of 2022 was characterized by a surge of enthusiasm as OpenAI unveiled ChatGPT powered by GPT-3.5 as part of a free research preview. This introduction marked a milestone in the GPT journey as ChatGPT quickly amassed a significant user base, reaching 100 million users faster than even the social media giants, TikTok and Instagram. The adoption and success of ChatGPT, rapidly penetrating the tech sphere, provided a glimpse into the acceptance and utility of AI in our everyday lives.

As the world was still coming to terms with GPT-3.5's transformative potential, OpenAI wasted no time in broadening its horizons. In February 2023, OpenAI introduced ChatGPT Plus, a premium subscription model that offered users enhanced access and minimized downtime. This announcement signaled a shift in the operational paradigm, hinting at the vast economic potential and novel business models that AI and specifically, LLMs, could unlock.

OpenAI's partnership with Microsoft brought further validation to the power and promise of the GPT series. By incorporating ChatGPT-powered features in Bing, OpenAI successfully extended the utility and influence of its models into the mainstream digital infrastructure and Microsoft announced the recreation of search as we know it while pointing the gun to Google's search engine market share. The rollout of these features, along with the introduction of the ChatGPT API for developers to integrate ChatGPT functionality into their applications, transformed the digital landscape. AI was no longer confined to the realm of labs and research papers; it was reshaping the very way we interact with our digital world.

A landmark moment arrived on March 14, 2023, with the release of GPT-4. The fourth iteration of the GPT series brought to the fore an even more sophisticated and versatile model. Touted for its superior reliability, creativity, and problem-solving skills, GPT-4 was not merely an enhancement; it was a quantum leap.

With its powerful capabilities, GPT-4 emerged as a paragon of AI advancement. Its creative prowess shone bright in its ability to generate, edit, and iterate with users on an array of creative and technical writing tasks, ranging from composing songs to learning a user's writing style. The reasoning capabilities of GPT-4 surpassed even its ChatGPT predecessor, underscoring the considerable strides made in AI.

GPT-4's exceptional performance was demonstrable in its test scores, as it outperformed older GPT models, even in high-stakes academic exams. Scoring at the 90th percentile on the Uniform Bar exam, 88th percentile on the LSAT, 89th percentile on the Math SAT, and 80th percentile on the GRE Quantitative exam, GPT-4 showcased its cognitive prowess and its ability to engage in complex problem-solving tasks.

GPT-4's capabilities stretched far beyond conventional tasks, allowing it to find a common theme between two articles, code a website from an image of the outline, and handle the complex language in legal documents. The last feat, in particular, encapsulates GPT-4's remarkable ability to comprehend and navigate the labyrinthine intricacies of legal jargon and syntax.

One of the key improvements over GPT-3 was GPT-4's ability to handle longer prompts. The model could analyze, read, and generate up to 25,000 words. This increase in capacity heralded new possibilities, expanding the scope of tasks GPT-4 could undertake and the complexities it could grapple with.

GPT-4 was also noted for its improved steerability. While GPT-3 responded in a uniform tone and style, users could instruct GPT-4 on the tone and style they preferred, making GPT-4 a more adaptable, personalized, and engaging AI companion.

The crowning glory of GPT-4, however, was perhaps its ability to learn from its predecessor's limitations. GPT-4 showcased improved mathematical abilities, even without being connected to a calculator. It also had a more robust ethical framework, refusing to respond to requests for disallowed content, indicating a significant leap in AI's sensitivity toward potential misuse.

The odyssey of the GPT series is a testament to AI's transformative potential. With GPT-4 at its helm, the GPT series is poised to redefine our world in unprecedented ways, illuminating the vast expanse of what AI can achieve. Yet, the narrative of GPT is far from over. As we peer into the future, we can only imagine the incredible possibilities that the next chapters of this odyssey hold.

Possible Use Cases in Education

As artificial intelligence continues its inexorable march, transforming industries and altering the way we live and work, its influence stretches far and wide. From finance to health care, transportation to entertainment, AI's imprint can be seen everywhere. Yet, among these myriad fields, one sector stands out for its potential for profound transformation—education. The opportunity for AI, and specifically advanced AI models like generative models, in the education sector is not just in its sheer scale, given the significant number of students in every country, but also in its capacity for societal impact. The influence of education extends beyond the present, molding the architects of the future, shaping the contours of society, and propelling us toward a more enlightened world. Therefore, the application of AI in this sector could have far-reaching implications, revolutionizing not just education, but also the very fabric of our future societies. As we embark on this exciting journey of AI-driven educational transformation, we envision a future that's more inclusive, more personalized, and exponentially more innovative.

Before we delve into the fascinating world of AI-driven education, it is critical to understand the distinct ways in which technologies like ChatGPT and enterprise GPT applications can be utilized. At the heart of this differentiation is the source and application of the training data.

ChatGPT operates as a conversational interface that leverages pre-trained data selected by OpenAI. It is like a well-read scholar, having been taught a wide array of topics using a broad spectrum of data sources. It uses this knowledge to generate human-like text, assisting users in various tasks and conversations. While ChatGPT possesses a vast repertoire of knowledge, it isn't specifically trained on any particular dataset.

Conversely, enterprise GPT applications, facilitated through APIs or Microsoft Azure's OpenAI service, offer a more customized approach. Educational institutions can utilize these platforms to train the AI on their specific data—curriculum, books, previous exams, institution documents, and laws. This is akin to hiring a private tutor, one who has been specifically educated using the institution's unique data, and therefore, can provide personalized guidance based on that precise knowledge base. The opportunities here are immense, unlocking a new realm of possibilities for educational advancement.

The bespoke nature of enterprise GPT applications paves the way for a plethora of use cases in the educational sphere. One of the most promising applications is the creation of a personalized tutor through a GPT-powered chatbot. Imagine a virtual tutor that understands the curriculum as well as any experienced educator, but with the ability to cater to a student's individual learning style, pace, and preferences. Such a tutor can provide personalized explanations, adapt to changing learner needs, and even assess a learner's progress, providing real-time, individualized feedback.

Beyond personalized tutoring, GPT models could also serve as AI advisors for university students. The college journey is often rife with complexities—from applying and selecting courses to navigating program requirements and institutional laws. A GPT-powered AI advisor, trained on the specific information and policies of an institution, could streamline this process. It could guide students on application procedures, help them choose and register for courses that align with their degree requirements, and offer advice tailored to the university's rules and regulations.

Another exciting prospect is the potential for GPT to serve as an AI assessment generator and feedback system. By being trained on a range of exams, assessments, and grading criteria, AI could revolutionize the way we design and evaluate tests. It could generate customized exams for students, ensuring a fair evaluation of their understanding. Furthermore, it could provide immediate, comprehensive feedback on their performance, identifying areas of strength and those needing improvement.

The world of education stands on the brink of a transformative era, fueled by the power of AI. The applications of AI in education extend far beyond what we have discussed here, and it's thrilling to think of the potential that lies ahead. The future of education promises to be more personalized, more accessible, and more innovative, driven by the intelligent capabilities of AI technologies like GPT. The journey is just beginning, and the destination holds unimaginable promise.

Diving Deeper: Personalized Learning as a Use Case

Why Personalized Learning

As we traverse the vast landscape of opportunities that AI can introduce to the field of education, one use case captures our attention more than others. This is the concept of personalized tutoring, facilitated by a GPT-powered chatbot that is meticulously trained on a specific curriculum.

The reasons for our focus on this particular use case are manifold, spanning both global and regional scopes.

From a global standpoint, personalized tutoring via AI-powered chatbots presents an ingenious solution to two monumental challenges faced by the education sector today. The first is the Two Sigma Problem, which we discussed earlier. AI-powered tutoring could bridge the gap between traditional classroom instruction and personalized tutoring, potentially raising the average performance of students by two standard deviations—thereby replicating the 'Two Sigma' effect. The second is the issue of accessibility and equity in education. Personalized AI-powered tutors, accessible via simple digital devices, could democratize education, making high-quality, personalized education a reality for students across socio-economic strata and geographical divides.

Narrowing our focus to the Middle East and North Africa (MENA) region, the value proposition of AI-powered tutoring becomes even more compelling. The region, marred by political instability and ongoing crises, is grappling with significant educational challenges. A large number of students are denied access to consistent, high-quality education due to the prevailing circumstances. AI-powered personalized tutors could provide a cost-effective and readily accessible solution to this critical issue, offering on-demand, high-quality education to students irrespective of their geographical location or personal circumstances. Such a solution could keep education going even amidst unrest, ensuring that the future generation's learning isn't collateral damage to the prevailing geopolitical climate.

Returning to our earlier classification of educational challenges, we identified 'Equity and Accessibility' and 'High Cost of Education' as the most pressing and impactful issues. Interestingly, AI-powered personalized tutoring stands at the intersection of these challenges, offering a promising way forward. Further, we also recognized 'High Cost of Personalized/Adaptive Learning' as a significant barrier to the advancement of education quality. Despite its immense benefits, the implementation of personalized learning at a large scale has been hindered by prohibitive costs and logistical complexities. With the advent of AI-powered personalized tutors, this challenge could soon become a relic of the past. By offering a cost-effective and logistically feasible way of providing personalized learning, AI could potentially usher in an era of widespread adaptive learning, elevating educational outcomes like never before.

A Practical Overview of Building an AI Personalized Tutor

Designing a GPT-powered personalized tutor might seem like a complex undertaking, but the reality is surprisingly different. Thanks to the advancements in AI and related technologies, setting up such a system is less complex than many other programming scenarios. Here is a broad overview of how this can be achieved.

The foundation of any GPT-powered system is data. For a personalized tutor, the primary data sources would be the specific educational content and curriculum materials relevant to the institution and the course. These could include textbooks, course notes, supplementary materials, past examinations, marking rubrics, and institutional policies and procedures. These sources could be in various formats—databases, PDFs, Word documents, and even physical documents.

For physical documents, an initial step of digitization would be needed, which could be achieved using Optical Character Recognition (OCR) technologies. The OCR system can convert different types of documents, such as scanned paper documents, PDF files, or images captured by a digital camera, into editable and searchable data.

Once all the data is ready in a digital format, the next step is ingesting it into a system that is set up for reinforcement learning. The process involves breaking down the large-scale data into manageable chunks that the GPT model can be trained on, an approach commonly referred to as "chunking."

Semantic ranking can then be applied to optimize the responses generated by the AI. This is a technique used to ensure the relevance of the generated output, by ranking the possible outputs based on how closely they align semantically with the input prompt and the targeted response.

The AI system responsible for generating responses—the GPT model—can then be integrated with the institution's chosen interface, which could range from an interactive website to a mobile application or a simple chatbot interface. Communication between the interface and the GPT model happens via APIs or similar services.

This might seem like a lot to comprehend, but the good news is that many cloud-based AI platforms offer an integrated environment that simplifies much of this process. These platforms provide tools for managing and processing data, training AI models, and deploying the AI-powered chatbots.

Moreover, the beauty of GPT models like ChatGPT lies in the fact that they are already trained on a vast corpus of data. This means that, when trained with specific educational content, the GPT model can effectively 'understand' and 'generate' meaningful responses based on that content. However, it's important to remember that the output of GPT models will only be as good as the quality of data they are trained on. Therefore, data preparation, including quality assurance and relevancy checks, is a crucial step in the process.

In essence, developing a GPT-powered personalized tutor involves a synergistic blend of data management, AI training, semantic optimization, and user interface design. With the right planning and resources, it's a perfectly feasible venture that is both cost and time efficient.

What Would the Solution Look Like

In a world increasingly defined by digital interaction, the GPT-powered tutor is poised to fit seamlessly within the fabric of modern educational institutions. Accessible at a student's convenience, it can become an indispensable part of their learning journey, ready to clarify, explain, and explore course material at a moment's notice. This AI tutor could be integrated directly into existing university portals, using established student credentials for secure and straightforward access. It becomes a constant companion to the student's academic exploration, available anytime, anywhere—through the simplicity of a mobile app, a website, or even via voice-activated AI assistants.

Now imagine a scenario where a student, who we'll call Sarah, interacts with this virtual tutor after a lecture, during exam preparation, or when she's seeking assistance with an assignment. Sarah, just home from a lecture on organic chemistry, finds herself puzzled over the concept of chirality. Unfazed, she reaches for her phone and types into her university app, "I didn't understand chirality in today's lecture. Can you explain?" The AI tutor, proficient in the course curriculum, provides a clear, detailed explanation, using examples and analogies that make the complex concept understandable.

As semester finals approach, the AI tutor proves to be an even more invaluable resource. Sarah asks it to generate a practice test based on her mathematics curriculum. Upon completion, the AI not only grades the test but also offers detailed feedback on areas of strength and those needing more work. It then adapts its teaching to address these weaker areas, breaking down complex concepts into manageable parts and providing additional problems for practice.

The same AI tutor could also support Sarah in her coursework. When tasked with a research paper on the economic impacts of climate change, she turns to the tutor for guidance on how to approach it. It responds with a clear breakdown of how she could structure her argument, offers key points to consider, and even suggests potential sources for her research.

To further illustrate the interaction, consider this extended dialogue:

> **Sarah:** "I am struggling with solving quadratic equations. Can you help me?"

> **GPT-powered Tutor:** "Of course, Sarah. Quadratic equations can be solved using several methods. The simplest one is factoring. A quadratic equation is of the form $ax^2 + bx + c = 0$. To factorize it, we need to find two numbers that multiply to give 'ac' (product of a and c) and add up to 'b'. Does that make sense?"

> **Sarah:** "I think so. Could you show me an example?"

> **GPT-powered Tutor:** "Absolutely, Sarah. Let's consider the equation $2x^2 + 7x + 3 = 0$. Here, 'a' is 2, 'b'

is 7, and 'c' is 3. We need two numbers that multiply to 6 (since 2*3=6) and add up to 7. The numbers that meet these conditions are 1 and 6. Therefore, the factors of the equation are $(2x + 1)$ and $(x + 3)$. Setting these equal to zero gives us the solutions x $= -1/2$ or x $= -3$. Does this process make more sense now?"

> **Sarah:** "I'm starting to get it. But how do I know which method to use when solving quadratic equations?"

> **GPT-powered Tutor:** "That's a great question, Sarah. The method to use often depends on the specific equation. Factoring, as we just used, is often the simplest approach, but it may not always be possible or the most efficient. Other methods include completing the square, using the quadratic formula, or graphing. Can you tell me what you know about these methods?"

> **Sarah:** "I know the quadratic formula, but I'm not sure about the others."

> **GPT-powered Tutor:** "That's a good start, Sarah. Let's delve deeper into these methods one by one, so you will have a range of tools at your disposal when facing different quadratic equations."

This virtual conversation between a student and the AI tutor demonstrates how the tool can interactively and effectively respond to student queries, providing a personalized, adaptive learning experience at all times. It showcases an exciting vision of the future of education—one that is adaptable, accessible, and student-centered.

Ethical and Governance Considerations

As we chart our course toward the future of education, radiant with the transformative possibilities of artificial intelligence, we find ourselves navigating a landscape layered with ethical and governance considerations. Our journey to redefine education is replete with challenges that command meticulous attention, thoughtful deliberation, and above all, an unwavering commitment to the values fundamental to education.

Immersed in an era defined by the ubiquity of digital data, concerns surrounding data privacy and security thrust themselves into the limelight. When educational institutions harness AI's might, they dive into a vast ocean of data—information that extends beyond academic borders and encroaches upon personal and potentially sensitive domains. The assurance of students' data privacy and security becomes a priority we cannot compromise on. An additional layer of security, designed to deter AI systems from catering to harmful or inappropriate requests, is necessary. As we stride forward, embracing AI's role in education, we must remain committed to fostering an environment that respects privacy, protects data, and builds trust.

Yet, as we navigate these digital waters, we encounter another pressing ethical concern—the risk of algorithmic bias. AI's allure lies in its capacity to learn from data and emulate human intelligence. But this strength could mutate into a weakness if AI reflects and amplifies existing biases. In the world of education, where fairness and impartiality are sacrosanct, we must ensure that these biases find no foothold in AI applications. The journey toward integrating AI in education demands an understanding of the potential for bias and a commitment to creating systems that are both fair and impartial.

The integration of AI systems into education brings to light another crucial aspect—transparency and accountability. We must ensure that AI's decisions are intelligible to students, teachers, and administrators. Furthermore, we need to identify who bears the responsibility when an AI system falters in its judgment or offers misguided recommendations. These considerations are paramount to maintaining trust and confidence in an education system powered by AI. Transparency is not just about unveiling the inner workings of AI; it is about clearly articulating the role AI occupies in education.

Education rests on the twin pillars of accessibility and equity. Our quest to enhance learning through AI cannot undermine these principles. AI's promise is its ability to revolutionize education, offering quality learning to everyone. But we must ensure that this promise doesn't fall short, contributing to further educational disparities. As we tread the path of AI-driven education, we must ensure that this transformative technology acts as a beacon of equity, illuminating the path to education for all.

The unfolding narrative of AI and education brings the student–teacher relationship into sharp focus. The intention behind AI's incorporation into the classroom is not to supplant teachers but to bolster their capabilities, facilitating their evolution from information providers to enablers of learning. AI could aid teachers in optimizing time spent on preparation, freeing them to foster critical thinking, facilitate project-based learning, enhance communication skills, and craft enriching educational experiences. The dawn of AI in education does not signal the end of teaching; instead, it heralds a new era brimming with opportunities.

As we conclude, we turn our attention to the necessity of a robust and updated regulatory framework accompanying the introduction of AI into the education sector. This framework must oversee AI's ethical use in education, ensuring that this potent technology is harnessed responsibly and effectively. This could necessitate revising existing legislation or even crafting new regulations, tailor-made for the unique challenges and opportunities presented by AI in education.

As we look toward a future steeped in AI, these ethical and governance considerations offer themselves as guiding principles. Our journey to this future, while intricate, holds the promise that with careful deliberation and adherence to these principles, we can align our destination with the loftiest ideals of education.

Concluding Remarks and Recommendations

As our exploration of the intersection between artificial intelligence and higher education draws to a close, it seems appropriate to revisit the central themes and dilemmas that formed the bedrock of our journey. We embarked on this voyage with a keen focus on the intricate web of challenges facing the global education sector, particularly within the MENA region. These dilemmas, such as the need for increasing equity and access, personalized learning, the judicious allocation of instructor time, and the educational disparities highlighted by the Two Sigma Problem, paint a vivid picture of an education system in dire need of transformative solutions.

In the midst of these challenges, we encountered a glimmer of hope in the realm of AI, a technology ripe with potential and primed to challenge the status quo. It promises a new era of education that could weave innovation into its very fabric. The transformative capacity of AI across several applications and particularly in the arena of personalized learning that we thoroughly discussed is palpable. Our exploration led us to envision a future where a GPT-powered chatbot could cater to individual learning styles and needs, thereby offering a solution to the pervasive challenge of personalized education.

Our attempt toward classification revealed that challenges, such as 'Equity and Accessibility,' 'High Cost of Education,' 'Standardized Teaching and Assessment,' and 'Higher Education Institutions Focusing on Content and Not Skills,' while significant, are by no means insurmountable. What AI offers is a realistic possibility of addressing these challenges simultaneously, something that no other single intervention has ever promised before. AI's potential to make personalized learning economically viable could finally address the urgency and the institutional difficulty that the chart highlights in these areas.

This brings us to the crucial ethical and governance considerations that we must bear in mind as we venture further into the AI era. Issues ranging from data privacy and security, algorithmic bias, transparency and accountability, to accessibility and equity—these guiding principles must form the bedrock of our policies as we navigate the labyrinthine world of AI integration in education. An updated and comprehensive regulatory framework that ensures responsible and ethical use of AI is no longer an option—it is an imperative.

Standing at the crossroads of the AI revolution, we see the need for close collaboration between educational institutions, technology companies, and policymakers. Such a partnership could bridge the divide between policy, technology, and education, truly harnessing the transformative power of AI. We also find that experimentation is key. A willingness from educational institutions to explore the capabilities of AI and launch smaller pilot projects can pave the way for large-scale transformations and invaluable insights.

Furthermore, investment in training is paramount to ensure teachers and students are equipped with the necessary skills and knowledge to navigate the AI-enabled educational landscape. And finally, AI's introduction into the education sector is a clarion call for an updated regulatory framework. This will ensure the ethical use of AI, effective data privacy management, and the maintenance of accountability.

As we stand at the threshold of this exciting confluence of AI and education, our outlook is one of hope and anticipation. The challenges before us are significant, yet the potential of AI to transform education is vast and inspiring. As we move forward, we are guided by our learnings from the past and the possibilities of the future, steering toward a horizon where AI in education fosters innovation, inclusivity, and excellence. Let us step forward into this future, undeterred by the complex landscape that lies ahead, and driven by the promise of what could be.

References

Baum, S., Ma, J., & Payea, K. (2013). *The benefits of higher education for individuals and society.* College Board.

Bloom, B. S. (1984). https://www.insidehighered.com/news/2014/04/09/res earch-shows-professors-work-long-hours-and-spend-much-day-meetings. *Educational Researcher* (pp. 4–16).

Devarajan, S. (2016). *The paradox of higher education in MENA.* Brookings.

Flaherty, C. (2014, April 8). *So much to do, so little time*. Retrieved from Inside Higher Ed. https://www.insidehighered.com/news/2014/04/09/research-shows-professors-work-long-hours-and-spend-much-day-meetings

Hall, S., Schmautzer, D., Tmiri, S., & Tschupp, R. (2022). *Reimagining higher education in MENAP*. McKinsey & Company.

Østergaard, S. F., & Nordlund, A. G. (2019). *The 4 biggest challenges to our higher education model—And what to do about them*. World Economic Forum.

Truitt, E. (2021, November 24). *Surveillance, companionship, and entertainment: The Ancient history of intelligent machines*. Retrieved from The MIT Press Reader. https://thereader.mitpress.mit.edu/the-ancient-history-of-intelligent-machines/

UNESCO. (2023, April 20). *The United Nations educational, scientific and cultural organization*. Retrieved from UNESCO. https://www.unesco.org/en/higher-education/need-know

World Bank. (2014). *Equity, access and success in higher education*. World Bank.

13

Conclusion

Georges Yahchouchi

This book has examined two pivotal axes that are vital for success in education today: the shift and challenges in governance along with the shift in education. The first axis explored the governance of educational institutions, including the organizational structures, decision-making processes, and policies that enable educational institutions to adapt to the changing landscape. The second axis focused on the changing face of education, with a particular emphasis on the new tools, assignments, and methodologies that are now available to educators and how to juggle between them and the governance of the university. Accordingly, governance in educational institutions has become increasingly challenging. Furthermore, the changing and challenging environment has demanded a shift in the approaches; the education is delivered, via new tools, assignments, and teaching methodologies.

The main objective of this book was to provide a comprehensive and up-to-date analysis of these two axes, offering valuable insights as well as

G. Yahchouchi (✉)
American University of the Middle East, Egaila, Kuwait
e-mail: georges.yahchouchi@aum.edu.kw

N. Azoury and G. Yahchouchi (eds.), *Governance in Higher Education*,
https://doi.org/10.1007/978-3-031-40586-0_13

practical advice for educational professionals, policymakers, and students alike. Through addressing the challenges and opportunities presented by the evolving educational landscape, this book aimed to equip readers with the knowledge and skills required to navigate this new terrain and hence succeed in the world of education.

Throughout the book, key topics in Higher Education Global Reform have been overviewed, and various perspectives have been discussed. The comprehensive analysis covered the future of education, inclusion, and diversity, E-Education and grading systems, the higher education system in the MENA region, hybrid learning modes, and challenges and opportunities for students and faculty; altogether collectively contributing to the existing knowledge in the field.

Regarding the future of education, it is apparent that the adoption of new technologies and innovative approaches will form education in the future. The metaverse, a virtual world enabling real-time interaction, represents a new frontier for education. However, effective implementation and governance are essential. In terms of inclusion and diversity, there is a growing recognition of the need of addressing issues of diversity and inclusion within the education system. Creating an inclusive and supportive learning environment is a key goal. Strategies such as affirmative action policies, diversity training programs, and targeted recruitment efforts have been implemented, but their effectiveness and the challenges faced in promoting diversity and inclusion need to be examined. As for E-Education and grading systems, with the growing prevalence of e-learning and online education platforms, the question of how to effectively grade and evaluate student work has become increasingly important. A balance between strict and lenient grading systems may be necessary to ensure quality education while supporting student motivation and engagement. Regarding the higher education system in the MENA region, both public and private universities face challenges and opportunities. Understanding the complexities of the system, including its governance and management, is crucial for its success in a rapidly changing environment.

The shift from traditional in-person learning to hybrid learning modes has significant implications for educational institutions. Effective governance in this new environment, including reassessing organizational structures, policies, and decision-making processes, is vital. The changing landscape of higher education presents new challenges and opportunities for students and faculty. The role of governance in shaping their experiences needs to be explored.

In closing, this book reveals the revolutionary potential of innovative tools, diverse pedagogies, and effective governance in higher education and has created opportunities for future research. The perceptions gathered from this exploration can guide educators, policymakers, and other stakeholders toward the required changes to proactively respond to the dynamic educational developments in the MENA region and beyond. As a final note, in light of the ever-changing factors, namely artificial intelligence (AI) and COVID-19, it has become imperative more than ever to take into account their disruptive impacts on higher education.

Index

N. Azoury and G. Yahchouchi (eds.), *Governance in Higher Education*,
https://doi.org/10.1007/978-3-031-40586-0